Preface

From the Secretary of State for Education and Skills, the Rt Hon Estelle Morris MP

The Government's education policy is focused on helping all children release their potential. We are committed to developing an education service that provides equality of opportunity and high achievement for all children.

This new Special Educational Needs Code of Practice plays an important role in delivering that commitment. It promotes a consistency of approach to meeting children's special educational needs and places the rights of children with special educational needs at the heart of the process, allowing them to be heard and to take part in decisions about their education.

The focus is on preventative work to ensure that children's special educational needs are identified as quickly as possible and that early action is taken to meet those needs. The Code of Practice sets out a framework for effective school based support with less paper work for teachers and an emphasis on monitoring the progress of children with special educational needs towards identified goals. It covers the special educational needs provisions of the Special Educational Needs and Disability Act 2001 and provides a framework for developing the strong partnerships between parents, schools, Local Education Authorities, health and social services and voluntary organisations that are crucial to success in removing barriers to participation and learning.

I am confident that this Code of Practice will build on the success of its predecessor and help us to raise the achievement of all children.

Estelle Morris

Estelle Morris

Foreword

Introduction

1 The SEN Code of Practice provides practical advice to Local Education Authorities, maintained schools, early education settings and others on carrying out their statutory duties to identify, assess and make provision for children's special educational needs.

2 The Education Act 1993 placed a duty on the Secretary of State to issue a Code of Practice and the power to revise it from time to time. The first Code of Practice came into effect in 1994. Since then, the rights and duties contained in the 1993 Act have been consolidated into Part IV of the 1996 Education Act. This Code of Practice replaces the 1994 Code in England. It follows consultation in January 1999 on proposals for changes to the Code of Practice and subsequent consultation between July and October 2000 with LEAs, schools, SEN voluntary bodies, the health and social services, and others on a draft of a revised Code. The draft was then revised in the light of comments from all interested parties, and subsequently laid before and approved by Parliament.

3 This Code, like its predecessor, will help schools and LEAs obtain the best value from the considerable resources and expertise they invest in helping children with special educational needs. It retains much of the guidance from the original Code. But it takes account of the experiences of schools and LEAs in using the original Code and developments in education since 1994. It includes new rights and duties introduced by the SEN and Disability Act 2001 and Regulations.

4 This foreword explains the status of this Code of Practice, highlights related developments and summarises the main differences from the 1994 Code. It is not formally part of the Code itself.

The Status of the SEN Code of Practice

5 This Code of Practice is effective from 1 January 2002. From that date LEAs, schools, early education settings and those who help them – including health and social services – must have regard to it. They must not ignore it. That means that whenever settings, schools and LEAs decide how to exercise their functions relating to children with special educational needs, and whenever the health and social services provide help to settings, schools and LEAs in this, those bodies must consider what this Code says. These bodies must fulfil their statutory duties towards children with special educational needs but it is up to them to decide how to do so – in the light of the guidance in this Code of Practice. The Code is designed to help them to make effective decisions but it does not – and could not – tell them what to do in each individual case. The duty to have regard to this Code will continue for its lifetime.

Implementation

6 New statutory duties on LEAs, schools and early education settings introduced by the Special Educational Needs and Disability Act 2001 and revised Regulations come into force on 1 January 2002. Key statutory duties are paraphrased in boxes throughout the text. The Regulations set out transitional provisions dealing with assessments, statements and reviews commenced under the old system. During the transitional period, whilst schools and LEAs must have regard to this Code, they will need to do so in the light of those transitional arrangements. It would be unrealistic to expect them to have in

place on 1 January procedures matching every aspect of the arrangements described in this Code. They must however, have regard to this Code from that date and thereafter.

Changes from the Original SEN Code of Practice

7 This Code takes account of the SEN provisions of the Special Educational Needs and Disability Act 2001:

- a stronger right for children with SEN to be educated at a mainstream school
- new duties on LEAs to arrange for parents of children with SEN to be provided with services offering advice and information and a means of resolving disputes
- a new duty on schools and relevant nursery education providers to tell parents when they are making special educational provision for their child
- a new right for schools and relevant nursery education providers to request a statutory assessment of a child

It contains separate chapters on provision in the early years, primary and secondary phases and new chapters on:

- working in partnership with parents
- pupil participation
- working in partnership with other agencies

8 The Code recommends that, to help match special educational provision to children's needs, schools and LEAs should adopt a graduated approach through *School Action* and *School Action Plus* and *Early Years Action* and *Early Years Action Plus* in early education settings.

Monitoring the SEN Code of Practice

9 The operation of Part IV of the 1996 Act, including the effect of this Code, will be closely monitored. Ofsted inspectors will look closely at schools' SEN policies and practices. Through their examination of and reports on the education system, they will also monitor and evaluate the impact of this Code and other measures on schools and LEAs. The Secretary of State will consider, in the light of this evaluation and all other relevant factors, whether and when the Code should be revised again.

The SEN Tribunal

10 When considering an appeal from a parent, the SEN Tribunal **must** have regard to any provision of this Code relevant to any question arising on the appeal. The Tribunal does not exercise a general oversight of LEAs' adherence to the Code's provisions. Its task is to consider whether LEAs have reached the right decision in the light of the particular circumstances of each appeal. Nonetheless, the Tribunal will expect LEAs, schools and early education settings to be able to explain the rationale for any departure from this Code where such a departure was relevant to the decision in question.

Relevant Regulations

11 The following Regulations are relevant to matters covered in the Code:

- The Education (Special Educational Needs) (England) (Consolidation) Regulations 2001.
- The Special Educational Needs (Provision of Information by Local Education Authorities) (England) Regulations 2001.
- The Education (Special Educational Needs) (Information) (England) Regulations 1999.

Other Guidance

Guidance on inclusion

12 Section 316A of the Education Act 1996 requires maintained schools and local education authorities to have regard to guidance on the statutory framework for inclusion. The separate guidance "Inclusive Schooling – Children with Special Educational Needs" provides advice on the practical operation of the new framework. It gives examples of the reasonable steps that maintained schools and LEAs could consider taking to ensure that the inclusion of a child with a statement of special educational needs in a mainstream school is not incompatible with the efficient education of other children.

The Disability Rights Code of Practice for Schools

13 Part 2 of the Special Educational Needs and Disability Act 2001 amends the Disability Discrimination Act 1995 to prohibit all schools from discriminating against disabled children in their admissions arrangements, in the education and associated services provided by the school for its pupils or in relation to exclusions from the school. The reasonable adjustments duty on schools does not require the provision of auxiliary aids and services or the removal or alteration of physical features. Decisions about the provision of educational aids and services for children with SEN will continue to be taken within the SEN framework.

14 From September 2002, schools will be required not to treat disabled pupils less favourably for a reason relating to their disability and to take reasonable steps to ensure that they are not placed at a substantial disadvantage to those who are not disabled. A Disability Rights Code of Practice for schools, prepared by the Disability Rights Commission, will explain these new anti-discrimination duties to schools. LEAs and relevant schools will also be required from September 2002 to plan strategically and make progress in improving accessibility for disabled pupils to schools' premises and to the curriculum, and to improve the delivery of written information in an accessible way to disabled pupils. The Department will prepare separate guidance for LEAs and schools in England on the practical steps they can take to improve their accessibility to a wide range of disabled pupils.

15 When the Disability Rights Code of Practice for Schools and the planning duty guidance are published they will go alongside this SEN Code of Practice and cross-refer to it where appropriate.

SEN Toolkit

16 Additional guidance to be read in conjunction with this Code of Practice is available in the "SEN Toolkit." The additional guidance and this Code cross-refer to each other.

Contents

4 Identification, assessment and provision in early education settings

5 Identification, assessment and provision in the primary phase

6 Identification, assessment and provision in the secondary sector

7 Statutory assessment of special educational needs

1 Principles and Policies

Introduction

1:1 The purpose of the Code of Practice is to give practical guidance on the discharge of their functions under Part IV of the Education Act 1996 to LEAs, the governing bodies of maintained schools and settings in receipt of government funding to provide early education – and to those who help them, including the health services and social services. It also provides general practical guidance to such settings about the provision of nursery education to children with special educational needs. All these parties are required to have regard to this Code.

1:2 The Code sets out guidance on policies and procedures aimed at enabling pupils with special educational needs (SEN) to reach their full potential, to be included fully in their school communities and make a successful transition to adulthood. For the vast majority of children their mainstream setting will meet all their special educational needs. Some children will require additional help from SEN services or other agencies external to the school. A very small minority of children will have SEN of a severity or complexity that requires the LEA to determine and arrange the special educational provision their learning difficulties call for.

1:3 These challenging objectives present teachers, and all the professionals and administrators involved, with some of the most rewarding work the education service can offer.

Definition of Special Educational Needs

Children have special educational needs if they have a *learning difficulty* which calls for *special educational provision* to be made for them.

Children have a *learning difficulty* if they:

a) have a significantly greater difficulty in learning than the majority of children of the same age; or

(b) have a disability which prevents or hinders them from making use of educational facilities of a kind generally provided for children of the same age in schools within the area of the local education authority

(c) are under compulsory school age and fall within the definition at (a) or (b) above or would so do if special educational provision was not made for them.

Children must not be regarded as having a learning difficulty solely because the language or form of language of their home is different from the language in which they will be taught.

***Special educational provision* means:**

(a) for children of two or over, educational provision which is additional to, or otherwise different from, the educational provision made generally for children of their age in schools maintained by the LEA, other than special schools, in the area

(b) for children under two, educational provision of any kind.

See Section 312, Education Act 1996

Definitions in the Children Act 1989 and the Disability Discrimination Act 1995

> **A child is disabled if he is blind, deaf or dumb or suffers from a mental disorder of any kind or is substantially and permanently handicapped by illness, injury or congenital deformity or such other disability as may be prescribed.**
>
> Section 17 (11), Children Act 1989

> **A person has a disability for the purposes of this Act if he has a physical or mental impairment which has a substantial and long-term adverse effect on his ability to carry out normal day-to day activities.**
>
> Section 1(1), Disability Discrimination Act 1995

1:4 A child may fall within one or more of the definitions. This Code helps early education settings, schools and LEAs meet their responsibilities for children with SEN. Guidance relating to Part 4 of the Disability Discrimination Act 1995 will help them meet their responsibilities for disabled children.

Fundamental Principles

1:5 The detailed guidance in this Code is informed by these general principles and should be read with them clearly in mind:

- a child with special educational needs should have their needs met
- the special educational needs of children will normally be met in mainstream schools or settings[1]
- the views of the child should be sought and taken into account
- parents[2] have a vital role to play in supporting their child's education
- children with special educational needs should be offered full access to a broad, balanced and relevant education, including an appropriate curriculum for the foundation stage and the National Curriculum.

Critical Success Factors

1:6

- the culture, practice, management and deployment of resources in a school or setting[3] are designed to ensure **all children's needs are met**

---

1 See Glossary.

2 Here, and throughout this Code, 'parents' should be taken to include all those with parental responsibility including corporate parents and carers.

3 Here, and throughout this Code, 'setting' should be taken to include those settings in receipt of Government funding to provide nursery education (other than LEAs maintained nursery schools).

- LEAs, schools and settings work together to ensure that any child's special educational needs are **identified early**
- LEAs, schools and settings exploit **best practice** when devising interventions
- those responsible for special educational provision take into account **the wishes of the child** concerned, in the light of their age and understanding
- special education professionals and **parents** work in **partnership**
- special education professionals take into account the **views of individual parents** in respect of **their child's particular needs**
- interventions for each child are **reviewed regularly** to assess their impact, the child's progress and the views of the child, their teachers and their parents
- there is close co-operation between all the agencies concerned and a **multi-disciplinary approach** to the resolution of issues
- LEAs make assessments in accordance with the **prescribed time limits**
- where an LEA determines a child's special educational needs, statements are **clear and detailed**, made within **prescribed time limits, specify monitoring arrangements**, and are **reviewed annually.**

Strategic planning partnerships

1:7 Meeting the needs of children and young people with SEN successfully requires partnership between all those involved – LEAs, schools, parents, pupils, health and social services and other agencies. Partnerships can only work when there is a clear understanding of the respective aims, roles and responsibilities of the partners and the nature of their relationships, which in turn depends on clarity of information, good communication and transparent policies.

1:8 A range of formal planning opportunities exist which relate to all pupils including those with SEN such as the Education Development Plan (EDP), the School Organisation Plan, the Early Years Development and Childcare Plan, the Connexions Plan and the Health Improvement Programme. Children's Service Plans and Behaviour Support Plans have a statutory basis, whilst some other plans open the way to resources via, for example, special grants. Some apply to services for all children; others to services for children with particular needs.

1:9 In all cases, LEAs should work together with their partner agencies to agree local protocols for information collection and management so as to inform planning of provision for children with SEN at both individual and strategic levels.

The role of the LEA

1:10 The Local Education Authority – School Relations Code of Practice[4] provides broad guidance on the relationships between LEAs, governing bodies and head teachers in their respective roles in achieving excellence for all children. That Code expects LEAs, in

---

4 DfEE February 2001

partnership with schools, to place the highest priority on their statutory duty to promote high standards of education for all children, including those with SEN.

1:11 An essential function of the LEA is to make effective arrangements for SEN by ensuring that:

- the needs of children and young people with SEN are identified and assessed quickly and matched by appropriate provision
- high quality support is provided for schools and early education settings – including, through educational psychology and other support services, and arrangements for sharing good practice in provision for children and young people with SEN
- children and young people with SEN can benefit from co-ordinated provision – by developing close partnerships with parents, schools, health and social services and the voluntary sector
- strategic planning for SEN is carried out in consultation with schools and others to develop systems for monitoring and accountability for SEN
- LEA arrangements for SEN provision are kept under review as required under section 315 of the Education Act 1996.

1:12 As part of their role in ensuring that needs are matched by appropriate provision, LEAs should work with schools to evaluate the effectiveness of their school funding arrangements in supporting and raising the achievement of children with SEN.

LEA policy framework

1:13 The Special Educational Needs (Provision of Information by Local Education Authorities) (England) Regulations 2001 set out at Annex A, require LEAs to publish their policies on SEN and information about how the authority is:

- promoting high standards of education for children with SEN
- encouraging children with SEN to participate fully in their school and community and to take part in decisions about their education
- encouraging schools in their area to share their practice in providing for children with SEN
- working with other statutory and voluntary bodies to provide support for children with SEN.

1:14 LEAs must also publish their general arrangements, including any plans setting out objectives, targets and timescales covering local arrangements for:

- identifying children with SEN
- monitoring the admission of children with SEN (whether or not those children have a statement) to maintained schools in their area
- organising the assessment of children's SEN statements, including any local protocols for so doing
- providing support to schools with regard to making provision for children with SEN

- auditing, planning, monitoring and reviewing provision for children with SEN (generally and in relation to individual pupils)
- supporting pupils with SEN through *School Action* and *School Action Plus*
- securing training, advice and support for staff working in SEN
- reviewing and updating the policy and development plans on a regular basis
- explaining that element of provision for children with SEN (but without statements) which the LEA expects normally to be met from maintained schools' budget shares and that element of such provision that the authority expects normally to be met from funds which it holds centrally.

1:15 To fulfil their role effectively, LEAs' planning should provide for the inclusion of children with SEN in mainstream schools. They should monitor and review the role and quality of central SEN support services and parent partnership services; take account of current and predicted pupil numbers; monitor the kinds of needs that are identified and where children are placed; and should develop their SEN policies in consultation with schools and their other partners and keep them under review.

The duties of governing bodies[5]

1:16 All maintained school governing bodies have important statutory duties towards pupils with special educational needs. Governing bodies should, with the head teacher, decide the school's general policy and approach to meeting pupils' special educational needs for those with and without statements. They must set up appropriate staffing and funding arrangements and oversee the school's work.

1:17 Governors of community, voluntary and foundation schools, and LEAs in relation to maintained nursery schools, have a duty under s317 of the Education Act 1996 to do their best to ensure that the necessary provision is made for pupils with SEN. The School Standards and Framework Act 1998 requires governors to conduct the school with a view to promoting high standards. These high standards relate to all the pupils in the school including those with SEN.

1:18 Through the performance management framework the governors should secure that objectives are set for the head teacher. These should include objectives for leadership, management, pupil achievement and progress, and will also relate to priorities in the school development plan. All these objectives should include SEN.

1:19 Every school must have a 'responsible person' who makes sure that all those who are likely to teach a pupil with a statement of special educational needs are told about the statement. The person is generally the head teacher, but may be the chair of the governing body or a governor appointed by the governing body to take that responsibility.

1:20 Most governing bodies appoint a governor or sub-committee to have specific oversight of the school's arrangements and provision for meeting special educational needs. The SEN governor's remit does not necessarily need to include the role of 'responsible person.'

---

5 These duties apply to all maintained schools including those with nursery classes.

1:21 The governing body of a community, voluntary or foundation school must:

- **do its best to ensure that the necessary provision is made for any pupil who has special educational needs**
- **ensure that, where the 'responsible person' – the head teacher or the appropriate governor – has been informed by the LEA that a pupil has special educational needs, those needs are made known to all who are likely to teach them**
- **ensure that teachers in the school are aware of the importance of identifying, and providing for, those pupils who have special educational needs**
- **consult the LEA and the governing bodies of other schools, when it seems to be necessary or desirable in the interests of co-ordinated special educational provision in the area as a whole**
- **ensure that a pupil with special educational needs joins in the activities of the school together with pupils who do not have special educational needs, so far as is reasonably practical and compatible with the child receiving the special educational provision their learning needs call for and the efficient education of the pupils with whom they are educated and the efficient use of resources**
- **report to parents on the implementation of the school's policy for pupils with special educational needs**

See Section 317, Education Act 1996

- **have regard to this Code of Practice when carrying out its duties toward all pupils with special educational needs**

See Section 313, Education Act 1996

- **ensure that parents are notified of a decision by the school that SEN provision is being made for their child.**

See Section 317A, Education Act 1996

(LEAs have these duties, where relevant, in relation to maintained nursery schools)

1:22 Governors play a major part in school self-review and should establish mechanisms to ensure that they are fully informed about the school, including the systems for and the outcomes of in-school monitoring and evaluation. In relation to SEN, the governing body should make sure that:

- they are fully involved in developing and monitoring the school's SEN policy
- all governors, especially any SEN governors, are up-to-date and knowledgeable about the school's SEN provision, including how funding, equipment and personnel resources are deployed

- SEN provision is an integral part of the school development plan
- the quality of SEN provision is continually monitored.

SEN Policies in Early Education Settings and Schools

1:23 These educational settings and schools **must** have a written SEN policy:

- settings in receipt of government funding for early education[6]
- maintained nursery schools
- community, foundation and voluntary schools
- community and foundation special schools
- City Academies
- City Technology Colleges
- City Colleges for the Technology of the Arts.

1:24 The SEN policy **must** contain the information as set out in the Education (Special Educational Needs) (Information) (England) Regulations 1999 at Annex A or, in the case of early education settings and City Academies, as set out in the conditions of grant.

1:25 LEAs are responsible for ensuring that Pupil Referral Units have appropriate SEN policies.

1:26 As part of their statutory duties, governing bodies of all maintained mainstream schools must publish information about, and report on, the school's policy on special educational needs. This information must be freely available to parents. While the governing body and the head teacher will take overall responsibility for the school's SEN policy, the school as a whole should be involved in its development. Governing bodies of maintained special schools must also publish information about, and report on, their school policies. Schools may also wish to consult the LEA and neighbouring schools in reviewing and revising their policy, in the interests of co-ordinated special educational provision within the area as a whole.

1:27 As with all policies, the SEN policy should be subject to a regular cycle of monitoring, evaluation and review. Thus governing bodies **must**, on at least an annual basis, consider, and report on, the effectiveness of the school's work on behalf of children with special educational needs. In drawing up their annual report they may wish to consult support services used by the school, other schools and parents. In the light of evaluation and the response to consultation the school should consider whether the policy needs amending.

1:28 Regulations made under Section 42 of the School Standards and Framework Act 1998 require that the governing body's annual report **must** include information on the implementation of the governing body's policy on pupils with special educational needs and any changes to the policy during the last year.

---

6 Providers, in particular accredited childminders who are part of an approved network, may work together to develop their SEN policy.

Roles and Responsibilities in Early Education Settings

1:29 Provision for children with special educational needs is a matter for everyone in the setting. In addition to the setting's head teacher or manager and the SEN coordinator (SENCO)[7] all other members of staff have important responsibilities. In practice, the division of day-to-day responsibilities is a matter for individual settings.

1:30 Whatever arrangements are made for meeting the needs of children with SEN in a particular setting, the general duty to identify and make provision for children with SEN remains with the LEA.

Roles and Responsibilities in Maintained Mainstream Schools[8]

1:31 Provision for pupils with special educational needs is a matter for the school *as a whole*. In addition to the governing body, the school's head teacher, the SENCO[9] or SEN team and all other members of staff have important responsibilities. In practice the division of day-to-day responsibilities is a matter for individual schools, to be decided in the light of a school's circumstances and size, priorities and ethos.

Roles and Responsibilities in Special Schools

1:32 Provision for the pupils is a matter for the school *as a whole*. In addition to the governing body, the school's head teacher and all other members of staff have important day-to-day responsibilities. Whatever arrangements are made for meeting the needs of children with SEN in a particular special school, the statutory duties remain with the governing body rather than with the school staff.

School Admissions and Inclusion

1:33 All schools should admit pupils with already identified special educational needs, as well as identifying and providing for pupils not previously identified as having SEN. Admission authorities may not refuse to admit a child because they feel unable to cater for their special educational needs. Pupils with special educational needs but without statements must be treated as fairly as all other applicants for admission. Admission authorities must consider applications from parents of children who have special educational needs but no statement on the basis of the school's published admissions criteria. Such children should be considered as part of the normal admissions procedures. Admission authorities cannot refuse to admit children on the grounds that they do not have a statement of special educational needs or are currently being assessed.

---

7 In the case of accredited childminders that are part of an approved network, the SENCO role may be shared between individual childminders and the coordinator of the network.

8 Maintained Mainstream schools include maintained nursery schools where the LEA has ultimate responsibility for carrying out the same functions as undertaken by the Governing Body in a maintained primary or secondary school.

9 See Glossary.

1:34 LEAs and school governing bodies, where they are the admissions authority, have a duty to comply with the statutory infant class size limit of 30 pupils.[10] No infant class containing 5, 6 or 7 year olds in a maintained school may contain more than 30 pupils with one qualified teacher except in certain limited circumstances. These include:

- pupils attending mainstream lessons and registered at a special school normally educated in a resourced SEN unit in a mainstream school
- pupils admitted outside the normal admission round to an infant class in a mainstream school with a statement of SEN naming that school may be counted as an exception for the remainder of the academic year of admission.

1:35 There is a clear expectation within the Education Act 1996 that pupils with statements of special educational needs will be included in mainstream schools. A parents' wish to have their child with a statement educated in the mainstream should only be refused in the small minority of cases where the child's inclusion would be incompatible with the efficient education of other children.

1:36 If a child has a statement of special educational needs maintained by the LEA, that LEA is responsible for arranging the special educational provision and, in finalising the statement, considering the school's suitability. Where a maintained school is named in a statement of special educational needs, the governing body of the school must admit the child to the school. Further details on the considerations that apply when LEAs name a school in a child's statement are given in Chapter 8.

Scope for Flexibility

1:37 The Code advises the adoption of a range of strategies that recognise the various complexities of need, the different responsibilities to assess and meet those needs, and the associated range and variations in provision, which will best reflect and promote common recognition of the continuum of special educational needs.

1:38 There is scope for flexibility and variation in the responses adopted by schools, early education settings and LEAs. However, early education settings, schools and LEAs will need to be able to demonstrate, in their arrangements for children with special educational needs, that they are fulfilling their statutory duty to have regard to this Code. OFSTED will consider the effectiveness of their policies and practices and the extent to which they have had regard to this Code.

---

10 The infant class size limit became statutory from September 2001. In recognition of the particular challenge faced by LEAs and schools in managing the transition in September 2001 from the non-statutory to the statutory basis of the limit, financial support has been made available to local education authorities that need it to help to ensure all infant classes have 30 or fewer pupils in September 2001 – including those classes that would be breaching the limit as a result of excepted pupils.

1:39 Table of Roles and Responsibilities

In Maintained Mainstream Schools	In Maintained Special Schools	In Early Education Settings
• **the governing body** should, in co-operation with the head teacher, determine the school's general policy and approach to provision for children with SEN, establish the appropriate staffing and funding arrangements and maintain a general oversight of the school's work	• **the governing body** should, in co-operation with the head teacher, determine the school's general policy and approach to provision for all pupils, establish the appropriate staffing and funding arrangements and maintain a general oversight of the school's work	• **the setting's management group** should work with practitioners to determine the setting's general policy and approach to provision for children with SEN
• **the governing body** may appoint a **committee** to take a particular interest in and closely monitor the school's work on behalf of children with SEN		
• the **governing body must** report to parents annually on the school's policy on SEN	• the **governing body must** report to parents annually on the school's policy on SEN	
• **the head teacher** has responsibility for the day-to-day **management** of all aspects of the school's work, including provision for children with SEN. The head teacher should keep the governing body fully informed and also work closely with the school's SEN coordinator or team	• **the head teacher** has responsibility for the day-to-day **management** of all aspects of the school's work, and will keep the governing body informed	• **the head of the setting** has responsibility for the day-to-day **management** of all aspects of the setting's work, including provision for children with SEN. The head of the setting should keep the management group fully informed and also work closely with the SENCO
• **all teaching and non teaching staff** should be involved in the development of the school's SEN policy and be fully aware of the school's procedures for identifying, assessing and making provision for pupils with SEN	• **all teaching and non teaching staff** should be involved in the development of the school's policy and be fully aware of the school's procedures for making SEN provision, and monitoring and reviewing that provision in line with the guidance in the Code.	• **all practitioners**[11] should be involved in the development of the SEN policy and be fully aware of the procedures for identifying, assessing and making provision for children with special educational needs
• **the SENCO (or team)**, working closely with the head teacher, senior management and fellow teachers, should be closely involved in the strategic development of the SEN policy and provision. The SENCO has responsibility for day-to-day **operation** of the school's SEN policy and for coordinating provision for pupils with SEN, particularly through *School Action* and *School Action Plus*.		• **the SENCO** working closely with the head of the setting and colleagues, has responsibility for the day-to-day **operation** of the setting's SEN policy and for coordinating provision for children with SEN, particularly through *Early Years Action* and *Early Years Action Plus*.

11 Practitioners refers to all those in early education settings who act as educators.

2 Working in Partnership with Parents

Introduction

2:1 Partnership with parents plays a key role in promoting a culture of co-operation between parents, schools[12], LEAs and others. This is important in enabling children and young people with SEN to achieve their potential.

2:2 Parents[13] hold key information and have a critical role to play in their children's education. They have unique strengths, knowledge and experience to contribute to the shared view of a child's needs and the best ways of supporting them. It is therefore essential that all professionals (schools, LEAs and other agencies) actively seek to work with parents and value the contribution they make. The work of professionals can be more effective when parents are involved and account is taken of their wishes, feelings and perspectives on their children's development. This is particularly so when a child has special educational needs. All parents of children with special educational needs should be treated as partners. They should be supported so as to be able and empowered to:

- recognise and fulfil their responsibilities as parents and play an active and valued role in their children's education
- have knowledge of their child's entitlement within the SEN framework
- make their views known about how their child is educated
- have access to information, advice and support during assessment and any related decision-making processes about special educational provision.

2:3 These partnerships can be challenging, requiring positive attitudes by all, and in some circumstances additional support and encouragement for parents.

Defining Parental Responsibility

2:4 It is important that professionals understand who has parental responsibility for a child. The Children Act 1989 introduced the concept of parental responsibility. The Act uses the phrase "parental responsibility" to sum up the collection of duties, rights and authority that a parent has in respect of a child. In the event of family breakdown (i.e. separation or divorce) both married parents will normally retain parental responsibility for the child and the duty on both parents to continue to play a full part in the child's upbringing will not diminish. This means that parental responsibility will be shared, often with the parents living in different households. In relation to unmarried parents, only the mother will have parental responsibility unless the father has been granted parental responsibility by the Court or has made a parental responsibility agreement with the mother. Where a Residence Order is in place in respect of a non-parent (i.e. grandparent), that person will have parental responsibility for the duration of the Order.

2:5 If a child is 'looked after' by a local authority, they may either be on a care order or be voluntarily accommodated. A **Care Order** places a child in the care of a local authority and gives the local authority parental responsibility for the child. The local authority will have the power to determine the extent to which this responsibility will continue to be

---

12 Early education settings as well as schools should work in partnership with parents as described in this Chapter.

13 Here, and throughout this Code, "parents" should be taken to include all those with parental responsibility, including corporate parents and carers.

shared with the parents. A child may also be **accommodated** by the local authority under voluntary arrangements with the child's parents. In these circumstances the parents will retain parental responsibility acting so far as possible as partners of the local authority. Where a child is looked after by a local authority day-to-day responsibility may be with foster parents, residential care workers or guardians.

Key principles in communicating and working in partnership with parents

2:6 Positive attitudes to parents, user-friendly information and procedures and awareness of support needs are important. There should be no presumption about what parents can or cannot do to support their children's learning. Stereotypic views of parents are unhelpful and should be challenged. All staff should bear in mind the pressures a parent may be under because of the child's needs.

2:7 To make communications effective professionals should:

- acknowledge and draw on parental knowledge and expertise in relation to their child
- focus on the children's strengths as well as areas of additional need
- recognise the personal and emotional investment of parents and be aware of their feelings
- ensure that parents understand procedures, are aware of how to access support in preparing their contributions, and are given documents to be discussed well before meetings
- respect the validity of differing perspectives and seek constructive ways of reconciling different viewpoints
- respect the differing needs parents themselves may have, such as a disability, or communication and linguistic barriers
- recognise the need for flexibility in the timing and structure of meetings.

2:8 LEAs and schools should always seek parental permission before referring them to others for support (for example the local parent partnership service). Where parents do not wish to have their details passed on to third parties their wishes should be respected.

2:9 When a child attends a residential school, or is 'looked after' by the local authority and is living away from home, every effort should be made to ensure that parents are encouraged to continue to play an active role in their children's education. Parents' participation in assessment and reviews when a child is away from home is particularly important, because of the need to forward plan for when the child or young person returns to their own community.

Schools working in partnership with parents

2:10 The school is often the first point of contact for parents. Parents should be fully involved in the school-based response for their child, understand the purpose of any intervention or programme of action, and be told about the parent partnership service when SEN are identified. Schools **must** tell parents when they first identify that a child has SEN. It is vitally important that schools welcome and encourage parents to participate from the outset and throughout their child's educational career at the school. Schools need to regularly review their policies to ensure that they encourage active partnership with parents and do not present barriers to participation. Schools should seek to actively work with their local parent partnership service.

2:11 Parents also have a responsibility to communicate effectively with professionals to support their children's education. In working with schools they should:

- communicate regularly with their child's school and alert them to any concerns they have about their child's learning or provision
- fulfil their obligations under home-school agreements which set out expectations of both sides.

Supporting parents during statutory assessment

2:12 The statutory assessment process can be difficult and challenging for parents. Parents should be fully involved in the discussion leading up to a school's decision to request a statutory assessment. In a minority of cases, the proposal to request a statutory assessment may be unexpected and create alarm or anxiety in the family. Whether the school or the parents make a request for a statutory assessment, when a proposed statement is issued the parents will need comprehensive information on the full range of local provision. They may also need additional information and support in visiting schools in order to make an informed choice.

LEAs working in partnership with parents

2:13 LEAs need to ensure that:

- they are accessible, welcoming and value the views and involvement of parents
- information is available in a range of appropriate languages and variety of mediums, so that all parents for whom English is not their first language, and those with a disability or learning difficulties can access the information.

2:14 LEAs should work in partnership with local parent and voluntary organisations, as well as the parent partnership service, to produce such materials and ensure that parents receive comprehensive, neutral, factual and appropriate advice.

Working in partnership with the voluntary sector

2:15 The voluntary sector has a unique and important contribution to make in supporting parents and providing a range of services for parents. Schools, LEAs and parent partnership services should ensure that families have information on the full range of support services in the voluntary sector within their area. In order that voluntary organisations can play an effective role, LEAs and schools should regularly involve the voluntary sector in consultations, training days and information exchanges. Voluntary groups can be represented on Early Years Development and Child Care Partnerships and participate in a range of consultative activities on local steering or advisory groups relating to the parent partnership service.

Parent partnership services

> **A local education authority must arrange for the parent of any child in their area with special educational needs to be provided with advice and information about matters relating to those needs.**
>
> **LEAs must take whatever steps they consider appropriate to make parent partnership services known to parents, head teachers, schools and others they consider appropriate.**
>
> See Section 332A, Education Act 1996

2:16 All LEAs **must** make arrangements for parent partnership services. It is essential that parents are aware of the parent partnership service so that they know where they can obtain the information and advice they need. LEAs **must** therefore inform parents, schools and others about the arrangements for the service and how they can access it. LEAs **must** also remind parents about the parent partnership service and the availability of disagreement resolution services at the time a proposed statement or amendment notice is issued (see Chapter Eight).

2:17 LEAs do not necessarily have to provide a parent partnership service themselves. They may provide an entirely LEA-based parent partnership service if they wish, or 'buy-in' the service from another provider, or they may choose a mix of the two. In establishing parent partnership services, LEAs are encouraged to work with voluntary groups and organisations to deliver the services which best meet the needs of parents. Where the service is provided 'in-house', LEAs are encouraged to nevertheless ensure they are run at arms' length to ensure parental confidence. However the service is provided, LEAs should meet the **minimum standards** set out below.

2:18 In delivering effective parent partnership services LEAs are expected to:

- take responsibility for setting and monitoring the overall standard of the service and ensure it is subject to Best Value principles
- set out their funding and budgeting plans for the service (where appropriate the budget should be delegated to the parent partnership service)
- ensure adequate resources and staffing to meet the needs of the parents in their area
- ensure appropriate management structures for the service
- ensure that the service has a development plan which sets out clear targets and is regularly reviewed; such plans should specify short, medium and long term strategies and arrangements for evaluation and quality assurance
- ensure that the service is flexible and responsive to local changes
- ensure that parents and schools are provided with clear information about the parent partnership service, and about the various other sources of support in their area, including statutory and voluntary agencies
- ensure that the service is provided with accurate information on all SEN processes as set out in the Education Act 1996, relevant Regulations, the SEN Code of Practice and relevant information about the Disability Discrimination Act 1995
- ensure, where the service is provided in-house, that the staff receive appropriate initial and ongoing training and development to enable them to carry out their role effectively
- establish, where the service is outsourced either wholly or partially, a service level agreement for delivering the service which ensures sufficient levels of resources and training, and clearly set out the quality standards expected of, and the responsibilities delegated to, the provider
- have, irrespective of whether it is outsourced or provided in-house, appropriate arrangements for overseeing and regularly monitoring and reviewing the service, taking account of best practice both locally and nationally
- develop co-operative arrangements with the voluntary sector to ensure the mutual exchange of information and expertise
- promote and facilitate arrangements for the service to work in partnership with other agencies such as health and social services, using local planning structures such as the Education Development Plan, Early Years Development and Childcare Plan, Connexions Plan and Children's Service Plan. Provisions under the Health Act 1999 allow LEAs and health and social services to pool budgetary and management resources; such arrangements might therefore include the provision of joint information services
- actively seek feedback from the service and service users to inform and influence decisions on SEN policies, procedures and practices in order to improve communications and minimise the potential for misunderstandings and disagreements.

2:19 The aim of parent partnership services is to ensure parents of children with additional needs – including the very young – have access to information, advice and guidance in relation to the special educational needs of their children so they can make appropriate, informed decisions. The service should provide advice to the parents of all children with special educational needs not only those with statements. The prime role of parent partnership services is to help parents whose children have been identified as having special educational needs. However, there will be cases where parents believe that their child has special educational needs, but the school takes a different view. Parent partnership services should be flexible in their approach and handle such cases sensitively and sympathetically. They should consider parents' concerns carefully, try to help and support parents who want information, and not dismiss out of hand any enquiries for assistance or information.

2:20 Parent partnership services are expected to provide a range of flexible services, including access to an Independent Parental Supporter for all parents who want one, and referral to other agencies, voluntary organisations or parent support groups, which can offer advice and support. However, such referrals should only be made when there is prior agreement with the parent, and with the organisation or support group concerned about the nature and level of the service to be offered.

2:21 An effective parent partnership service is expected to meet the following **minimum standards** and ensure:

- the provision of a range of flexible services including using their best endeavours to provide access to an Independent Parental Supporter for all parents who want one
- that practical support is offered to parents, either individually or in groups, to help them in their discussions with schools, LEAs and other statutory agencies
- that parents (including all those with parental responsibility for the child) are provided with accurate, neutral information on their rights, roles and responsibilities within the SEN process, and on the wide range of options that are available for their children's education
- that parents are informed about other agencies, such as Health Services, Social Services and voluntary organisations, which can offer information and advice about their child's particular SEN. This may be particularly important at the time the LEA issues a proposed statement
- that, where appropriate and in conjunction with their parents, the ascertainable views and wishes of the child are sought and taken into consideration
- that information about the available services is publicised widely in the area using a variety of means
- the provision of neutral, accurate information for parents on all SEN procedures as set out in SEN legislation and the SEN Code of Practice
- the interpretation of information published by schools, LEAs and other bodies interested in SEN

- that a wide range of information for parents is available in community languages, and to parents who may not be able to gain access to information through conventional means
- that advice on special educational needs procedures is made available to parents through information, support and training
- they use their best endeavours to recruit sufficient Independent Parental Supporters to meet the needs of parents in their area, including arrangements for appropriate training, ensuring that they are kept up to date with all relevant aspects of SEN policy and procedures so that they can fulfil their role effectively
- that training on good communication and relationships with parents is made available to teachers, governors and staff in SEN sections of the LEA
- they work with schools, LEA officers and other agencies to help them develop positive relationships with parents
- they establish and maintain links with voluntary organisations
- that parents' views are heard and understood, and inform and influence the development of local SEN policy and practice
- the regular review of the effectiveness of the service they provide, for instance by seeking feedback from users.

Preventing and resolving disagreements

A local education authority must make arrangements, that include the appointment of independent persons, with a view to avoiding or resolving disagreements between authorities (on the one hand) and parents of children in their area (on the other) about the way LEAs and maintained schools carry out their responsibilities towards children with special educational needs.

A local education authority must also make arrangements with a view to avoiding or resolving disagreements between parents and certain schools about the special educational provision made for their child.

LEAs must take whatever steps they consider appropriate to make disagreement resolution services known to parents, head teachers, schools and others they consider appropriate.

See Section 332B, Education Act 1996

2:22 Parent partnership services can help to prevent difficulties from developing into disagreements. LEAs may helpfully see their parent partnership service as the main approach to preventing disagreements from arising. Using this service is purely voluntary.

2:23 Parents may wish to access the local disagreement resolution procedures at any time during the SEN process, including where there is a disagreement with the school about any aspect of their child's special educational provision.

2:24 All LEAs must provide disagreement resolution services. They should demonstrate independence and credibility in working towards early and informal resolution of disagreements. It is essential that parents are aware of the arrangements and how and when they can access them. LEAs must therefore inform parents, schools, and others about the arrangements for the service and how they can access it. Parents who have a right of appeal to the SEN Tribunal continue to be able to exercise that right at any stage. LEAs must inform parents in writing that their legal right to appeal is not affected by entering into disagreement resolution. Disagreement resolution can run alongside the appeals process.

2:25 In delivering an effective disagreement resolution service, and in meeting the following **minimum standards**, LEAs:

- should take responsibility for the overall standard of the service and ensure it is subject to Best Value principles
- should have clear funding and budgeting plans for the service
- should ensure that the service is neutral and must involve an independent element
- should ensure that the service, whether outsourced or provided in-house, has a development plan which sets out clear targets and is regularly reviewed. Such plans should specify arrangements for evaluation and quality assurance
- must make the arrangements for disagreement resolution and how they will work known to parents, schools and others they consider appropriate
- must inform parents about the arrangements for disagreement resolution at the time a proposed statement or amended statement is issued, and that entering disagreement resolution does not affect their right of appeal to the SEN Tribunal
- should ensure that the independent persons appointed as facilitators have the appropriate skills, knowledge and expertise in disagreement resolution; an understanding of SEN processes, procedures and legislation; have no role in the decisions taken about a particular case, nor any vested interest in the terms of the settlement; are unbiased; maintain confidentiality; carry out the process quickly and to the timetable decided by the parties
- should establish protocols and mechanisms for referring parents to disagreement resolution
- should ensure that those providing the service receive appropriate initial and ongoing training and development to enable them to carry out their role effectively
- should establish a service level agreement for delivering the service which ensures sufficient levels of resources and training, and sets out the appropriate standards expected of, and the responsibilities delegated to, the provider

- should have appropriate arrangements for overseeing, regularly monitoring and reviewing the service, taking account of local and national best practice whether the service is provided in-house or bought-in
- should actively seek feedback from the service to inform and influence decisions on SEN policies, procedures and practices
- should monitor and evaluate the performance of the service.

2:26 The aim of informal disagreement resolution arrangements is to prevent the development of long-term problems thus reducing, in time, the number of appeals going to the SEN Tribunal. Confidence in disagreement resolution arrangements will be greatest when all concerned consider that the service offered is genuinely independent. Most importantly disagreement resolution should ensure that practical educational solutions – acceptable to all parties – are reached as quickly as possible ensuring the minimum disruption to the children's education.

2:27 It is envisaged that a facilitator will bring together all of the parties in a non-threatening environment, to seek to resolve the disagreement through discussion and negotiation. The facilitator is not there to determine the outcome. Rather all parties need to openly discuss the issues and the full range of options available, and seek to agree how to resolve the disagreement. Disagreement resolution can be entered into at any point, but will be more commonly used when parents are dissatisfied with the proposed provision for their children. It is not envisaged that the various parties would require legal representation at this stage; that would be contrary to the spirit of informal disagreement resolution. All participants, including the child, need to feel confident that their views and concerns will receive equal respect. The purpose of disagreement resolution is not to apportion blame but to achieve a solution to a difference of views in the best interest of the child.

2:28 It is essential that independent persons appointed to facilitate disagreement resolution have a range of experience, knowledge and qualifications, for instance:

- training and experience in disagreement resolution
- counselling and negotiation skills
- the ability to establish and maintain communications
- knowledge of SEN legislation and framework, the SEN Code of Practice and other educational issues.

2:29 There are a number of models that LEAs might adopt to include an independent element in their disagreement resolution arrangements, for instance:

- using a panel of trained facilitators, affiliated to a recognised body in the field of disagreement resolution. LEAs could then buy the services as they were required
- expanding existing disagreement resolution services that cover a wide range of areas across the work of the authority to include SEN expertise

- using regional panels funded by a number of neighbouring LEAs, perhaps using the SEN Regional Partnerships LEAs within the region would then have access to a pool of facilitators.

2:30 Many organisations have expertise in disagreement resolution and can be a valuable resource in providing trained and experienced independent facilitators. LEAs should therefore consider working in partnership with other organisations in making their arrangements for disagreement resolution services.

Roles and responsibilities

2:31 The following table sets out the different roles and responsibilities of local authorities, schools and the voluntary sector. The text in bold denotes statutory duties. Additional guidance about parent partnerships and disagreement resolution can be found in the SEN Toolkit. Detailed guidance about roles and responsibilities concerning parents and particular circumstances is included throughout subsequent chapters of this Code.

Roles and Responsibilities of Local Education Authorities:

All LEAs have a statutory duty to provide parent partnership services, but they do not have to deliver the services themselves.

- Parents and schools should receive clear information about services and providers (including where relevant the involvement of voluntary groups).
- LEAs may wish to develop consultation arrangements with voluntary organisations and parent support groups to ensure that they are aware of local policies and procedures for children with SEN. They should be aware that voluntary groups can make a positive contribution to the development and review of SEN policies and practices.
- LEAs have responsibility for the provision of a wide range of information material for parents.
- LEAs should inform all parents that all maintained schools are required to publish their SEN policy.

All LEAs must provide disagreement resolution arrangements that can demonstrate independence and credibility in working towards early and informal dispute resolution. The early resolution of disputes can prevent long-term problems.

- Disagreement resolution arrangements must include the appointment of persons who are independent of the LEA, the parents, and the professionals involved.

Roles and Responsibilities of the Voluntary Sector:

- Voluntary groups could encourage schools and local authorities to develop partnerships with them, by explaining what services they can offer parents and carers.
- Voluntary groups can facilitate information and explain procedures to parents and talk them through the options available to them.
- Voluntary groups could take a proactive role in parent partnerships. They could develop a sense of ownership, seeking representation on advisory groups and other consultative activities. They could share their experiences of best practice and encourage schools and LEAs to adopt them.

Roles and responsibilities of Schools:

- Teachers, SENCOs, pastoral and other staff all have an important role in developing positive and constructive relationships with parents.
- Schools should accept and value the contribution of parents and encourage their participation. Every effort should be made to identify how parents prefer to work with schools, with the recognition that some families will require both practical help and emotional support if they are to play a key role in the education of their children.
- Schools should seek to develop partnerships with local parent support groups or voluntary organisations.

All maintained schools must publish their SEN policy.

- Schools should have a clear and flexible strategy for working with and encouraging parents to play an active role in the education of their children.
- In publishing the school's SEN policy, the school should seek to ensure it is presented in parent friendly formats.

Roles and responsibilities of the Parent Partnership Service

- Provision of flexible services for parents, including access to other agencies and organisations, and, for all parents who want one, access to an Independent Parental Supporter.
- Provision of accurate, neutral information on parents rights, roles and responsibilities within the SEN process, and on the wide range of options available, to enable them to make informed decisions.
- Training for parents, Independent Parental Supporters and school staff.
- Working with schools, LEA officers and other agencies to help them develop positive relationships with parents.
- Establishing and maintaining links with voluntary organisations.
- Ensuring that parents' views inform and influence the development of local SEN policy and practice.

3 Pupil Participation

Introduction

> **Children, who are capable of forming views, have a right to receive and make known information, to express an opinion, and to have that opinion taken into account in any matters affecting them. The views of the child should be given due weight according to the age, maturity and capability of the child.**
>
> See Articles 12 and 13, The United Nations Convention on the Rights of the Child

3:1 All children and young people have rights. Most references to rights are about what is due to children from others, particularly from their parents and the state and its agencies. This chapter is about the right of children with special educational needs to be involved in making decisions and exercising choices.

3:2 Children and young people with special educational needs have a unique knowledge of their own needs and circumstances and their own views about what sort of help they would like to help them make the most of their education. They should, where possible, participate in all the decision-making processes that occur in education including the setting of learning targets and contributing to IEPs, discussions about choice of schools, contributing to the assessment of their needs and to the annual review and transition processes. They should feel confident that they will be listened to and that their views are valued. However there is "a fine balance between giving the child a voice and encouraging them to make informed decisions, and overburdening them with decision-making procedures where they have insufficient experience and knowledge to make appropriate judgements without additional support."[14]

3:3 Ascertaining the child's views may not always be easy. Very young children and those with severe communication difficulties, for example, may present a significant challenge for education, health and other professionals. But the principle of seeking and taking account of the ascertainable views of the child or young person is an important one. Their perceptions and experiences can be invaluable to professionals in reaching decisions. LEAs, schools and early education settings should make arrangements to enable this to happen.

Pupils and parents

3:4 Many schools have already developed policies and procedures that encourage pupil involvement. This may be easier to achieve where there are strong and explicit procedures for involving children and their families at all levels in the life of the school. Home – School, agreements offer an important opportunity to ensure that pupils as well as parents understand their rights and responsibilities with regard to their schools.

3:5 Some parents may need support in seeing their children as partners in education; they may be reluctant to involve their child in education decision-making perhaps considering them ill-equipped to grasp all the relevant factors. If the parents' experience of working with professionals has been disappointing, or they perceive their views as being marginalised, they may suspect that professionals may give undue weight to the views

14 From The Children Act 1989 Guidance and Regulations, Vol. 6. Children with Disabilities (1991), HMSO.

of their children. LEAs, schools and settings should show sensitivity, honesty and mutual respect in encouraging pupils to share concerns, discuss strategies and see themselves as equal partners with the school. In instances where parents and pupils may have different views about the origins of and provision for a special educational need these principles will be even more essential to ensure constructive discussions.

Pupil participation in schools and other settings

3:6 All children should be involved in making decisions where possible right from the start of their education. The ways in which children are encouraged to participate should reflect the child's evolving maturity. Participation in education is a process that will necessitate all children being given the opportunity to make choices and to understand that their views matter. Very young children can be encouraged to choose and to share their wishes and feelings with families and staff. The Early Learning Goals recognise the importance of children's ability to develop competency and confidence progressively and to have opportunities to develop a range of social as well as educational skills. Confident young children, who know that their opinions will be valued and who can practice making choices, will be more secure and effective pupils during the school years.

3:7 Practitioners should ensure that where an Individual Education Plan (IEP) is developed the child is involved at an appropriate level. Consultation with young children will necessitate a range of communication strategies, including the use of play, art, audio and video as well as verbal communication. Child development centres, therapy services, social services family centres, day care or other non-educational provision will already know many young children with special educational needs. Partnership between providers will be important in ensuring that the child is encouraged to share their views through the most appropriate adult, and to address any special communication needs.

3:8 Classroom organisation in the primary phase should include opportunities for choice and decision-making for all children for at least some part of the school day. Such opportunities should ensure that children have sufficient time and encouragement to state their views and to learn how to explain the reasons for their preferences.

3:9 Pupil participation should be the goal for all children and opportunities for such participation should expand as pupils develop. From an early age, children with SEN should be actively involved at an appropriate level in discussions about their IEPs, including target setting and review arrangements and have their views recorded. Children should be encouraged to share in the recording process and in monitoring and evaluating their own performance.

3:10 Children and young people who attend special schools should be offered the same opportunities for involvement and participation as their peers in mainstream schools. They may need additional support or time to practice expressing their views. Teachers will need to be sensitive to their views and wishes and ensure that as they mature their opportunities to participate are fully exploited.

3:11 Many children will have their special educational needs first identified during the primary phase of education. Schools should be sensitive to the level of understanding and feelings of the child, and provide appropriate information in a non-stigmatising way. If children are involved in the IEP process, then achievements can be noted and celebrated as well as any difficulties clarified and addressed. Recognition of success for all children is integral to the life of all primary schools and successes in meeting targets in IEPs should also be acknowledged.

3:12 Some children will have contact with a range of professionals such as support and advisory teachers, educational psychologists, therapists, social workers and health professionals, who should listen to the child's views and record those views within any reports or reviews.

3:13 Where children have attended a primary school that encouraged pupil participation and sought their views on a range of issues, it will be possible to build upon these positive experiences in the secondary sector. Pastoral programmes should ensure that all pupils are involved in and can contribute to both their own education and the wider life of the school. Many schools have school councils or other mechanisms for including and representing all pupils in the organisation and management of the school. All schools should ensure that pupils with special educational needs are fully involved in all aspects of the life of the school and are enabled to have an equal voice. Some young people may need additional support and encouragement, either from a peer or from an adult, in order to participate fully.

3:14 Pupils with special educational needs should become progressively more involved in setting and evaluating targets within the IEP process. Young people with special educational needs may have low self-esteem and lack confidence. Actively encouraging these pupils to track their own progress and record achievement within a programme of action designed to meet their particular learning or behavioural difficulty will contribute to improved confidence and self-image.

3:15 Pupils' views should be sought and recorded as part of the statutory annual review process where possible, as well as within the IEP and any other assessment and review. Some young people may wish for personal support and may prefer to express their views through a parent or other family member or an independent supporter such as an advocate, Connexions Personal Adviser, counsellor, social worker or health professional or through peer support. These preferences should be taken seriously. This flexible approach will be effective so long as the school ensures that the support is properly co-ordinated.

3:16 A child's views can be ascertained at other times as well as during consultation, formal choice and decision-making. Adults can encourage self-advocacy by responding to the messages the child gives. For example, if a pupil's choice of subjects in year 9 does not reflect their expressed interests and aptitudes staff should notice and follow this up. Pupils who are experiencing discrimination or particular barriers to learning because of their special needs should be encouraged to discuss what they would like done about this. By year 9 when the Transition Plan is prepared for those young people with a statement, most young people should be ready to play a constructive role in the transition review process. For some pupils, this may still be through an appropriate adult who records their views. But many pupils will be able and eager to attend the review meeting and to express their views and preferences directly, if they have had relevant information and time for preparation beforehand. Planning for transition necessitates young people being offered accurate information on the options available to them.

3:17 Relationships between parents and pupils may be sensitive at the time of the year 9 review where transition planning is an integral part of the process. Many parents will feel anxious about post-school options and may be worried about their children's expectations being raised unreasonably about post-school provision and career choices. Other parents may be anxious about the level of support available in the post-school sector. Parents and pupils should have their views listened to and recorded separately and with respect for any differences of opinion. The year 9 annual review offers an opportunity for all concerned to address concerns and to identify any special support in order to achieve the pupil's goals. Planning for transition necessitates young people being encouraged to have high aspirations, offered accurate information on the options available to them, and invited to say what other options they would like considered. Connexions Personal Advisers (PAs) will have particular skills in working with young people and their parents, encouraging participation post-16 and in identifying suitable post-16 opportunities.

Involving pupils in assessment and decision making

3:18 Children and young people may feel anxious and confused about the purpose of an assessment. They may be concerned about the particular practicalities or possible stigma attached to any special support or programme of work and they may be worried about their longer-term future. Schools and professionals therefore need to:

- provide clear and accurate information about the child's special educational needs and the purpose of any assessment, individual education plan or any intervention
- help the pupil to understand the agreed outcomes of any intervention and how they can be a partner in working towards the goals. Pupils who play an active part in assessment and in developing and monitoring agreed targets will also have greater self esteem and feel confident that they are making progress
- explain clearly what additional support or assessment arrangements are being made and how the pupil can contribute to them
- consult pupils who need individual support (whether through equipment or a learning support assistant) to ensure that such support is provided in a timely and sensitive way and enables them to fully participate in learning
- recognise the potential stress of assessment and review arrangements and do their best to ensure that the pupil understands the role and contribution of any other professionals from the educational psychology service, child health or social services and Connexions Service, who may be involved
- draw upon the experience of any local pupil support or advocacy services for children which might offer additional advice and assistance
- ensure that the pupil has access to a designated member of staff with whom they can discuss any difficulties or concerns. It is important that they can feel confident to share any anxieties at an early stage
- be aware that many pupils may already be in contact with other professionals in child health, mental health, social services or other agencies.

3:19 Parents can assist staff with these goals. In some instances, a pupil may be 'looked after' by the local authority and may not have natural parents to provide support.[15] Good communication with the local authority in question will be essential to ensure that the pupil is given positive support and that carers are able and willing to contribute to any educational assessment or programme. The pupil will need to know and understand when the social worker or carer is acting as the corporate parent and when they are acting as advocate for the child.

3:20 Schools and education authorities should be aware of the wider range of participation and advocacy services for children and young people and their families being developed in partnership with health and social services departments.

The LEA's role in pupil participation

3:21 The LEA has a critical role in encouraging and supporting pupil participation across all phases of education. Some LEAs already consult children and young people with special educational needs about how the whole system of assessment, planning and review might be improved to make it more user-friendly, and how they wish to be consulted. LEAs may wish to discuss consultation with children and young people with the relevant health and social services departments and local voluntary organisations.

3:22 Both school and LEA staff will need information and training on consulting children and young people with communication difficulties. LEAs may wish to develop training options to build the confidence and competence of all staff in working with children, however complex their needs. Learning support staff have a critical role in supporting many children and their training should include an element on pupil participation and the development of communication skills.

3:23 Participation of pupils will be facilitated if the LEA works with all concerned, including schools, pupils and parents, in order to develop user-friendly information for children and young people. Such information may take the form of printed, video or taped information and may be provided in alternative and augmentative communication systems.

3:24 Because some children will need additional support in order to participate in any education decision-making, it is important that the LEA can signpost schools and relevant professionals to different sources.

Providing special support

3:25 It is important to avoid making assumptions about levels of understanding, particularly amongst very young children and older children with learning, communication or sensory difficulties. These children may need additional help to be able to make their views and wishes known and efforts should be made to arrange for this help to be provided where it is needed.

3:26 Pupil participation will not only depend upon the quality of educational experience and support offered. Children's progress may be directly affected by anxieties about a special health need or the management of personal care. Pupils should be given the opportunity to talk in private if necessary about their concerns and appropriate action should be taken.

3:27 Further advice on ways of enabling pupil participation is set out in the SEN Toolkit.

---

15 DfEE/DH Guidance on the Education of Children and Young People in Public Care. May 2000

4 Identification, Assessment and Provision in Early Education Settings

Introduction

4:1 Early Years Development and Childcare Partnerships (EYDCP) bring together private, voluntary and independent settings in receipt of Government funding to provide early education, with LEAs, Social Services departments, health services and parent representatives in the planning and provision of services in the early education sector.

4:2 There is a diverse range of early education providers eligible for Government funding including maintained mainstream and special schools, maintained nursery schools, independent schools, non-maintained special schools, local authority daycare providers such as day nurseries and family centres, other registered daycare providers such as pre-schools, playgroups and private day nurseries, local authority Portage schemes and accredited childminders working as part of an approved network.

4:3 All early education settings in receipt of government funding are required to have regard to the Code of Practice. This duty is set out in section 313(2) of the Education Act 1996 (in relation to governing bodies and LEAs), and section 4(1) of the Nursery Education and Grant Maintained Schools Act 1996 and section 123 of the School Standards and Framework Act 1998 (in relation to other early education providers).

4:4 All providers delivering Government funded early education are expected to have a written SEN policy. Partnerships with schools and between early education settings are an excellent method of sharing best practice. Such partnership arrangements will be particularly supportive for accredited childminders who are part of an approved network who may wish to work together to develop their SEN policy.

Provision in the early years

4:5 Wherever it occurs, early education provision is part of the foundation stage of education for children aged 3–5 years. During this time most children experience rapid physical, emotional, intellectual and social growth. For many children the early education setting will provide their first experience of learning within a peer group. The QCA publication 'Curriculum guidance for the foundation stage'[16] provides advice for early education practitioners on providing learning and teaching experiences of the highest quality throughout the foundation stage, whilst allowing a flexible response to the particular needs of the children.

4:6 Practitioners should work closely with all parents to listen to their views so as to build on children's previous experiences, knowledge, understanding and skills, and provide opportunities to develop in six areas of learning:

- personal, social and emotional development
- communication, language and literacy
- mathematical development
- knowledge and understanding of the world

---

16 QCA/00/587

- physical development
- creative development.

4:7 The Government's Early Learning Goals set out what most children will have achieved in each of these areas by the end of the foundation stage/school reception year. They represent the expected outcomes of a planned approach to early education that integrates play and learning. Children will progress at different rates during the foundation stage. By the end of the stage, some will have achieved beyond the expectations set out in the Early Learning Goals, whilst others may still be working towards the goals.

4:8 Children making slower progress may include those who are learning English as an additional language or who have particular learning difficulties. It should not be assumed that children who are making slower progress must, therefore, have special educational needs. But such children will need carefully differentiated learning opportunities to help them progress and regular and frequent careful monitoring of their progress.

Graduated response

4:9 Monitoring of individual children's progress throughout the foundation stage is essential. Where a child appears not to be making progress either generally or in a specific aspect of learning, then it may be necessary to present different opportunities or use alternative approaches to learning. Ongoing difficulties may indicate the need for a level of help above that which is normally available for children in the particular early education setting.

4:10 Good practice can take many forms. It is for individual settings to decide the exact procedures they should adopt, and the nature and content of the special educational provision. Early education settings should adopt a graduated response so as to be able to provide specific help to individual young children. This approach recognises that there is a continuum of special educational needs and, where necessary, brings increasing specialist expertise to bear on the difficulties a child may be experiencing.

4:11 The graduated approach, as described in this Code, should be firmly based within the setting. Once practitioners have identified that a child has special educational needs, the setting should intervene through *Early Years Action*. If the intervention does not enable the child to make satisfactory progress the SENCO may need to seek advice and support from external agencies. These forms of intervention are referred to below as *Early Years Action Plus*.

4:12 As most settings are in day-to-day contact with parents they are best placed to judge how to tell parents that their child is receiving special educational provision because their child has SEN. It should be done in a way that encourages parents to contribute their knowledge and understanding of their child, and raise any concerns they may have about their child's needs and the provision that is being made for them.

4:13 The key test for action is evidence that the child's current rate of progress is inadequate. There should not be an assumption that all children will progress at the same rate. A judgement has to be made in each case as to what it is reasonable to expect that particular child to achieve. Where progress is not adequate, it will be necessary to take some <u>additional</u> or <u>different</u> action to enable the child to learn more effectively. Whatever the level of pupils' difficulties, the key test of how far their learning needs are being met is whether they are making adequate progress.

4.14 Adequate progress can be defined in a number of ways. It might, for instance, be progress that:

- closes the attainment gap between the child and the child's peers
- prevents the attainment gap growing wider
- is similar to that of peers starting from the same attainment baseline, but less than that of the majority of peers
- matches or betters the child's previous rate of progress
- ensures access to the full curriculum
- demonstrates an improvement in self-help, social or personal skills
- demonstrates improvements in the pupil's behaviour.

The Role of the SENCO

4:15 Early education settings, except specialist SEN provision, will need to identify a member of staff to act as the special educational needs coordinator (SENCO)[17]. In the case of accredited childminders who are part of an approved network, the SENCO role may be shared between individual childminders and the coordinator of the network. The SENCO should have responsibility for:

- **ensuring liaison with parents and other professionals in respect of children with special educational needs**
- **advising and supporting other practitioners in the setting**
- **ensuring that appropriate Individual Education Plans are in place**
- **ensuring that relevant background information about individual children with special educational needs is collected, recorded and updated.**

4:16 The SENCO should take the lead in further assessment of the child's particular strengths and weaknesses; in planning future support for the child in discussion with colleagues; and in monitoring and subsequently reviewing the action taken. The SENCO should also ensure that appropriate records are kept including a record of children at *Early Years Action* and *Early Years Action Plus* and those with statements. The practitioner usually responsible for the child should remain responsible for working with the child on a daily basis and for planning and delivering an individualised programme. Parents should always be consulted and kept informed of the action taken to help the child, and of the outcome of this action.[18]

---

17 The reference to the SENCO should be taken to mean any practitioner who acts in the capacity of SEN coordinator; this may be the head of the setting.

18 The role of the SENCO set out in this chapter applies to all settings in receipt of Government funding to provide early education except for LEA maintained nursery schools where the SENCO role will be similar to that in the primary phase.

Time required for SEN Coordination

4:17 The setting's management group and the head of the setting should give careful thought to the SENCO's time allocation in the light of the Code and in the context of the resources available to the setting. Settings may find it effective for the SENCO to be a member of the senior management team.

Individual Records

4:18 In addition to the information that all settings will record for all children, the pupil record or profile for a child with SEN should include information about the child's progress and behaviour from the early education setting itself, from the parents, and from health and social services. It might also include the child's own perception of any difficulties and how they might be addressed. It may also be necessary to record in the profile information about the child's needs in relation to the general strategies to be used to enable access to an appropriate curriculum and, in a reception class, the school day.

4:19 The information collected should reveal the different perceptions of those concerned with the child, any immediate educational concerns and an overall picture of the child's strengths and weaknesses.

Early Years Action

4:20 When an early education practitioner who works day-to-day with the child, or the SENCO, identifies a child with special educational needs, they should devise interventions that are additional to or different from those provided as part of the setting's usual curriculum offer and strategies (*Early Years Action*).

4:21 The triggers for intervention through *Early Years Action* could be the practitioner's or parent's concern about a child who despite receiving appropriate early education experiences:

- makes little or no progress even when teaching approaches are particularly targeted to improve the child's identified area of weakness
- continues working at levels significantly below those expected for children of a similar age in certain areas
- presents persistent emotional and/or behavioural difficulties, which are not ameliorated by the behaviour management techniques usually employed in the setting
- has sensory or physical problems, and continues to make little or no progress despite the provision of personal aids and equipment
- has communication and/or interaction difficulties, and requires specific individual interventions in order to access learning.

4:22 If practitioners in consultation with parents conclude that a child may need further support to help them progress, staff should seek the help of the SENCO.

4:23 As an important part of the *Early Years Action* the SENCO and colleagues should collect all known information about the child and seek additional new information from the parents. In some cases outside professionals from health, social services or the education psychology service may already be involved with the child. The SENCO should build on the existing knowledge of the child; multi-agency input is often very significant for young children. The educational psychologist can have a key role in assessment and intervention and in providing support and advice to parents. Educational psychologists can help teachers and parents *notice* children's individual needs and help them to adjust their response accordingly. In such cases it is good practice for these professionals to liaise with the early education settings and keep them informed of the work in progress. Where these professionals have not already been working with practitioners, the SENCO should contact them if parents agree.

4:24 Parents are the prime source of information in many cases. The information collected can be maintained as part of the child's individual record that will also include previous observations on the child made as part of the regular assessment and recording systems within the early education setting. Settings should make sure that parents are as fully involved as possible with their child's education and should always be kept fully informed about how the setting is seeking to meet their child's needs.

4:25 Children with a learning difficulty or developmental delay, and whose parents do not have English as a first language, do not have fluent English, or are disabled are likely to be particularly disadvantaged if any special educational needs are not identified at the earliest possible stage. Parents may be unable to voice their own concerns because of a lack of a means of communication with the early education provider. Where such difficulties occur, LEAs should ensure that parents and relevant professionals are provided with access to signers or interpreters and translated information material, so that early concerns may be shared about the child's behaviour, health and development. Bilingual support staff, teachers of English as an additional language and teachers of the deaf may be able to help. Parent partnership services, discussed fully in Chapter Two, will also be a source of advice and support. Without such support early identification and intervention may be delayed or ineffective.

Nature of intervention

4:26 The SENCO and the child's teacher, in consultation with parents, should decide on the *Action* needed to help the child to progress in the light of their earlier assessment. There is sometimes an expectation that *Action* will comprise support in the form of the deployment of extra staff to enable one-to-one tuition to be given to the child. This may not be the most appropriate way of helping the child. The *Action* should enable the very young child with special educational needs to learn and progress to the maximum possible. The key lies in effective individualised arrangements for learning and teaching. The resources might be extra adult time in devising the nature of the planned intervention and monitoring its effectiveness; the provision of different learning materials or special equipment; some individual or group support or staff development and training to introduce more effective strategies. Speedy access to LEA support services for one-off or occasional advice on strategies or equipment or for staff training may make it possible to provide effective intervention without the need for regular or ongoing input from external agencies.

Individual Education Plans

4:27 Strategies employed to enable the child to progress should be recorded within an Individual Education Plan (IEP); this should include information about the short-term targets set for the child, the teaching strategies and the provision to be put in place, when the plan is to be reviewed, and the outcome of the action taken. The IEP should only record that which is additional to or different from the differentiated curriculum plan that is in place as part of normal provision. The IEP should be crisply written and focus on three or four key targets. IEPs should be discussed with parents and the child.

Reviewing IEPs

4:28 Ideally IEPs should be continually kept 'under review,' and in such circumstances there cannot simply be a 'fixed term' or a formal meeting for reviews. However IEPs should be reviewed regularly and at least three times a year. Reviews need not be unduly formal, but parents' views on the child's progress should be sought, and they should be consulted as part of the review process. Further advice on IEPs and on involving pupils can be found in the SEN Toolkit.

Early Years Action Plus

4:29 *Early Years Action Plus* is characterised by the involvement of external support services who can help early education settings with advice on new IEPs and targets, provide more specialist assessments, give advice on the use of new or specialist strategies or materials, and in some cases provide support for particular activities. The kinds of advice and support available to early education settings will vary according to local policies. LEAs have the power, under section 318(3) of the Education Act 1996 to supply goods and services to assist early education settings outside the maintained sector in supporting children eligible for Government funding who have special educational needs but do not have a statement.

4:30 A request for help from external services is likely to follow a decision taken by the SENCO and colleagues, in consultation with parents, at a meeting to review the child's IEP. The review should consider:

- has progress been made?
- what are the parents' views?
- is there a need for more information or advice about the child?

4:31 The triggers for referral for seeking help from outside agencies could be that, despite receiving an individualised programme and/or concentrated support, the child:

- continues to make little or no progress in specific areas over a long period
- continues working at an early years curriculum substantially below that expected of children of a similar age
- has emotional or behavioural difficulties which substantially and regularly interfere with the child's own learning or that of the group, despite having an individualised behaviour management programme

- has sensory or physical needs, and requires additional equipment or regular visits for direct intervention or advice by practitioners from a specialist service
- has ongoing communication or interaction difficulties that impede the development of social relationships and cause substantial barriers to learning.

4:32 Where an early education setting seeks the help of external support services, those services will need to see the records on the child held by the setting, in order to establish which strategies have already been employed and which targets have been set and achieved. They will usually then observe the child, in their educational setting if that is appropriate and practicable, so that they can advise on new and appropriate targets for the child's IEP and accompanying strategies.

Requests for statutory assessment

4:33 For a very few children the help given by the early education setting through *Action Plus* will not be sufficiently effective to enable the child to progress satisfactorily. It will then be necessary for the setting, in consultation with the parents and any external agencies already involved, to consider whether a statutory multi-disciplinary assessment may be appropriate.

4:34 Parents, schools and settings can make a request to the LEA for a statutory assessment. Settings in receipt of Government funding to provide early education, other than maintained nursery schools or nursery classes in maintained schools, currently only have a statutory right to request an assessment for four and five year olds for whom they provide nursery education (those children for whom the LEA must secure education under section 118 of the School Standards and Framework Act).[19] The LEA is then responsible for determining whether a statutory assessment is required.

4:35 Where a request for statutory assessment is made to an LEA, the child will have demonstrated significant cause for concern. The LEA will generally seek evidence that any strategy or programme implemented for the child in question has been continued for a reasonable period of time without success. The LEA will need clear documentation in relation to the child's special educational needs and any action taken to deal with those needs. Each LEA will have its own system of referral. In deciding whether to make an assessment for a particular child, LEAs should, wherever possible, take into account existing information including IEPs rather than asking for further fresh written evidence.

4:36 In a very few cases where there are severe and complex needs the extent of the child's needs will be evident. In such cases requests for assessment might be made prior to any early education intervention, and there should be no need for reports from all the agencies involved with the child before the LEA can reach a decision. The LEA should act on reports from the professionals most closely involved with the child.

19 By September 2004 LEAs' duties under section 118 will extend to three year olds. When this happens, the right to request assessments will automatically be extended to cover requests in respect of three year olds.

Child Health Services in the early years

> **Health Authorities and National Health Service (NHS) Trusts must inform the parents and the appropriate LEA when they form the opinion that a child under compulsory school age may have special educational needs. They must also inform the parents if they believe that a particular voluntary organisation is likely to be able to give the parents advice or assistance in connection with any special educational needs that the child may have.**
>
> See Section 332, Education Act 1996

4:37 The child health services must alert the parents and the LEA to the child's potential difficulties. A child development centre or team may provide a multi-professional view at an early stage. Early contact with child health services will be important in order to ensure that there is no physical cause for the difficulty in question (such as a hearing or visual impairment) or to secure advice on the possible cause and the effective management of difficult behaviour. Children's development and subsequent progress in school will also be affected by their general health status. All early education settings should be aware of how to obtain information and advice on health related matters, using the school health service, the child's general practitioner or a relevant member of the child development centre or team. Where a setting wants advice about a particular child they should ensure that parents have given consent to this being obtained.

4:38 Where a health authority or Trust (perhaps on the basis of information provided by a general practitioner) consider that a child might have special educational needs, they **must** inform the parents of their views and give the parents an opportunity to discuss those views with an officer of the health authority or Trust (usually a doctor who has appropriate knowledge and experience). They **must** then inform the relevant LEA.

Statutory assessment of children under compulsory school age

4:39 Chapter Seven sets out the statutory procedures for assessment. The time limits and other statutory procedures for deciding whether to carry out a multi-disciplinary assessment for a child under compulsory school age (and over two) and for making the assessment and producing a statement are the same as for children of school age.

4:40 The parents' perspective is particularly important when assessing the special educational needs of young children. LEAs should consider using explanatory leaflets or guidelines for parents to encourage their participation. Such information could also include an explanation of the support available for children within early education settings through *Early Years Action* and *Action Plus*, an explanation of parents' rights in relation to requesting a statutory assessment, and information about the circumstances in which the LEA would consider giving a child a statement. LEAs should also ensure that parents are offered the full range of parent partnership services as described in Chapter Two of this Code.

Criteria for statutory assessment of children under compulsory school age and over two

4:41 In deciding whether a statutory assessment is necessary for a child over two but under compulsory school age, where the child is attending an early education setting, the LEA should ask the following questions:

a. what difficulties have been identified by the setting? Have the practitioners provided individualised strategies through *Early Years Action* and *Early Years Action Plus* to assist the child?

b. has outside advice been sought, regarding the child's:

- physical health and functioning
- communication skills
- perceptual and motor skills
- self-help skills
- social skills
- emotional and behavioural development
- responses to learning experiences.
- have parental views been considered?

4:42 Where a child is not attending an early education setting the LEA should try to collect as much information as is possible before deciding whether to assess.

4:43 The LEA will then assess the evidence and decide whether the child's difficulties or developmental delays are likely to be addressed only through a statement of special educational needs. Where a child's educational needs appear to be sufficiently severe or complex as to require attention for much of the child's school life, or that the evidence points to the need for specialist early intervention that cannot be provided in the current setting, then the LEA is likely to conclude that an assessment is necessary.

Statements for children under compulsory school age and over two

4:44 Where children aged between two and five have such severe and complex needs that statutory procedures are essential in order to maximise their opportunities, the statement will follow the same format as for any other children. The contributions of non-educational service providers are likely to be of key importance.

4:45 LEAs should note that parents of children under five and over two may express a preference for a maintained school to be named in their child's statement. The LEA must name the school the parents name so long as it meets the criteria set out in Schedule 27 of the Education Act 1996. (See 8:58). A key issue is likely to be whether a school is suitable for the child's age. The parents may also make representations in favour of an independent, private or voluntary early education setting for their child. If the LEA considers such provision appropriate, it is entitled to specify this in the statement and if it does, must fund the provision. There is, however, no point in doing this for settings outside the maintained sector unless the setting agrees as the LEA cannot require an independent or voluntary setting to admit a child. The LEA should ensure that parents have full information on the range of provision available within the authority and may wish to offer parents the opportunity to visit such provision and discuss any aspect of the provision with the Named LEA Officer (see Glossary).

4:46 LEAs should consider informally reviewing a statement for a child under five at least every six months to ensure that the provision continues to be appropriate to the child's needs. Such reviews would complement the statutory duty to carry out an annual review in accordance with the Regulations but would not necessarily require the same range of documentation so long as they reflected the significant changes which can take place in the progress of a child under the age of five. If necessary the statement should be amended following a six monthly review.

Statutory assessment of children under two

If an LEA believe that a child in their area who is under the age of two may have special educational needs for which the LEA should determine the special educational provision, the LEA may make an assessment of their educational needs if the parent consents to it, and must make such an assessment if the parent requests it. Such an assessment shall be made in such a manner as the authority consider appropriate. Following such an assessment, the LEA may make and maintain a statement of the child's special educational needs in such manner, as they consider appropriate.

See Section 331, Education Act 1996

4:47 When a child under two is referred to the LEA, it is probable that their parents or the child health services will have first identified any special needs. In some areas of the country Sure Start programmes will have not only identified the child but also co-ordinated access to relevant services. They will continue to offer support to the family after the child has been made known to statutory services. The child is likely to have a particular condition or to have a major health problem that has caused concern at an early stage. Assessment of children under two need not follow the statutory procedures that are applicable to assessments of children who are aged two and over.

Statements for children under two

4:48 Statements will be rare for children under two. The LEA should first consider individual programmes of support according to the child's particular needs. The procedures are not specified in legislation. But while LEAs may prefer to make voluntary agreements to cover such arrangements, they should be aware that a parental request for a statutory assessment could indicate that those arrangements are insufficient. For very young children LEAs should consider home-based programmes such as Portage, if available, or peripatetic services for children with hearing or visual impairment. Parents should be consulted about the nature of the help and support that they would like to receive; some may prefer to attend a centre or to combine home-based with centre-based support.

4:49 If a decision is made to issue a statement, usually because of the child's complex needs or to allow access to a particular service such as a home-based teaching or a developmental play programme, it should include:

- **all available information about the child, with a clear specification of the child's special educational needs**
- **a record of the views of the parents and any relevant professionals**
- **a clear account of the services being offered, including the contribution of the education service and the educational objectives to be secured and the contribution of any statutory and voluntary agencies**
- **a description of the arrangements for monitoring and review.**

4:50 LEAs should ensure that any specific educational targets are regularly reviewed and, if necessary, revised. Any action will require close collaboration with child health services and social services.

Special educational provision for children under compulsory school age

4:51 For very young children, access to a home-based learning programme, such as the Portage Home Teaching Programme, or the services of a peripatetic teacher for the hearing or visually impaired, may provide the most appropriate support or advice. In the case of a child with a behavioural difficulty, the advice of the clinical psychologist at a child development centre or an educational psychologist may enable the child to remain within an existing setting. In most instances there should be a decision that the child can attend, or continue to attend, mainstream early education provision, but with additional support or resources. For some children it may be more appropriate for them to transfer to a specialist provision. Parents should be kept informed and consulted throughout the process of such decisions.

4:52 The Early Years Development and Childcare Partnership and the LEA should have information on nursery school or class places for children with special educational needs, and about places in independent and voluntary play or opportunity groups, family centres, day nurseries or other provision for young children in that authority. Partnerships are required to include this information in the EYDCP Plan. Social services departments will be able to provide information on provision for young children 'in need'.

4:53 If a child is on a local authority child protection register, or where there is concern about a child's welfare, the LEA and social services department should consider jointly agreeing an arrangement for identifying a child's needs and specifying and monitoring the provision to meet such needs. This should be done sensitively and with regard for the confidentiality of the information. If the child is looked after by the local authority – living with a foster parent or in a residential setting – the LEA's assessment could form part of the child's Care Plan and be regularly reviewed.

Moving to primary school

4:54 In some instances a child under five may have received considerable support without the necessity of making a statement. If it is decided that the child's needs are such that they will require a statement prior to entering primary school, careful attention should be paid to the parents' views and to information available from the full range of assessment arrangements within all the relevant agencies making provision for young children with special needs. Particular attention should be given to the child's general health and development and home circumstances to ensure that a learning difficulty is not directly related to wider family problems. Any record drawn up by an early education setting for a child with a possible special need should be passed on to the school with the parent's consent. The importance and benefits to their child of providing these records to schools should be carefully explained to parents.

4:55 The LEA should ensure that appropriate support is provided for parents in order that they can make a full contribution to their child's progress at school. Parents should be provided with full information to enable them to express a preference for an appropriate primary school or to make representations for an independent or non-maintained special school. Detailed consideration of the kinds of provision that may be appropriate at the primary phase should be undertaken as part of the annual review process as described in Chapter Nine.

5 Identification, Assessment and Provision in the Primary Phase

Introduction

5:1 Most children admitted to an infant or primary school will already have attended an early education setting. Some will not. Children with special educational needs who have attended a nursery class, playgroup or other early education setting should have had their needs identified already. Others may not. Schools should therefore be aware that any child admitted to the reception class might have unidentified special educational needs. The same applies to children who transfer from one school to another during the primary phase.

5:2 Provision for children with special educational needs is a matter for the school as a whole. In addition to the governing body, the school's head teacher, the SENCO and all other members of staff have important day-to-day responsibilities. *All teachers are teachers of children with special educational needs*. Teaching such children is therefore a whole school responsibility. In practice, the way in which this responsibility is exercised by individual staff is a matter for schools, to be decided in the light of a school's circumstances and size, priorities and ethos.

5:3 At the heart of the work of every primary school class is a continuous cycle of planning, teaching and assessing which takes account of the wide range of abilities, aptitudes and interests of children. The majority of children will learn and progress within these arrangements.

5:4 The National Curriculum programmes of study for key stages 1 and 2 set out the knowledge, understanding and skills expected of children in this age group. As part of the normal school arrangements, teachers plan from the National Curriculum programmes of study, using all the available flexibilities[20] and make judgements about children's performance in relation to the appropriate level descriptions.

5:5 Assessment against the National Curriculum level descriptions for each subject will enable the school to consider the individual child's attainment and progress against the expected levels for the majority of their peers. The National Literacy and Numeracy Strategy Frameworks for teaching also provide a basis for assessment against national norms. Those children whose overall attainments or attainment in specific subjects fall significantly outside the expected range may have special educational needs.

5:6 The assessment process should always be fourfold. It should focus on the child's learning characteristics, the learning environment that the school is providing for the child, the task and the teaching style. It should be recognised that some difficulties in learning may be caused or exacerbated by the school's learning environment or adult/child relationships. This means looking carefully at such matters as classroom organisation, teaching materials, teaching style and differentiation in order to decide how these can be developed so that the child is enabled to learn effectively.

---

20 National Curriculum Handbook for Primary Teachers in England (QCA/99/457) incorporates a statement entitled 'Inclusion: Providing effective learning opportunities for all children.' The National Curriculum is statutory unless formally disapplied through an appropriate regulation. For further information, see *Disapplication of the National Curriculum* 0118/2000 (www.dfes.gov.uk/natcurr/disapplyprimary).

Provision in primary schools[21]

5:7 All schools will wish to assess each child's current levels of attainment on entry in order to ensure that they build upon the pattern of learning and experience already established during the child's pre-school years. Schools should make full use of information passed to them when the child transfers from early education provision. Early education settings will maintain records on every child, and these will be a useful starting point for all children. This also applies to children who transfer between schools within the primary phase. Some children's performance can be exceptionally varied across settings. Therefore, where possible, it is important to look for multiple sources of evidence of children's performance in different roles and situations.

5:8 Schools should bear in mind that early education settings are required to have regard to this Code of Practice and are expected to plan for children with special educational needs but without statements through *Early Years Action* and *Early Years Action Plus*. Thus where a child starting school has already been identified as having special educational needs, the school should have access to records that will include the child's earlier IEPs. The child's IEPs will have been written in the context of the foundation stage curriculum, recording aspects that were additional to or different from the differentiated approaches and learning arrangements normally provided for all children.

5:9 The outcome of baseline assessment, which is considered in relation to all children shortly after they start primary school, may indicate areas of concern. Although the assessment is not specifically designed to identify those children with special educational needs, it should alert teachers to children who have particular difficulties, some of whom *might* have special needs.

5:10 Thus if a child has an identified special educational need when they start primary school, the head teacher, SENCO and the child's class teacher should:

- **use information arising from the child's previous educational experience to provide starting points for the development of an appropriate curriculum for the child**
- **identify and focus attention on the child's skills and highlight areas for early action to support the child within the class**
- **use the curricular and baseline assessment processes to allow the child to show what they know, understand and can do, as well as to identify any learning difficulties**
- **ensure that ongoing observation and assessment provide regular feedback to teachers and parents about the child's achievements and experiences and that the outcomes of such assessment form the basis for planning the next steps of the child's learning**
- **involve parents in developing and implementing a joint learning approach at home and in school.**

---

21 The term 'primary school' in this Chapter refers to any maintained primary or middle school that is a community, foundation or voluntary school. It also includes those community or foundation special schools with pupils of the relevant age group (other than special schools established in hospitals).

Early identification

5:11 The importance of early identification, assessment and provision for any child who may have special educational needs cannot be over-emphasised. The earlier action is taken, the more responsive the child is likely to be, and the more readily can intervention be made without undue disruption to the organisation of the school. Assessment should not be regarded as a single event but rather as a continuing process.

5:12 If a child's difficulties prove to be transient, the child will subsequently be able to learn and progress normally. If the child's difficulties prove less responsive to the provision made by the school, then an early start can be made in considering the additional help the child may need.

5:13 To help identify children who may have special educational needs, schools can measure children's progress by referring to:

- their performance monitored by the teacher as part of ongoing observation and assessment
- the outcomes from baseline assessment results
- their progress against the objectives specified in the National Literacy and Numeracy Strategy Frameworks
- their performance against the level descriptions within the National Curriculum at the end of a key stage
- standardised screening or assessment tools.

5:14 Schools should also be open and responsive to expressions of concern by parents, and take account of any information that parents provide about their child.

English as an additional language

5:15 The identification and assessment of the special educational needs of children whose first language is not English, requires particular care. It is necessary to consider the child within the context of their home, culture and community. Where there is uncertainty about an individual child, schools should make full use of any local sources of advice relevant to the ethnic group concerned, drawing on community liaison arrangements wherever they exist.

5:16 Lack of competence in English must not be equated with learning difficulties as understood in this Code. At the same time, when children who have English as an additional language make slow progress, it should not be assumed that their language status is the only reason; they may have learning difficulties. Schools should look carefully at all aspects of a child's performance in different subjects to establish whether the problems they have in the classroom are due to limitations in their command of the language that is used there or arise from special educational needs. At an early stage a full assessment should be made of the exposure they have had in the past to each of the languages they speak, the use they make of them currently and their proficiency in them. The information about their language skills obtained in this way will form the basis of all further work with them both in assisting their learning difficulties and in planning any additional language support that is needed.

National Curriculum

5:17 The National Curriculum is a statutory requirement for all[22] maintained schools[23] that sets out the areas and content of learning in each key stage. It secures access to essential areas of learning and provides for the development of the knowledge, understanding and skills that children will need in order to become active and responsible citizens.[24] All children in the primary sector should have access to the National Literacy and Numeracy Strategy Frameworks alongside the National Curriculum. All schools will through their cycle of observation, assessment, planning and review make provision for increased curriculum differentiation, curricular adaptations, and pastoral or disciplinary procedures dependent on the individual child's strengths and weaknesses. A variety of approaches should be employed to maximise the achievement of all pupils. These kinds of arrangements apply to all children and are not part of special educational provision.

5:18 Effective management, school ethos and the learning environment, curricular, pastoral and discipline arrangements can help prevent some special educational needs arising, and minimise others. Differentiation of learning activities within the primary curriculum framework will help schools to meet the learning needs of all children. The National Literacy and Numeracy Strategy Frameworks provide efficient planning models that allow every teacher to match teaching objectives to the needs of their pupils. They also provide guidance on including children with SEN in the Literacy Hour and the daily mathematics lesson. Schools should not assume that children's learning difficulties always result solely, or even mainly, from problems within the child. A school's own practices make a difference – for good or ill. The governing body, head teacher and SENCO should be alert to any particular patterns in the school's identification and recording of children's special educational needs or parents' expressions of concern, and should examine the school's general practices and policies in the light of any such patterns.

5:19 Thus all primary schools should consider the kinds of options and the variety of activities available within the class setting to enable children to access the National Curriculum. Teachers' planning should be flexible in order to recognise the needs of all children as individuals and to ensure progression, relevance and differentiation. The National Curriculum Inclusion Statement[25] emphasises the importance of providing effective learning opportunities for all pupils and offers three key principles for inclusion:

- setting suitable learning challenges
- responding to pupils' diverse needs
- overcoming potential barriers to learning and assessment for individuals and groups of pupils.

---

22 The statutory framework is set out in Part V of the Education Act 1996 and orders made under those provisions.

23 The National Curriculum is not a requirement for Pupil Referral Units or hospital special schools.

24 Additional guidance can be found in 'Planning, teaching and assessing the curriculum for pupils with learning difficulties.' QCA March 2000.

25 'Inclusion: Providing effective learning opportunities for all children.' QCA/99/458.

Graduated response

5:20 In order to help children who have special educational needs, schools in the primary phase should adopt a graduated response that encompasses an array of strategies. This approach recognises that there is a continuum of special educational needs and, where necessary, brings increasing specialist expertise to bear on the difficulties that a child may be experiencing. However the school should, other than in exceptional cases, make full use of all available classroom and school resources before expecting to call upon outside resources.

5:21 This Code sets out a model of action and intervention that is designed to help children towards independent learning, in particular the procedures community, voluntary and foundation schools might adopt in order to fulfil their duty to use their best endeavours[26] on behalf of children with special educational needs. In many cases the action taken will mean that the child's needs are resolved. Only for those children whose progress continues to cause concern should additional action be taken. For children in the primary phase this Code recommends that when a child is identified as having special educational needs the school should intervene as described below at *School Action* and *School Action Plus*.

5:22 These interventions will not usually be steps on the way to statutory assessment. Nor are they hurdles to be crossed before a statutory assessment can be made. Some children will require less rather than more help if the interventions work successfully. The interventions are a means of matching special educational provision to the child's needs, and are therefore part of the continuous and systematic cycle of planning, action and review within the school to enable all children to learn and progress.

5:23 Good practice can take many different forms. Even those schools that decide to follow the Code's model closely may need to make adjustments to reflect their particular circumstances. The model applies to maintained primary schools other than special schools but might be adopted differently in, for example, a small rural primary school and a large inner-city junior school. The model nonetheless embodies the principles set out below, which are central to this Code and to which all schools should have regard:

- **provision for a child with special educational needs should match the nature of their needs**
- **there should be regular recording of a child's special educational needs, the action taken and the outcomes.**

Record keeping

5:24 Schools should record the steps taken to meet the needs of individual children. The school's SENCO should have responsibility for ensuring that the records are properly kept and available as needed. If schools refer a child for a statutory assessment, they should provide the LEA with a record of their work with the child including the resources or special arrangements they have already made available. LEAs and schools may wish to consider the use of an agreed style for IEPs at *School Action* and *School Action Plus*. This may be particularly helpful in ensuring that information effectively transfers between

26 See paragraph 1:21

schools. The Education (Pupil Information) Regulations 2000 require schools to provide full pupil records to the receiving school even if the new school does not lodge a request. Such records should include all the information held by the SENCO including IEPs.

5:25 In addition to the information that all schools will record for all children, the pupil record or profile for a child with SEN should include information about the child's progress and behaviour from the school setting itself, from the child's early education setting or a previous school, from the parents, and from health and social services. It should also include the child's own perception of any difficulties and how they might be addressed. It may also be necessary to record in the profile information about the child's needs in relation to the general strategies to be used to enable access to the curriculum and the school day.

5:26 The information collected should reveal the different perceptions of those concerned with the child, any immediate educational concerns and an overall picture of the child's strengths and weaknesses.

Working with other providers of support

5:27 Many children with special educational needs have a range of difficulties and the achievement of educational objectives is likely to be delayed without partnership in the child's education between all concerned. Thus support for children with special educational needs requires a concerted approach from healthcare professionals, social services departments, specialist LEA support services and other providers of support services. All these services should aim to provide an integrated service for the child so that parents perceive the provision as 'seamless'. They should keep one another fully informed about the action taken in support of the child. Under the Children Act 1989 and the Education Act 1996 schools, LEAs, the health services and the social services departments of local authorities are required to help each other in various ways. Further guidance on other agencies is set out in Chapter Ten.

Involvement of social services

5:28 Schools should be aware of the full range of local services provided by social services departments (SSDs). SSDs have duties under section 17 of the Children Act 1989 to provide a range of services for children regarded as being 'in need' (see Glossary). While a child with special educational needs will not necessarily be 'in need' as defined in the Children Act 1989, that Act allows an integrated approach to the educational, health and welfare needs of children with special educational needs who are 'in need'. It also requires LEAs and others to assist social services departments if a child is suffering or at risk of suffering significant harm (section 47 of the Children Act 1989).[27]

5:29 The designated teacher for 'looked after' children should work closely with the SENCO when the child also has SEN. Schools should also ensure that where a child is 'looked after'[28] by the local authority both the child's social worker, and where possible, the parents are involved in their child's education and all processes relating to special educational needs.

---

27 DH et al 'Framework for Assessment of Children in Need.' April 2000.

28 DfEE/DH Guidance on the Education of Children and Young People in Public Care. May 2000.

The role of the SENCO in mainstream primary schools[29]

5:30 The SEN Coordinator (SENCO), in collaboration with the head teacher and governing body, plays a key role in determining the strategic development of the SEN policy and provision in the school in order to raise the achievement of children with SEN. The SENCO takes day-to-day responsibility for the operation of the SEN policy and co-ordination of the provision made for individual children with SEN, working closely with staff, parents and carers, and other agencies. The SENCO also provides related professional guidance to colleagues with the aim of securing high quality teaching for children with SEN.

5:31 The SENCO, with the support of the head teacher and colleagues, seeks to develop effective ways of overcoming barriers to learning and sustaining effective teaching through the analysis and assessment of children's needs, by monitoring the quality of teaching and standards of pupils' achievements, and by setting targets for improvement. The SENCO should collaborate with curriculum coordinators so that the learning for all children is given equal priority, and available resources are used to maximum effect.

5:32 In mainstream primary schools the key responsibilities of the SENCO may include:

- **overseeing the day-to-day operation of the school's SEN policy**
- **coordinating provision for children with special educational needs**
- **liaising with and advising fellow teachers**
- **managing learning support assistants**
- **overseeing the records of all children with special educational needs**
- **liaising with parents of children with special educational needs**
- **contributing to the in-service training of staff**
- **liaising with external agencies including the LEA's support and educational psychology services, health and social services, and voluntary bodies.**

Time required for SEN coordination

5:33 Governing bodies and head teachers will need to give careful thought to the SENCO's timetable in the light of the Code and in the context of the resources available to the school. Experience shows that SENCOs require time for: planning and coordination away from the classroom; maintaining appropriate individual and whole school records of children at *School Action* and *School Action Plus* and those with statements; teaching pupils with SEN; observing pupils in class without a teaching commitment; managing, supporting and training learning support assistants; liaising with colleagues and with early education settings and secondary schools. Access to a telephone and an interview room is also desirable where possible. In many schools the governing body has been able to allocate some administrative staff time to help the SENCO, thus releasing the SENCO to use their expertise more effectively.

29 TTA 'National Standards for Special Educational Needs Coordinators' provides guidance on training and development for SENCOs.

5:34 In schools the SENCO duties will be a specific responsibility for one member of staff. In terms of responsibility the SENCO role is at least equivalent to that of curriculum, literacy or numeracy coordinator. The role is time consuming and therefore it is usually inappropriate for the SENCO to have other school-wide responsibilities. Many schools find it effective for the SENCO to be a member of the senior leadership team. However although in very small schools the head or deputy may need to take on the role of SENCO, such a decision should be considered very carefully.

5:35 It is good practice for the costs of the SENCO (or those parts of the post holder's work devoted to SENCO duties) to be set against the core or base budget of the school rather than against additional funds delegated to the school for the purpose of meeting the particular needs of children with SEN.

5:36 Head teachers and governors should support the SENCO in the use of Information and Communications Technology (ICT) for SEN management systems and for preparing and recording IEPs. Head teachers should also ensure where possible that the SENCO is able to communicate with other SENCOs through, for example, the SENCO Forum coordinated by the British Educational and Technology Communications Agency (BECTa).[30]

Monitoring children's progress

5:37 The way in which a school meets the needs of **all** children has a direct bearing on the nature of the additional help required by children with special educational needs, and on the point at which additional help is required. The key to meeting the needs of all children lies in the teacher's knowledge of each child's skills and abilities and the teacher's ability to match this knowledge to finding ways of providing appropriate access to the curriculum for every child.

5:38 It is for individual schools to decide the procedures they should adopt for meeting the needs of all children, for observing and assessing their progress, and for deciding the nature of the special educational provision that they should make. It is essential that these procedures are carefully managed and monitored, and that there are effective internal communication and liaison arrangements between staff.

5:39 A school's system for observing and assessing the progress of individual children should provide information about areas where a child is not progressing satisfactorily even though the teaching style has been differentiated. These observations should be enhanced by knowledge built up over time of an individual child's strengths and weaknesses. Using this evidence, class teachers may come to feel that the strategies they are currently using with the child are not resulting in the child learning as effectively as possible. Under these circumstances, they will need to consult the SENCO to consider what else might be done. The starting point will always be a review of the strategies currently being used and the way in which these might be developed. The review may lead to the conclusion that the pupil requires help over and above that which is normally available within the particular class or subject. Consideration should then be given to helping the pupil through *School Action*.

---

30 The SENCO Forum can be found at www.becta.org.uk/senco/sources/senfor

> **The school has a duty to inform the child's parents that special educational provision is being made for the child because the child has SEN.**
>
> See Section 317A , Education Act 1996

5:40 As most schools are in day-to-day contact with parents they are best placed to judge how to tell parents that because their child has SEN they are receiving special educational provision. It should be done in a way that encourages parents to contribute their knowledge and understanding of their child, and to raise any concerns they may have about their child's needs and the provision which is being made for them. Although it is the responsibility of the governing body to ensure that parents are informed, in practice it should usually be delegated to the head teacher who will decide how to involve other members of staff in informing parents.

5:41 The key test of the need for action is evidence that current rates of progress are inadequate. There should not be an assumption that all children will progress at the same rate. A judgement has to be made in each case as to what it is reasonable to expect a particular child to achieve. Where progress is not adequate, it will be necessary to take some <u>additional</u> or <u>different</u> action to enable the pupil to learn more effectively. Whatever the level of pupils' difficulties, the key test of how far their learning needs are being met is whether they are making *adequate progress*.

5:42 Adequate progress can be defined in a number of ways. It might, for instance, be progress which:

- closes the attainment gap between the child and their peers
- prevents the attainment gap growing wider
- is similar to that of peers starting from the same attainment baseline, but less than that of the majority of peers
- matches or betters the child's previous rate of progress
- ensures access to the full curriculum
- demonstrates an improvement in self-help, social or personal skills
- demonstrates improvements in the child's behaviour.

School Action

5:43 When a class teacher or the SENCO identifies a child with SEN the class teacher should provide interventions that are <u>additional to</u> or <u>different from</u> those provided as part of the school's usual differentiated curriculum offer and strategies (*School Action*).

5:44 The triggers for intervention through *School Action* could be the teacher's or others' concern, underpinned by evidence, about a child who despite receiving differentiated learning opportunities:

- makes little or no progress even when teaching approaches are targeted particularly in a child's identified area of weakness

- shows signs of difficulty in developing literacy or mathematics skills which result in poor attainment in some curriculum areas
- presents persistent emotional or behavioural difficulties which are not ameliorated by the behaviour management techniques usually employed in the school
- has sensory or physical problems, and continues to make little or no progress despite the provision of specialist equipment
- has communication and/or interaction difficulties, and continues to make little or no progress despite the provision of a differentiated curriculum.

5:45 If a child's class teacher in consultation with parents concludes that a child may need further support to help their progress, the teacher should seek the help of the SENCO. The teacher and the SENCO should consider the teacher's reasons for concern alongside any information about the child already available to the school.

5:46 To help inform the decision on the nature of the additional help that might be needed by the child through *School Action* the class teacher together with the SENCO should collect all the available information about the child and seek additional information from the parents. In some cases outside professionals from health or social services may already be involved with the child. In such instances it is good practice for these professionals to liaise with the school and keep them informed of their input. Where these professionals have not already been working with the school staff, the SENCO should contact them if the parents agree.

5:47 The SENCO should take the lead in the further assessment of the child's particular strengths and weaknesses; planning future support for the child in discussion with colleagues; and monitoring and subsequently reviewing the action taken. The child's class teacher should remain responsible for working with the child on a daily basis and for planning and delivering an individualised programme. Parents should always be consulted and kept informed of the action taken to help the child, and of the outcome of this action.

5:48 The information collected about the child, and details of the extra help given to them, can be incorporated in the child's individual record. The record should also include previous observations on the child made as part of the assessment and recording systems in place for all children.

Nature of intervention

5:49 The SENCO and the child's class teacher should decide on the *Action* needed to help the child to progress in the light of their earlier assessment. There is sometimes an expectation that this help will take the form of the deployment of extra staff to enable one-to-one tuition to be given to the child. However, this may not be the most appropriate way of helping the child. A more appropriate approach might be to provide different learning materials or special equipment; to introduce some group or individual support; to devote extra adult time to devising the nature of the planned intervention and to monitoring its effectiveness; or to undertake staff development and training to introduce more effective strategies. Speedy access to LEA support services for one-off or occasional advice on strategies or equipment or for staff training may make it possible to provide effective intervention without the need for regular or ongoing input from external agencies.

Individual Education Plans

5:50 Strategies employed to enable the child to progress should be recorded within an Individual Education Plan (IEP). Further information on managing IEPs and Group Education Plans can be found in the SEN Toolkit. The IEP should include information about:

- the short-term targets set for or by the child
- the teaching strategies to be used
- the provision to be put in place
- when the plan is to be reviewed
- success and/or exit criteria
- outcomes (to be recorded when IEP is reviewed).

5:51 The IEP should only record that which is additional to or different from the differentiated curriculum plan, which is in place as part of provision for all children. The IEP should be crisply written and focus on three or four individual targets, chosen from those relating to the key areas of communication, literacy, mathematics, and behaviour and social skills that match the child's needs. The IEP should be discussed with the child and the parents.

5:52 Where a child with identified SEN is at serious risk of disaffection or exclusion the IEP should reflect appropriate strategies to meet their needs[31]. A Pastoral Support Programme should not be used to replace the graduated response to special educational needs.

Reviewing IEPs

5:53 IEPs should be reviewed at least twice a year. Ideally they should be reviewed termly, or possibly more frequently for some children. At least one review in the year could coincide with a routine Parents' Evening, although schools should recognise that some parents will prefer a private meeting. Reviews need not be unduly formal, but parents' views on the child's progress should be sought and they should be consulted as part of the review process. Wherever possible, the child should also take part in the review process and be involved in setting the targets. If the child is not involved in the review, their ascertainable views should be considered in any discussion.

School Action Plus

5:54 A request for help from external services is likely to follow a decision taken by the SENCO and colleagues, in consultation with parents, at a meeting to review the child's IEP. Schools should always consult specialists when they take action on behalf of a child through *School Action Plus*. But the involvement of specialists need not be limited to such children. Outside specialists can play an important part in the very early identification of special educational needs and in advising schools on effective provision designed to prevent the development of more significant needs. They can act as consultants and be a source for in-service advice on learning and behaviour management strategies for all teachers.

---

31 Guidance is set out in DfEE Circular 10/99 'Social Inclusion: Pupil Support.'

5:55 At *School Action Plus* external support services, both those provided by the LEA and by outside agencies, will usually see the child, in school if that is appropriate and practicable, so that they can advise teachers on new IEPs with fresh targets and accompanying strategies, provide more specialist assessments that can inform planning and the measurement of a pupil's progress, give advice on the use of new or specialist strategies or materials, and in some cases provide support for particular activities. The kinds of advice and support available to schools will vary according to local policies.

5:56 The triggers for *School Action Plus* could be that, despite receiving an individualised programme and/or concentrated support under *School Action*, the child:

- continues to make little or no progress in specific areas over a long period
- continues working at National Curriculum levels substantially below that expected of children of a similar age
- continues to have difficulty in developing literacy and mathematics skills
- has emotional or behavioural difficulties which substantially and regularly interfere with the child's own learning or that of the class group, despite having an individualised behaviour management programme
- has sensory or physical needs, and requires additional specialist equipment or regular advice or visits by a specialist service
- has ongoing communication or interaction difficulties that impede the development of social relationships and cause substantial barriers to learning.

5:57 Where schools seek the help of external support services, those services will need to see the child's records in order to establish which strategies have already been employed and which targets have been set and achieved. They can then advise on new and appropriate targets for the child's IEP and on accompanying strategies. The targets set may require specialist assessment arrangements to measure the child's progress. If so, outside specialists, for example educational psychologists may be required for this.

5:58 The SENCO and class teacher, together with curriculum, literacy and numeracy coordinators and external specialists, should consider a range of different teaching approaches and appropriate equipment and teaching materials, including the use of information technology. The external specialist may act in an advisory capacity, or provide additional specialist assessment or be involved in teaching the child directly. In some instances improved management or alternative arrangements based on advice from health professionals may considerably reduce the child's special educational needs.

5:59 The resulting new IEP for the child should set out fresh strategies for supporting the child's progress. Although developed with the help of outside specialists, the strategies specified in the IEP should usually be implemented, at least in part and as far as possible, in the normal classroom setting. The delivery of the interventions recorded in the IEP continues to be the responsibility of the class teacher.

5:60 If the SENCO and the external specialist consider that the information gathered about the child is insufficient, and that more detailed advice must be obtained from other outside professionals, then the consent of the child's parents must be sought.

5:61 The SENCO should note in the child's records:

- what further advice is being sought
- the support to be provided for the child pending receipt of the advice.

School request for a statutory assessment

5:62 Where a request for a statutory assessment is made by a school to an LEA, the child will have demonstrated significant cause for concern. The LEA will seek evidence from the school that any strategy or programme implemented for the child in question has been continued for a reasonable period of time without success and that alternatives have been tried, or the reasons why this has not occurred. The LEA will need information about the child's progress over time, and will also need clear documentation in relation to the child's special educational needs and any action taken to deal with those needs, including any resources or special arrangements put in place. In some cases there will be existing reports or written advice from external agencies that should be included in the documentation, however where there is no such evidence LEAs should not require it in order to decide whether an assessment is needed.

5:63 The evidence that the LEA will need to examine in deciding whether to make a statutory assessment is described in Chapter Seven. The criteria, which LEAs may adopt in deciding whether to issue a statement for a particular child, are set out in Chapter Eight. Regular liaison between the LEA and schools should ensure that there is clarity about the information required by the Authority when an assessment is requested.

5:64 By the time the head teacher considers asking for statutory assessment of a child's special educational needs, the school should be able to provide written evidence of or information about:

- **the school's action through *School Action* and *School Action Plus***
- **individual education plans for the pupil**
- **records of regular reviews and their outcomes**
- **the pupil's health including the child's medical history where relevant**
- **National Curriculum levels**
- **attainments in literacy and mathematics**
- **educational and other assessments, for example from an advisory specialist support teacher or an educational psychologist**
- **views of the parents and of the child**
- **involvement of other professionals**
- **any involvement by the social services or education welfare service.**

5:65 The description of the child's learning difficulty and progress together with information about the special educational provision made will form the basis on which the LEA can consider whether a statutory assessment is necessary. If the LEA's support services and, in particular, the LEA's educational psychologists have already been involved in assessing the child and reviewing provision, the LEA should be able to decide relatively quickly whether a statutory assessment is necessary. In the meantime – and whilst any subsequent statutory assessment is being made – the child should continue to be supported through *School Action Plus*.

School transfer

5:66 When children move schools, either at phase transfer or at any other time, primary schools are required to transfer school records for all pupils within 15 school days of the child ceasing to be registered at the school.[32] However when transfer arrangements are made in advance it is good practice for information to be provided in time for appropriate planning by the receiving school. Secondary schools or a new primary school should receive the school records of all pupils identified by their primary schools as having special educational needs. When such a pupil is admitted to a new school, the school should be in possession of a good deal of useful information about the child, including any detailed background information collated by the primary school SENCO; copies of IEPs prepared in support of intervention through *School Action* or *School Action Plus*; and any statements of special educational needs.

Working with children with statements of special educational needs

5:67 All children with statements of special educational needs, whether in mainstream or special schools, should have short-term targets set. In the majority of cases the strategies to meet these targets will be set out in an IEP. As at *School Action* and *School Action Plus* the IEP should record only that which is <u>additional to</u> or <u>different from</u> the differentiated curriculum plan.

Annual review

5:68 The procedures to be followed during annual reviews of statements are explained in Chapter Nine. There are however particular points in a child's school career when the arrangements for annual reviews might need to be varied.

5:69 All concerned with the child should give careful thought to transfer between phases. Advance planning is essential. The move should initially be considered at the review meeting prior to the last year in the current school. Thus consideration of transfer from primary to secondary education would need initial consideration at the review in year 5.

5:70 At the review in year 5 it should be possible, in most cases, to give clear recommendations as to the type of provision the child will require at the secondary stage. It will then be possible for the parents to visit secondary schools and to consider appropriate options within the same or similar timescales as other parents.

5:71 In a very few cases the options may not be clear at the year 5 review, in which case it may be necessary to hold an interim or early annual review in the autumn of year 6. Very rarely a child's needs may change after the year 5 review to such a great extent that the recommendations as to the type of provision will need amendment. This should take place through an interim or year 6 review.

---

32 Education (Pupil Information) Regulations 2000.

5:72 Thus for all children transferring between phases, except from early education settings, a provisional recommendation should be made in the year previous to transfer so that parents can consider options at the same time as other parents. The child's statement **must** then be amended by 15 February of the year of transfer in the light of the recommendations of the annual review, the parents' views and preferences and the response to consultation by the LEA with the school or schools concerned. There will be no need to require the annual review for such children to be brought forward since the information from the previous review can be used. All the arrangements for a child's placement should therefore be completed no later than the beginning of March before transfer. It is important for placements to be finalised as early as possible in order for any advance arrangements relating to that placement to be made and to ensure that parents and children feel confident and secure about the arrangements in question.

5:73 It is good practice for the SENCO of the receiving school, where possible, to attend the final annual review in primary school of pupils with statements for whom the particular school has been named. It will then be possible for the receiving school to plan a differentiated curriculum response and an appropriate IEP to start at the beginning of the new school year. It will also enable the pupil and the parents to be reassured that an effective and supportive transfer will occur.

6 Identification, Assessment and Provision in the Secondary Sector

Introduction

6:1 All mainstream secondary schools will admit pupils who have already been identified as having special educational needs. Some of the pupils will have been identified by their primary school and helped through *School Action* or *School Action Plus*, whilst a few may have statements. Secondary schools will need to be aware that any pupil admitted to year 7 may have unidentified special educational needs. They should also recognise that children's special educational needs are on a continuum and may also change over time; and that the period of transfer and adjustment to a new school, which is crucial to all pupils, may hold a particular challenge for a pupil with special educational needs.

6:2 Provision for pupils with special educational needs is a matter for the school as a whole. In addition to the governing body, the school's head teacher, SENCO and learning support team, and all other members of staff have important operational responsibilities. *All teachers are teachers of pupils with special educational needs*. Teaching such pupils is therefore a whole-school responsibility, requiring a whole-school response. In practice the way in which this responsibility is exercised by individual staff is a matter for schools, to be decided in the light of a school's circumstances and size, priorities and ethos.

6:3 Central to the work of every class and every subject is a continuous cycle of planning, teaching, assessment and evaluation that takes account of the wide range of abilities, aptitudes and interests of the pupils. The majority of pupils will learn and progress within these arrangements.

6:4 Each school is required to plan a curriculum that includes provision for those National Curriculum subjects that are statutory at key stages 3 and 4. Teachers should deliver the National Curriculum programmes of study in ways that meet the particular learning requirements of their pupils.[33] Some variations in the requirements at key stage 4 are permitted through the use of the regulations under Section 363 of the Education Act 1996 which permit disapplications of National Curriculum subjects for specific purposes.[34]

6:5 Assessment against the National Curriculum level descriptions for each subject will enable the school to consider the individual pupil's attainment and progress against the expected levels for the majority of their peers. Pupils whose overall attainments or attainment in specific subjects fall significantly outside the expected range may have special educational needs.

Provision in secondary schools[35]

6:6 All secondary schools will wish to assess **all** pupils' current levels of attainment on entry in order to ensure that they build upon the pattern of learning and experience already

---

33 The National Curriculum Handbook for Secondary Teachers in England (QCA/99/458) includes a statement entitled 'Inclusion: Providing effective opportunities for all children.' The National Curriculum is statutory unless formally disapplied through an appropriate regulation. For further information, see *Disapplication of the National Curriculum* 0118/2000 (www.dfes.gsi.gov.uk/natcurr/disapply).

34 The Education (National Curriculum) (Exceptions at Key Stage 4) (England) Regulations 2000.

35 The term "secondary school" refers to any maintained secondary school that is a community, foundation or voluntary school. It also includes maintained middle schools, and those community and foundation special schools (other than hospital special schools) with pupils of secondary age.

established during the child's primary years. Secondary schools should be aware that primary schools are required to transfer to them the school records for all pupils within 15 school days of pupils ceasing to be registered at the school. Secondary schools should therefore receive the school records of all pupils in year 7 identified by their primary schools as having special educational needs. They should also receive copies of the statements of pupils transferring to them.

6:7 When such a pupil is admitted to secondary school, the school should be in possession of a good deal of useful information about the child, including detailed background information collated by the primary school SENCO; copies of IEPs prepared in support of intervention through *School Action* or *School Action Plus*; and any statements of special educational needs. This information can help to shape curriculum and pastoral planning for the pupil in the first few months at secondary school. Many mainstream secondary schools supplement the information received from primary schools by carrying out their own assessments of new entrants.

6:8 Schools should make full use of information passed to them by primary schools. It is good practice for secondary schools to liaise closely with their feeder primary schools and to arrange induction days for transferring pupils in the summer term. This helps to achieve a smooth and successful transition for all pupils. Where possible secondary SENCOs should attend year 6 annual reviews of pupils with statements to ensure a smooth transition and appropriate planning of the pupil's curriculum and the first IEP in year 7.

6:9 If a pupil is known to have special educational needs when they arrive at the school, the head teacher, SENCO, literacy and numeracy coordinators, departmental and pastoral colleagues should:

- **use information from the pupil's primary school to provide starting points for the development of an appropriate curriculum for the pupil**
- **identify and focus attention on the pupil's skills and highlight areas for early action to support the pupil within the class**
- **ensure that ongoing observation and assessment provide regular feedback to all teachers and parents about the pupil's achievements and experiences, and that the outcomes of such assessment form the basis for planning the next steps of the pupil's learning**
- **ensure that appropriate informal opportunities for the pupil to show what they know, understand and can do are maximised through the pastoral programme**
- **involve the pupil in planning and agreeing targets to meet their needs**
- **involve parents in developing and implementing a joint learning approach at home and in school.**

Early Identification

6:10 The continued importance at secondary level of early identification and assessment for any pupil who may have special educational needs cannot be over-emphasised. The earlier action is taken, the quicker appropriate help can be provided without unduly disrupting the organisation of the school, and the more responsive the pupil is likely to be. Schools frequently make use of appropriate screening or assessment tools to assist them in early identification. Whatever systems are in place, however, assessment should not be regarded as a single event but as a continuing process.

6:11 If the pupil's difficulties prove to be temporary their rate of progress may be temporarily different although the pupil will be able to learn and progress alongside their peers. If the difficulties are less responsive to the intervention provided by the school, then an early start can be made in considering the kinds of additional help that might be required.

6:12 To help identify pupils who may have special educational needs, schools can measure children's progress by referring to:

- evidence from teacher observation and assessment
- their performance against the level descriptions within the National Curriculum at the end of a key stage
- their progress against the objectives specified in the National Literacy and Numeracy Strategy Frameworks
- standardised screening or assessment tools.

6:13 Schools should also be open and responsive to the expressions of concern by parents, and take account of any information that parents provide about their child. Schools should ensure that parents are aware of the local parent partnership service that will be able to offer parents advice and support. Some young people may also raise concerns about their own progress and their views should be treated seriously. In addition, other professionals such as the Connexions Personal Adviser may become aware of issues as they work with young people to address problems particularly associated with the teenage years.

English as an additional language

6:14 The identification and assessment of the special educational needs of young people whose first language is not English requires particular care. It is necessary to consider the young person within the context of their home, culture and community. Where there is uncertainty about an individual, schools should make full use of any local sources of advice relevant to the ethnic group concerned, drawing on community liaison arrangements wherever they exist.

6:15 Lack of competence in English must not be equated with learning difficulties as understood in this Code. At the same time, when pupils who have English as an additional language make slow progress, it should not be assumed that their language status is the only reason; they may have learning difficulties. Schools should look carefully at all aspects of a pupil's performance in different subjects to establish whether the problems they have in the classroom are due to limitations in their command of the language that is used there or arise from special educational needs.

6:16 At an early stage a full assessment should be made of the exposure they have had in the past to each of the languages they speak, the use they make of them currently and their proficiency in them. The information about their language skills obtained in this way will form the basis of all further work with them both in assisting their learning difficulties and in planning any additional language support that is needed. Where such information is available from a primary school in the case of children known to be at risk, every effort should be made to obtain it at the point of transfer.

National Curriculum

6:17 The National Curriculum is a statutory requirement for all pupils[36] in maintained schools that sets out the areas and content of learning in each key stage, securing access to essential areas of learning and providing for the development of the knowledge, understanding and skills necessary for self-development and for becoming active and responsible citizens. Children in the primary sector will have had access to the National Literacy and Numeracy Strategy Frameworks alongside the National Curriculum; and for some children it may be appropriate to continue to adopt these strategies at key stage 3.

6:18 Effective management, school ethos and the learning environment, curricular, disciplinary and pastoral arrangements can help prevent some special educational needs arising, and minimise others. Differentiation of learning activities in subjects within the secondary curriculum framework will help schools to meet the learning needs of all pupils. Schools should not assume that pupils' learning difficulties always result solely, or even mainly, from problems within the young person. Pupils' rates of progress can sometimes depend on what or how they are taught. A school's own practices make a difference – for good or ill. The governing body, head teacher, SENCO, heads of department and pastoral staff should be alert to any particular patterns in the school's identification of special educational needs or parents' expressions of concern. Schools may need to reconsider policies and practice in the light of the pattern and incidence of the special educational needs that are identified.

6:19 Teachers should use the National Curriculum programmes of study to teach knowledge, understanding and skills using a variety of methods that are appropriate to the abilities of individual pupils. For some pupils it will be necessary to choose work from earlier key stages so they are able to progress and demonstrate attainment.

6:20 The National Curriculum Inclusion Statement[37] emphasises the importance of providing effective learning opportunities for all pupils and offers three key principles for inclusion:

- setting suitable learning challenges
- responding to pupils' diverse needs
- overcoming potential barriers to learning and assessment for individuals and groups of pupils.

6:21 All secondary schools should consider the options available within the school's organisation to enable all pupils to access the National Curriculum. Differentiation can be addressed by considering the nature and variety of activities and the intellectual demands placed on the individual pupil. Subject teacher planning should be flexible so as to recognise the needs of all pupils as individuals and to ensure progression, relevance and differentiation. Many schools choose to aid curriculum planning and differentiation through the judicious use of setting and streaming of pupils. It should be noted that an individual pupil may progress at different rates in different subject areas and thus consideration of placement in a set should be made subject by subject. Where setting

---

36 The statutory framework is set out in Part V of the Education Act 1996 and orders made under those provisions.

37 'Inclusion: Providing effective learning opportunities for all children'. QCA/99/458.

and streaming occur, either the curriculum content or the speed of lesson presentation should still vary to reflect the needs of the particular class group.

Graduated response

6:22 In order to help pupils who have special educational needs, schools in the secondary sector should adopt a graduated response that includes a wide range of strategies. This approach will be very similar to that employed in primary schools. Although this response acknowledges that there is a continuum of special educational needs, it also requires that schools should make full use of available classroom and school resources before, where necessary, bringing increasing specialist expertise to bear on the difficulties that a pupil may be experiencing.

6:23 This Code sets out a model of action and intervention designed to help pupils towards independent learning; in particular the procedures schools might adopt in order to fulfil their duty to use their best endeavours[38] on behalf of pupils with special educational needs. In many cases the action taken will mean that the pupil's needs are resolved. Only for those pupils whose progress continues to cause concern should additional action be taken. For pupils in the secondary phase this Code recommends that, when a young person is identified as having special educational needs the school should intervene as described below at *School Action* and *School Action Plus*. The model recommended is very similar to that advocated for the primary phase, but takes into account the different organisation in secondary education.

6:24 These interventions will not usually be steps on the way to statutory assessment. Nor are they hurdles to be crossed before a statutory assessment can be made. Some pupils may gradually require less rather than more help if the interventions are a success. Such interventions are an appropriate means of helping schools and parents match special educational provision to individual pupil needs, and are therefore part of the continuous and systematic cycle of planning, action, review and evaluation within the school to enable all pupils to learn and progress.

6:25 Good practice can take many different forms. Even those schools that decide to follow the Code's model closely may need to make adjustments to reflect their particular circumstances. The model applies to maintained secondary schools other than special schools but might be adopted differently in, for example, a selective or partly selective school and a large inner-city comprehensive school. The model embodies the principles set out below, which are central to this Code and to which all schools should have regard:

- **provision for a pupil with special educational needs should match the nature of their needs**
- **there should be regular recording of a pupil's special educational needs, the action taken and the outcomes.**

38 See paragraph 1:21.

Time required for SEN coordination

6:36 Governing bodies and head teachers will need to give careful thought to the SENCO's timetable in the light of the Code and in the context of the resources available to the school. Experience shows that SENCOs require time for: planning and coordination away from the classroom; maintaining appropriate individual and whole school records of pupils at *School Action* and *School Action Plus* and those with statements; teaching pupils with SEN; observing pupils in class without a teaching commitment; managing the effective deployment of other teachers within the SEN team; managing, supporting and training learning support assistants; liaising with departmental and pastoral colleagues; liaising with feeder primary schools and working with the Connexions Personal Adviser in relation to transition planning. Access to a telephone and an interview room is also desirable where possible. In many schools the governing body has been able to allocate some administrative staff time to help the SENCO, thus releasing the SENCO to use their expertise more effectively.

6:37 In most secondary schools the SENCO role will be a specific responsibility for one member of staff. The role is time consuming and therefore it is usually inappropriate for the SENCO to have other school-wide responsibilities. In terms of the level of responsibility and the time required for the task, the SENCO's role is broadly equivalent to that of Head of Department or Faculty or Head of Year. Many schools find it effective for the SENCO to be a member of the senior leadership team.

6:38 It is good practice for the costs of the SENCO (or those parts of the post holder's work devoted to SENCO duties) to be set against the core or base budget of the school rather than against additional funds delegated to the school for the purpose of meeting the particular needs of children with SEN.

6:39 Head teachers and governors should support the SENCO in the use of Information and Communications Technology (ICT) for SEN management systems and for preparing and recording IEPs. Head teachers should also ensure where possible that the SENCO is able to communicate with other SENCOs through, for example, the SENCO Forum coordinated by the British Educational and Technology Communications Agency.[42] The management structures within a school should ensure that all the SENCO's functions can be carried out effectively.

6:40 There is a range of organisational structures in place in mainstream secondary schools, which aids the effective implementation of the SEN policy. As secondary schools are often very large, many schools have staff, additional to the SENCO, with SEN responsibilities. Whatever organisation is in place, all staff must know and understand their role, and management should ensure that it is an integral part of the job descriptions of the relevant personnel.

Monitoring pupil progress

6:41 The ways in which a secondary school meets the individual needs of **all** pupils has a direct bearing on the nature and frequency of the additional help required by pupils with special educational needs. The key to meeting the needs of all pupils lies in the teacher's

42 The SENCO Forum can be found at www.becta.org.uk/senco/sources/senfor

knowledge of each pupil's skills and abilities and the teacher's ability to match this knowledge to identifying and providing appropriate ways of accessing the curriculum for every pupil.

6:42 All schools will through their cycle of observation, assessment, planning and review make provision for increasing curriculum differentiation. They may decide that for some key stage 4 pupils more flexible arrangements would be appropriate.[43]

6:43 A variety of approaches should be employed to maximise the achievement of all pupils. The effective school will identify common strategies and responses across the secondary curriculum for all pupils designed to raise pupils' learning outcomes, expectations and experiences. The kinds of curriculum response available for **all** pupils will directly affect the need to intervene at an individual level.

6:44 All pupils should know what is expected of them. For example, secondary schools' general marking policies should therefore be consistent across all subjects. Schools should be similarly consistent in other areas, making clear, for example, how they expect all pupils to behave and to present their work. The emphasis on literacy across the curriculum will help to achieve consistency in handwriting, spelling, punctuation and presentation. Thus for all subject areas and for all pupils including those with SEN, there will be a common set of expectations across the school which are known to everyone, and a further commitment to support those pupils who have difficulty meeting those expectations.

6:45 It is for individual schools to decide the procedures they should adopt for meeting the needs of all pupils, for observing and assessing their progress, and for deciding the nature of the special educational provision that they should make. It is essential that these procedures are carefully managed and monitored, and that there are effective internal communication and liaison arrangements between staff.

6:46 School and departmental systems for observing and assessing the progress of individual pupils should provide information about areas where a pupil is not progressing even when the teaching style has been differentiated. These observations should be enhanced by knowledge built up over time of an individual pupil's strengths and weaknesses. Using this evidence, subject teachers may conclude that the strategies they are currently using with the pupil are not resulting in the pupil learning as effectively as possible. In these circumstances, they will need to consult the SENCO to consider what else might be done. The starting point will always be a review of the strategies being used and the way in which these might be developed. Evaluation of the strategies in place may lead to the conclusion that the pupil requires help over and above that which is normally available within the particular class or subject. Consideration should then be given to helping the pupil through *School Action*.

The school has a duty to inform the child's parents that special educational provision is being made for the child because the child has SEN.

See Section 317A, Education Act 1996

---

43 Flexibility in the Secondary Curriculum QCA/99/477.

expectation that this help will take the form of the deployment of extra staff to enable one-to-one tuition to be given to the pupil. However, this may not be the most appropriate way of helping the pupil. A more appropriate approach might be to provide different learning materials or special equipment, to introduce some group or individual support, to devote extra adult time to devising the nature of the planned intervention and to monitoring its effectiveness or to undertake staff development and training aimed at introducing more effective strategies. Speedy access to LEA support services for one-off or occasional advice on strategies or equipment or for staff training may make it possible to provide effective intervention without the need for regular or ongoing input from external agencies.

Individual Education Plans

6:58 Strategies employed to enable the pupil to progress should be recorded within an Individual Education Plan (IEP). Information on managing IEPs and Group Education Plans can be found in the SEN Toolkit. The IEP should include information about:

- the short-term targets set for or by the pupil
- the teaching strategies to be used
- the provision to be put in place
- when the plan is to be reviewed
- success and/or exit criteria
- outcomes (to be recorded when IEP is reviewed).

6:59 The IEP should only record that which is <u>additional to</u> or <u>different from</u> the differentiated curriculum provision, which is in place as part of provision for all pupils. The IEP should be crisply written and focus on three or four individual targets, chosen from those relating to the key areas of communication, literacy, mathematics, and behaviour and social skills to match the pupil's needs. Strategies may be cross curricular or may sometimes be subject specific. The IEP should be discussed with the pupil and the parents.

6:60 Where a pupil with identified SEN is at serious risk of disaffection or exclusion the IEP should reflect appropriate strategies to meet their needs[45]. A Pastoral Support Programme should not be used to replace the graduated response to special educational needs.

Reviewing IEPs

6:61 The IEP should be reviewed at least twice a year. Ideally it should be reviewed termly, or possibly more frequently for some pupils. At least one review a year could coincide with a routine Parents' Evening, although schools should recognise that some parents might prefer a more private meeting. Reviews need not be unduly formal, but parents' views on their child's progress should be sought and they should be consulted as part of the review process. The pupil should also take part in the review process and be involved in setting the targets. If the pupil is not involved in the review meeting, their ascertainable views

45 DfEE Circular 10/99 'Social Inclusion: Pupil Support'.

should be considered in any discussion. Further guidance on reviewing IEPs is to be found in the SEN Toolkit.

School Action Plus

6:62 A request for help from external services is likely to follow a decision taken by the SENCO and colleagues, in consultation with parents, at a meeting to review the child's IEP. Schools should always consult specialists when they take action on behalf of a pupil through *School Action Plus*. But the involvement of specialists need not be limited to such pupils. Outside specialists can play an important part in the very early identification of special educational needs and in advising schools on effective provision designed to prevent the development of more significant needs. They can act as consultants and be a source for in-service advice on learning and behaviour management strategies for all teachers.

6:63 At *School Action Plus* external support services, both those provided by the LEA and by outside agencies, will usually see the child, in school if that is appropriate and practicable, so that they can advise subject and pastoral staff on new IEPs, with fresh targets and accompanying strategies, provide more specialist assessments that can inform planning and the measurement of a pupil's progress, give advice on the use of new or specialist strategies or materials, and in some cases provide support for particular activities. The kinds of advice and support available to schools will vary according to local policies.

6:64 The triggers for *School Action Plus* could be that, despite receiving an individualised programme and/or concentrated support, the pupil:

- continues to make little or no progress in specific areas over a long period
- continues working at National Curriculum levels substantially below that expected of pupils of a similar age
- continues to have difficulty in developing literacy and mathematics skills
- has emotional or behavioural difficulties which substantially and regularly interfere with their own learning or that of the class group, despite having an individualised behaviour management programme
- has sensory or physical needs, and requires additional specialist equipment or regular advice or visits, providing direct intervention to the pupil or advice to the staff, by a specialist service
- has ongoing communication or interaction difficulties that impede the development of social relationships and cause substantial barriers to learning.

6:65 Where schools seeks the help of external support services, those services will need to see the pupil's records in order to establish which strategies have already been employed and which targets have been set and achieved. They can then advise on new and appropriate targets for the pupil's IEP and on accompanying strategies. They may also provide additional specialist assessment that can inform planning and the measurement of a pupil's progress.

6:66 The SENCO, link workers or subject specialists, and the literacy and numeracy coordinators, together with the external specialists, should consider a range of different teaching approaches and appropriate equipment and teaching materials, including the use of information technology. The external specialist may act in an advisory capacity, provide additional specialist assessment or be involved in teaching the pupil directly. In some instances better management or alternative arrangements in school, based on advice from health professionals, may considerably reduce the pupil's special educational needs.

6:67 The resulting IEP for the pupil will set out new strategies for supporting the pupil's progress. Although developed with the help of outside specialists, the strategies specified in the IEP should usually be implemented, at least in part and as far as possible, in the normal classroom setting. Hence delivery of the IEP will be the responsibility of subject teachers.

6:68 If the SENCO and the external specialist consider that the information gathered about the pupil is insufficient, and that more detailed advice must be obtained from other outside professionals, then the consent of the pupil's parents must be sought.

6:69 The SENCO should note in the pupil's records what further advice is being sought and the support to be provided for the pupil pending receipt of the advice.

School request for statutory assessment

6:70 For a very few pupils the help given by schools through *Action Plus* may not be sufficient to enable the pupil to make adequate progress. It will then be necessary for the school, in consultation with the parents and any external agencies already involved, to consider whether to ask the LEA to initiate a statutory assessment.

6:71 Where a request for a statutory assessment is made to an LEA, the pupil will have demonstrated significant cause for concern. The LEA will seek evidence from the school that any action implemented for the pupil has continued for a reasonable period of time without success and that alternatives have been tried. The LEA will need information about the pupil's progress over time, and will also need clear documentation in relation to the child's special educational needs and any action taken to deal with those needs, including any resources or special arrangements put in place. This information might in some cases include reports or written advice from external agencies. The evidence that the LEA will examine in deciding whether to make a statutory assessment is described in Chapter Seven. The criteria, which LEAs may adopt in deciding whether to issue a statement for a particular child, are set out in Chapter Eight. Regular liaison between the LEA and schools should ensure that there is clarity about the information required by the Authority when an assessment is requested.

6.72 By the time the head teacher considers requesting a statutory assessment of a pupils' special educational needs, the school should be in a position to provide written evidence of or information about:

- **the school's action through *School Action* and *School Action Plus***
- **individual education plans for the pupil**
- **records of regular reviews and their outcomes**
- **the pupil's health including the pupil's medical history where relevant**
- **National Curriculum levels**

- **attainments in literacy and mathematics**
- **educational and other assessments, for example from an advisory specialist support teacher or an educational psychologist**
- **views of the parents and of the pupil**
- **involvement of other professionals**
- **any involvement by the social services or education welfare service.**

6:73 The description of the pupil's learning difficulty and progress together with information about the special educational provision made will form the basis on which the LEA can consider whether a statutory assessment is necessary. If the LEA support services and, in particular, the LEA educational psychologist have already been involved in assessing the pupil and reviewing provision, the LEA should be able to decide relatively quickly whether a statutory assessment is necessary. In the meantime – and whilst any subsequent statutory assessment is being made – the pupil should continue to be supported through *School Action Plus*.

Working with children with statements of special educational needs

6:74 All pupils with statements of special educational needs, whether they are attending mainstream or special schools, should have short-term targets set. In the majority of cases the strategies to meet these targets will be set out in an IEP. As at *School Action* and *School Action Plus* the IEP should only record that which is additional to or different from the normal differentiated curriculum provision.

Annual review of a statement of special educational needs

6:75 The general procedures to be followed during annual reviews of statements and the particular arrangements for annual reviews held in year 9 and for transition planning are set out in Chapter Nine.

7 Statutory Assessment of Special Educational Needs

Introduction

> **LEAs must identify and make a statutory assessment of those children for whom they are responsible who have special educational needs and who probably need a statement.**
>
> See Sections 321 and 323, Education Act 1996.

7:1 The special educational needs of the great majority of children should be met effectively within mainstream settings through *Early Years Action* and *Early Years Action* Plus or *School Action* and *School Action Plus*, without the local education authority needing to make a statutory assessment. In a very small number of cases the LEA will need to make a statutory assessment of special educational needs and then consider whether or not to issue a statement.

7:2 Statutory assessment involves:

- consideration by the LEA, working co-operatively with parents, the child's school[46] and, as appropriate, other agencies, as to whether a statutory assessment of the child's special educational needs is necessary

and if so

- conducting the assessment, in close collaboration with parents, schools and other agencies.

7:3 The principles underpinning the carrying out of an assessment of special educational needs should be broadly similar to those adopted by the Department of Health for assessing children in need.[47]

7:4 An assessment under section 323 of the Education Act 1996 should **only** be undertaken if the LEA believe that the child probably has special educational needs and that the LEA needs or probably needs to determine the child's special educational provision itself by making a statement.

7:5 It may be that in considering whether the assessment is necessary the LEA will conclude that intervention at *Early Years Action Plus* or *School Action Plus* is appropriate; or the LEA might be able to identify different ways in which the school could help the child through such intervention. If so, the LEA would conclude that a statutory assessment was not necessary.

7:6 Statutory assessment itself will not always lead to a statement. The information gathered during an assessment may indicate ways in which the school can meet the child's needs without the need for any special educational provision to be determined by the LEA through a statement. It may be, that the provision of a particular piece of equipment

---

46 In this chapter 'schools' refers both to early education settings and all schools (including non-maintained schools).

47 DH et al 'The Framework for the Assessment of Children in Need and their Families'. April 2000.

would allow the school, guided as appropriate by expert help, to meet the child's needs or that alternative strategies, as advised by LEA support services, would enable the child to make progress.

Routes for referral

7:7 A child will be brought to the LEA's attention as possibly requiring an assessment through:

- **a request for an assessment by the child's school or setting**
- **a request for an assessment from a parent**

or

- **a referral by another agency.**[48]

7:8 It is important that all requests and referrals for assessment are considered as quickly as possible regardless of their source.[49]

Request by the child's school or setting

7:9 In some cases, schools or settings will conclude, after they have taken action to meet the learning difficulties of a child, that the child's needs remain so substantial that they cannot be met effectively within the resources normally available to the school or setting.

> **Schools and relevant nursery education providers have a statutory right to ask the LEA to conduct a statutory assessment or reassessment of a child's educational needs.**
>
> See Section 329A, Education Act 1996

7:10 In this context 'schools' include:

- maintained schools (mainstream and special, other than special schools established in a hospital)
- maintained nursery schools
- pupil referral units
- all independent schools including City Academies ,City Technology Colleges and City Colleges for Technology or the Arts
- schools approved under the Education Act 1996, section 342
- all early education settings who are in receipt of financial assistance from their LEA and are providers of relevant nursery education for the purposes of section 118 of the School Standards and Framework Act 1998 – effectively to four and five year olds.[50]

---

48 For example,health authorities and social services department can make referrals.

49 The Education (Special Educational Needs) (England) Regulations 2001 set out specific time limits in relation to requests for assessment.

50 Early education settings in receipt of financial assistance providing nursery education to a three year old, or a child under three, do not have a statutory right to request an assessment or reassessment but may refer a child. By September 2004 LEAs' duties under section 118 will extend to three year olds and settings' rights to request assessments will extend accordingly.

7:11 Schools and settings should consult the parents before requesting an assessment. The LEA must comply with such a request, unless it has made a statutory assessment within six months of the date of the request or unless it concludes, upon examining any evidence before it or representations made to it, that a statutory assessment is not necessary. If at this time the head teacher judges that the full National Curriculum is not meeting the pupil's needs then a temporary disapplication may be appropriate.[51]

7:12 If the LEA refuses to agree to the request, parents have the right of appeal to the SEN Tribunal. LEAs **must** make sure that parents are informed of their rights of appeal and the time limits for lodging an appeal, the availability of parent partnership and disagreement resolution services, and the fact that the parent's right of appeal cannot be affected by any disagreement resolution procedure.

Evidence to be provided by the school or early education setting

7:13 When making a request for a statutory assessment, the school or setting should state clearly the reasons for the request and submit the following evidence:

- **the views of parents recorded at *Early Years Action* and *Early Years Action Plus* or *School Action* and *School Action Plus***
- **the ascertainable views of the child**
- **copies of IEPs at *Early Years Action* and *Early Years Action Plus* or *School Action* and *School Action Plus***
- **evidence of progress over time**
- **copies of advice, where provided, from health and social services**
- **evidence of the involvement and views of professionals with relevant specialist knowledge and expertise outside the normal competence of the school or setting**
- **evidence of the extent to which the school or setting has followed the advice provided by professionals with relevant specialist knowledge.**

7:14 For some very young children with complex needs the LEA should accept as evidence one over-arching report from the lead professional involved with the child. This approach might also be appropriate for an older child who through an accident or ill health suddenly acquires easily identifiable complex needs that require the LEA to assess and make provision.

Referral by another agency

7:15 Health services and social services departments may draw children to the LEA's attention. This is particularly likely with children under five with complex needs who are not yet attending school but who may be in an early education setting. The LEA will then need to collect evidence before considering whether it is necessary to assess the child.

51 The Education (National Curriculum) Temporary Exceptions for Individual Pupils (England) Regulations 2000.

Notice that an LEA is considering whether to make a statutory assessment

7:16 Before deciding whether to make an assessment the LEA must issue a notice under section 323(1) or 329A(3) of the Education Act 1996. The LEA:

i. **must** write to the parents to give them notice that the LEA is considering whether to make a statutory assessment

ii. **must** set out for parents the procedures that will be followed if a statutory assessment is considered necessary and the procedures for subsequently drawing up a statement if it is considered necessary

iii. should explain the precise timing of each of the various stages of the assessments within the overall six-month time limit, indicate ways in which the parents can assist the LEA in meeting the time limits, and explain the exceptions to the time limits

iv. **must** tell parents the name of an officer of the LEA from whom further information may be obtained. (This person is often known as the Named LEA Officer)

v. **must** tell parents of their right to submit written evidence and make oral representations as to why they believe their child should or should not be assessed. The LEA **must** set a time limit for receipt of parental views, which must not be less than 29 days

vi. should encourage parents to respond and submit evidence, pointing out the importance of their contribution. When parents make oral representations, the LEA should agree a written summary with the parents. The LEA may invite parents to indicate formally if they do not wish to make or add to previous representations, in order that the LEA can then immediately start to consider whether a statutory assessment is necessary

vii. **must** give parents information about the local parent partnership service which should provide information about other sources of independent advice, such as local or national voluntary organisations and any local support group that may be able to help them consider what they feel about their child's needs

viii. should ask the parents whether they would like the LEA to consult anyone in addition to those whom the LEA must approach for educational, medical, psychological and social services advice, if the LEA decides to proceed with the statutory assessment

ix. should tell parents that they may also provide any private advice or opinions, which they have or can obtain, and that this advice will be taken into account.

7:17 This notice to parents should be written in plain language so that parents can readily understand its meaning. The notice **must** make clear that the LEA has not at this stage decided to go ahead with an assessment, rather it is considering whether it should do so. If the notice is not clear about this, some parents will, on reading all the documentation, believe the LEA has already begun to make an assessment, and may become confused if the LEA later informs them that it has decided not to make an assessment.

7:18 Statutory assessment will be a new and unknown experience for most parents. It is very important therefore that LEAs try to make the process as accessible as possible for all parents. Advice and suggestions as to support that might be given to parents throughout the statutory assessment process is contained in Chapter Two and in the SEN Toolkit.

Notification to other agencies of a proposal to assess

7:19 The LEA **must** send a copy of the notice to the designated officer of the Social Services department and the health authority. The LEA should explain that they will be asked for advice if the assessment proceeds. They should also copy it to their own educational psychology service and any other relevant agencies, such as the education welfare service, which might be asked for advice if the assessment proceeds.

7:20 LEAs are not at this point asking these agencies to provide advice, but alerting them to the possibility of a request for advice in the near future. This early information gives the agencies the opportunity to collate records and consult others who might be involved in providing advice. Early action at this stage within the health service and social services departments will in effect serve to extend the time available to those agencies for gathering advice, and thus help them meet the statutory time limits.

Request by a parent

7:21 Parents may ask the LEA to conduct a statutory assessment under section 328 or 329 of the Education Act 1996. The LEA **must** comply with such a request unless they have made a statutory assessment within six months of the date of the request or unless they conclude, upon examining all the evidence provided to them, that a statutory assessment is not necessary.

7:22 When schools, external specialists, including LEA support and educational psychology services, and parents have been working in partnership at *School Action Plus*, the parental request for a statutory assessment will usually have been discussed between them. Therefore the request is likely to be an approach agreed by all the parties involved. The parents may then, with the help of the school, be able to provide the LEA with the evidence listed at paragraph 7:13 above. Sometimes, however, a parental request for a statutory assessment may be a reflection of dissatisfaction with the action taken by the school. Whatever the reason, the LEA should take all parental requests seriously and take appropriate action.

7:23 Parents may decide to request an assessment if they believe that their child has needs which are either not being met through school-based intervention, or are so substantial that a mainstream school could not meet them effectively from within their own resources. Parents of very young children with complex needs may also request an assessment. It is helpful to the LEA if the parent can set out clearly the reason for the request, and provide information as to the provision the child has already received. In many cases the child's school or professionals already involved with the child can provide information for the parents to send to the LEA. The LEA should, where necessary, actively seek any additional appropriate evidence from the school.

7:24 Where a child attends an independent school (see Glossary), a parental request, or indeed a school request, for statutory assessment may be the first time that an LEA hears about that child. The procedure the LEA follows and the factors to consider in deciding whether to make an assessment should be the same as if the child were in a maintained school. The LEA will wish to consider evidence provided by the child's school and parents as to their learning difficulties, including evidence about any action taken by the school to meet those difficulties. LEAs may find it helpful to inform independent schools in their area of the LEA's duty to identify children for whom they are responsible and who may require statements of special educational needs. LEAs should explain to those schools the local arrangements for school-based provision, procedures for assessment and the information they would expect to be given.

7:25 Where parents are educating their child at home there will be occasions when parents may request an assessment. LEAs should seek evidence from the parents and professionals involved with the child so that they can consider whether it is necessary to assess.

7:26 When a child is brought to the attention of the LEA by a request for a statutory assessment, the LEA **must** decide within six weeks whether to carry out such an assessment. They are not required to issue a notice to the parents to say that they are considering whether to make an assessment under section 323(1). However the LEA should immediately contact the parents in order to:

- investigate further the nature of their concern
- ascertain the degree of their involvement and agreement with the special educational provision that has already been made for their child at school
- give them full details of the assessment process and the information set out at paragraph 7:16 above.

7:27 The LEA **must** inform the child's head teacher when the parents have made a request for a statutory assessment. If the parent has not already provided it, the LEA should ask the school for written evidence about the child, in particular, the school's assessment of the child's learning difficulty and the school's account of any special educational provision that has been made.

7:28 At the same time, the LEA must notify the educational psychology service, the designated officers of the Social Services department and the health authority and any other agencies that might later be asked for advice. They will thus be 'on notice' so that if a decision is later made to carry out an assessment they will be able to provide advice to the LEA within the prescribed time limits.

7:29 The LEA **must** then decide whether or not to make an assessment under section 323. The LEA should react consistently to requests from parents, schools and settings for assessments and should subsequently make open and objective judgements as to whether a statement should be issued. The LEA should reach decisions as quickly as thorough consideration of all the issues allows and always, subject to certain prescribed exceptions, within the statutory time limits. If the LEA refuses to agree to a parent's, school's or setting's request for assessment, parents have the right of appeal to the SEN Tribunal. LEAs must make sure that parents are informed of their rights of appeal and the time limits for lodging an appeal. They must also make sure that parents are informed of the availability of parent partnership and disagreement resolution services, and that disagreement resolution cannot affect the parent's right of appeal.

Children who may need immediate referral for statutory assessment

7:30 In the great majority of cases, before any request is made to the LEA for a statutory assessment, the school will have assessed a child's learning difficulties and will have made special educational provision to meet the child's needs. However, in a very small minority of cases, children may demonstrate such significant difficulties that the school may consider it impossible or inappropriate to carry out in full their chosen assessment procedure. For example, the school's concerns may have led to further diagnostic assessment or examination which demonstrates that a child has severe sensory or other impairment which, without immediate specialist intervention beyond the capacity of the school, will lead to increased learning difficulties, or a child may have severe emotional or behavioural difficulties which require an urgent outside-school response (see also 8:23). There is a need for a quick response from the LEA for such children.

7:31 Almost all pupils will remain at their mainstream school during the assessment process. There may be a very small number of exceptional cases where the child's needs mean that they would be better supported during the assessment by being placed in a special school. This will often be where immediate or emergency support is required or where any delay might further damage the child's development. Children who have special educational needs but do not have a statement must normally be educated in a mainstream school. Section 316A(2) provides flexibility to allow a child who does not have a statement to attend a special school in a number of exceptional circumstances. These are:

- where the child is being assessed to determine if a statement is needed
- where there has been a change in circumstances
- where the child is in hospital and is admitted to a special school within the hospital.

7:32 In order to place a child in a special school during the assessment process the child's parents, the head teacher of the special school at which the child will be placed, the local education authority and anyone who is providing advice as part of the assessment process **must** agree to the placement. Where a child is admitted to a special school following a change of circumstances, the child's parents, the head teacher of the special school at which the child will be placed and the local education authority **must** again agree. The LEA should make clear to parents the reason for such an assessment placement and its duration.

Considering whether a statutory assessment is necessary

7:33 The first task for the LEA, having notified the parents that a statutory assessment might be necessary or having received a request from the parents, school or setting for such an assessment, is to decide whether a statutory assessment must be made.

7:34 In deciding whether to make a statutory assessment, the critical question is whether there is convincing evidence that, despite the school, with the help of external specialists, taking relevant and purposeful action to meet the child's learning difficulties, those difficulties remain or have not been remedied sufficiently and may require the LEA to determine the child's special educational provision. LEAs will need to examine a wide range of evidence. They should consider the school's assessment of the child's needs, including the input of other professionals such as educational psychologists and specialist support teachers, and the action the school has taken to meet those needs. LEAs will always wish to see evidence of, and consider the factors associated with, the child's levels of academic attainment and rate of progress. The additional evidence that authorities should seek and the questions that need to be asked may vary according to the child's age and the nature of the learning difficulty.

Evidence for deciding whether to make a statutory assessment

7:35 In considering whether a statutory assessment is necessary, LEAs should pay particular attention to:

- evidence that the school has responded appropriately to the requirements of the National Curriculum, especially the section entitled 'Inclusion: Providing effective learning opportunities for all children'
- evidence provided by the child's school, parents and other professionals where they have been involved with the child, as to the nature, extent and cause of the child's learning difficulties
- evidence of action already taken by the child's school to meet and overcome those difficulties
- evidence of the rate and style of the child's progress
- evidence that where some progress has been made, it has only been as the result of much additional effort and instruction at a sustained level not usually commensurate with provision through *Action Plus*.

7:36 The following guidance therefore concentrates on the evidence LEAs should seek from schools, settings and parents and sets out key questions which LEAs should consider. The questions are not exhaustive: there will be other factors particular to an individual child that the LEA will wish to pursue. Nor does the guidance set out hard and fast rules whereby, if all the questions were answered in the affirmative, an assessment must always be made. Still less should an affirmative answer to any one question be taken as indicating that a statutory assessment is necessary. Decisions must be made by local education authorities in the light of all the circumstances of each individual case and, always, in the closest consultation with parents and schools.

7:37 In the interest of establishing agreed local interpretation, LEAs may operate moderating groups to support them in making consistent decisions. Such groups can include head teachers, SENCOs, governors, educational psychologists and colleagues from health and social services. LEAs may use similar groups of professionals to consider the evidence for all referrals for statutory assessment, so that the LEA have the advice and support of a multi-professional team in making decisions as to whether to carry out assessments. In the latter case, the group cannot take decisions on individuals without being fully informed about the particular child and having access to all the evidence. Locally agreed processes of these kinds are good practice, but the role of these groups must be clear, public and open to scrutiny. They can help to support consistent and transparent decision-making by schools and LEAs.

Evidence of attainment

7:38 LEAs will always require evidence of the child's academic attainment in all areas of learning. Key indicators are provided by the results of assessments and tests in the core subjects of the National Curriculum at the end of key stages, through the outcomes of baseline assessment or information about progress in the early learning goals where appropriate.

7:39 However, academic attainment is not in itself sufficient for LEAs to conclude that a statutory assessment is or is not necessary. An individual child's attainment must always be understood in the context of the attainments of the child's peers, the child's rate of progress over time and, where appropriate, expectations of the child's performance. A child's apparently weak performance may, on examination of the evidence, be attributable to wider factors associated with the school's organisation. Careful consideration of evidence of low attainment may reveal good progress from a low base.

7:40 Nonetheless, attainment is the essential starting point when considering the evidence. LEAs should always be alert to indications that a child's learning difficulties may be particularly complex or intractable. They should be alert, therefore, to significant discrepancies between:

- a child's attainments in assessments and tests in core subjects of the National Curriculum and the attainment of the majority of children of their age
- a child's attainments in assessments and tests in core subjects of the National Curriculum and the performance expected of the child as indicated by a consensus among those who have taught and observed the child, including their parents, and supported by such standardised tests as can reliably be administered
- a child's attainment within one of the core subjects of the National Curriculum or between one core subject and another
- a child's attainments in early learning goals in comparison with the attainments of the majority of their peers.

7:41 LEAs should therefore seek clear recorded evidence of the child's academic attainment and ask, for example, whether:

- the child is not benefiting from working on programmes of study relevant to the key stage appropriate to their age or from earlier key stages, or is the subject of any temporary exception from the National Curriculum under section 364 of the Education Act 1996
- the child is working at a level significantly below that of their contemporaries in any of the core subjects of the National Curriculum or the foundation stage curriculum
- there is evidence that the child is falling progressively behind the majority of children of their age in academic attainment in any of the National Curriculum core subjects, as measured by standardised tests and the teachers' own recorded assessments of a child's classroom work, including any portfolio of the child's work.

Other factors

7:42 While academic assessments will provide important evidence, LEAs should not delay their consideration of a child until up-to-date assessment results are available. LEAs should also have regard to teachers' own recorded assessments of a child's classroom work, the outcome of IEPs and any portfolio of the child's work compiled to illustrate their progress.

7:43 LEAs should also seek evidence of any other identifiable factors that could impact on learning outcomes including:

- clear, recorded evidence of clumsiness; significant difficulties of sequencing or visual perception; deficiencies in working memory; or significant delays in language functioning
- any evidence of impaired social interaction or communication or a significantly restricted repertoire of activities, interests and imaginative development
- evidence of significant emotional or behavioural difficulties, as indicated by clear recorded examples of withdrawn or disruptive behaviour; a marked and persistent inability to concentrate; signs that the child experiences considerable frustration or distress in relation to their learning difficulties; difficulties in establishing and maintaining balanced relationships with their fellow pupils or with adults; and any other evidence of a significant delay in the development of life and social skills.

7:44 **Some** factors, including significant problems in the child's home or family circumstances or their school attendance record, can contribute towards under-attainment but may not always be indicators of special educational needs. LEAs should therefore seek any evidence of such identifiable factors that could impact on learning outcomes including:

- any evidence that the child's performance is different in different environments
- evidence of contributory medical problems
- evidence from assessments or interventions by child health or social services.

7:45 LEAs will need to consider whether the evidence points to under-attainment rather than special educational needs and thus whether there are alternative and more appropriate ways to support the child's access to learning, such as referral to the education welfare service, or to health or social services.

The child's special educational provision

7:46 Having considered evidence about the child's attainment in conjunction with other factors referred to in the preceding paragraph, the LEA may be able to identify immediate remedies that would mean that a statutory assessment was not necessary. Such remedies could include enhancing school-based provision by a referral to external agencies not already involved with the child or devising alternative forms of teaching intervention through *Early Years Action Plus* or *School Action Plus*. On the other hand, consideration of all the evidence may suggest that a statutory assessment would help to fully identify the child's special educational needs.

7:47 In order to reach a decision, LEAs should evaluate the action already taken by the school or setting to help the child, in particular the special educational provision that has already been made. Except when the child's condition has suddenly changed, LEAs will wish to see clear evidence of the learning difficulties identified and the interventions made by the child's teachers and other professionals through *Early Years Action* and *Early Years Action Plus* or *School Action* and *School Action Plus*, together with the SENCO's evaluation of these interventions. LEAs should also ask to see evidence that information from, and the insights of, parents has been used and that, so far as possible, parents have been involved in the process of meeting the child's learning difficulties.

7:48 In cases where it is the parents who first express a concern to the school or setting about the child's progress, the LEA should ask to see evidence that the concerns have been investigated thoroughly, in the same way as if the child's teacher had expressed a concern. LEAs should also seek any medical advice which has been made available to the school or setting about the child, and will wish to seek information from the child's parents as to any medical condition that could be affecting the child's learning.

7:49 In the light of evidence about the child's learning difficulty, LEAs should consider the action taken and, in particular, should ask whether:

- the school or setting has, in consultation with outside specialists, formulated, monitored and regularly evaluated IEPs and whether the child's progress, measured by criterion referenced or standardised tests, continues to be significantly and consistently less than that which may be expected for the majority of children following such programmes
- the school or setting has sought the views of, and involved, the child's parents
- the school or setting has actively sought the views of the child, as appropriate to their age and understanding
- the school has, where appropriate, utilised structured reading and spelling programmes, and multi-sensory teaching strategies to enhance the National Literacy and Numeracy Frameworks
- the school has explored the possible benefits of, and where practicable, secured access for the child to appropriate information technology – for example word processing facilities (including spell-checkers), overlay keyboards and software, specialised switches and provision of training in the use of that technology for the child, their parents and staff – so that the child is able to use that technology across the curriculum in school, and where appropriate, at home
- the school has implemented its policy on pastoral care and guidance and sought external advice to meet any social, emotional or behavioural difficulties
- the school or setting has, with the parents' consent, notified and sought the assistance of the school doctor and/or the child's general practitioner, as appropriate.

7:50 Where the balance of evidence presented to, and assessed by, the LEA suggests that the child's learning difficulties:

- have not responded to relevant and purposeful measures taken by the school or setting and external specialists

and

- may call for special educational provision which cannot reasonably be provided within the resources normally available to mainstream maintained schools and settings in the area,

the LEA should consider very carefully the case for a statutory assessment of the child's special educational needs.

7:51 These considerations apply to all children referred to LEAs by their parents or by their schools or settings. But the precise nature of the evidence that LEAs should seek about the child's learning difficulty, its apparent cause and the special educational provision made, may depend in some part on the nature of the child's learning difficulty or disability, and on the child's age.

7:52 This guidance does not assume that there are hard and fast categories of special educational need. It recognises, as LEAs will recognise, that each child is unique and that the questions asked by LEAs should reflect the particular circumstances of that child. LEAs should recognise that there is a wide spectrum of special educational needs that are frequently inter-related, although there are also specific needs that usually relate directly to particular types of impairment. Children will have needs and requirements which may fall into at least one of four areas, many children will have inter-related needs. The impact of these combinations on the child's ability to function, learn and succeed should be taken into account. The areas of need are:

- communication and interaction
- cognition and learning
- behaviour, emotional and social development
- sensory and/or physical.

7:53 Although needs and requirements can usefully be organised into areas, individual pupils may well have needs which span two or more areas. For example, a pupil with general learning difficulties may also have behavioural difficulties or a sensory impairment. Where needs are complex in this sense it is important to carry out a detailed assessment of individual pupils and their situations. However, the accumulation of low-level difficulties may not in itself equate with a school being unable to meet the child's needs through school-based provision. In some cases pupils will have needs that are not only complex but also severe.

7:54 In considering evidence as to whether or not it is necessary to carry out a statutory assessment LEAs should bear in mind the particular requirements of the individual child, and whether these requirements can be met from the resources already available to mainstream maintained schools and settings in their area in the context of school-based intervention, monitoring and review arrangements

Communication and interaction

7:55 Most children with special educational needs have strengths and difficulties in one, some or all of the areas of speech, language and communication. Their communication needs may be both diverse and complex. They will need to continue to develop their linguistic competence in order to support their thinking as well as their communication. The range of difficulties will encompass children and young people with speech and language delay, impairments or disorders, specific learning difficulties, such as dyslexia and dyspraxia, hearing impairment and those who demonstrate features within the autistic spectrum; they may also apply to some children and young people with moderate, severe or profound learning difficulties. The range of need will include those for whom language and communication difficulties are the result of permanent sensory or physical impairment.

7:56 These children may require some, or all, of the following:

- flexible teaching arrangements
- help in acquiring, comprehending and using language
- help in articulation
- help in acquiring literacy skills
- help in using augmentative and alternative means of communication
- help to use different means of communication confidently and competently for a range of purposes, including formal situations
- help in organising and coordinating oral and written language
- support to compensate for the impact of a communication difficulty on learning in English as an additional language
- help in expressing, comprehending and using their own language, where English is not the first language.

7:57 If the LEA considers that some or all of these programmes could be provided for a child by the school in collaboration with LEA or external support services, then the LEA may conclude that intervention should be provided at *School Action Plus* and monitored to see if the action was effective. It would then be appropriate for the LEA to conclude that a statutory assessment was not necessary. If, on the other hand, the school and support services had already provided these interventions through *School Action Plus* and the child had not made acceptable progress, then a statutory assessment should be considered.

Cognition and learning

7:58 Children who demonstrate features of moderate, severe or profound learning difficulties or specific learning difficulties, such as dyslexia or dyspraxia, require specific programmes to aid progress in cognition and learning. Such requirements may also apply to some extent to children with physical and sensory impairments and those on the autistic spectrum. Some of these children may have associated sensory, physical and behavioural difficulties that compound their needs. These children may require some, or all, of the following:

- flexible teaching arrangements

- help with processing language, memory and reasoning skills
- help and support in acquiring literacy skills
- help in organising and coordinating spoken and written English to aid cognition
- help with sequencing and organisational skills
- help with problem solving and developing concepts
- programmes to aid improvement of fine and motor competencies
- support in the use of technical terms and abstract ideas
- help in understanding ideas, concepts and experiences when information cannot be gained through first hand sensory or physical experiences.

7:59 As indicated in paragraphs 7:46 and 7:47, the LEA will need to consider on an individual basis, whether these programmes can be provided through intervention at *School Action Plus* or whether the LEA should undertake a statutory assessment. The decision may depend on the severity of the child's cognitive ability and any associated needs that compound the child's difficulties in accessing the curriculum. If solutions for a child have moved beyond ordinary differentiation to a solution where specific input is necessary not just to provide access to learning but more importantly to secure learning or to develop strategies to overcome particular areas of weakness, then an assessment may be necessary.

Behaviour, emotional and social development

7:60 Children and young people who demonstrate features of emotional and behavioural difficulties, who are withdrawn or isolated, disruptive and disturbing, hyperactive and lack concentration; those with immature social skills; and those presenting challenging behaviours arising from other complex special needs, may require help or counselling for some, or all, of the following:

- flexible teaching arrangements
- help with development of social competence and emotional maturity
- help in adjusting to school expectations and routines
- help in acquiring the skills of positive interaction with peers and adults
- specialised behavioural and cognitive approaches
- re-channelling or re-focusing to diminish repetitive and self-injurious behaviours
- provision of class and school systems which control or censure negative or difficult behaviours and encourage positive behaviour
- provision of a safe and supportive environment.

7:61 The LEA will need to consider, on an individual basis, whether these interventions can be provided through *School Action Plus* or whether the LEA needs to undertake a statutory assessment.

Sensory and/or physical needs

7:62 There is a wide spectrum of sensory, multi-sensory and physical difficulties. The sensory range extends from profound and permanent deafness or visual impairment through to lesser levels of loss, which may only be temporary. Physical impairments may arise from physical, neurological or metabolic causes that only require appropriate access to educational facilities and equipment; others may lead to more complex learning and social needs; a few children will have multi-sensory difficulties some with associated physical difficulties. For some children the inability to take part fully in school life causes significant emotional stress or physical fatigue. Many of these children and young people will require some of the following:

- flexible teaching arrangements
- appropriate seating, acoustic conditioning and lighting
- adaptations to the physical environment of the school
- adaptations to school policies and procedures
- access to alternative or augmented forms of communication
- provision of tactile and kinaesthetic materials
- access to different amplification systems
- access to low vision aids
- access in all areas of the curriculum through specialist aids, equipment or furniture
- regular and frequent access to specialist support.

7:63 For the children with the most complex physical needs and the most severe sensory losses it is likely that the LEA will consider a statutory assessment to be necessary. The governing factors are probably the extent of specialist teaching or aids and adaptations which are required. However, for many children with a lesser level of sensory or physical needs, intervention at *School Action Plus* will be appropriate.

Medical conditions

7:64 A medical diagnosis or a disability does not necessarily imply SEN. It may not be necessary for a child or young person with any particular diagnosis or medical condition to have a statement, or to need any form of additional educational provision at any phase of education. It is the child's educational needs rather than a medical diagnosis that must be considered. Some pupils may not require statements or school-based SEN provision but they have medical conditions that, if not properly managed, could hinder their access to education.[52]

7:65 Medical conditions may have a significant impact on a child's experiences and the way they function in school. The impact may be direct in that the condition may affect cognitive or physical abilities, behaviour or emotional state. The impact may also be

52 DfEE/DH: 'Supporting Pupils with Medical Needs: a good practice guide' provides advice for schools on drawing up medication policies and putting in place effective management systems to support pupils with medical needs. DfEE/DH Circular 14/96 sets out the legal framework

indirect, perhaps disrupting access to education through unwanted effects of treatments or through the psychological effects that serious or chronic illness or disability can have on a child and their family. LEAs should consider the need for assessment in line with the guidance at 7:55–7:63. The effects of a medical condition may be intermittent and their impact on the child's function in school can vary at different stages of their school career. This may reflect changes in the school curriculum, changes in the individual child and changes in the peer group, for example, with the onset of puberty.

7:66 Consultation and open discussion between the child's parents, the school, the school doctor or the child's general practitioner, the community paediatrician and any specialist services providing treatment for the child will be essential to ensure that the child makes maximum progress. Such collaboration should also ensure that the child is not unnecessarily excluded from any part of the curriculum or school activity because of anxiety about their care and treatment.

7:67 Schools should ensure that their own pastoral care arrangements allow children and young people to discuss any health related and other problems with a relevant health professional, educational psychologist, education welfare officer, counsellor or other professional. The school and family should liaise in providing maximum support for the child.

Deciding that a statutory assessment is necessary

7:68 Within six weeks of notifying parents that a statutory assessment is being considered or within six weeks of parents, schools and settings requesting an assessment, the LEA **must** tell the parents and the school or setting (if they made the request) whether or not they will make a statutory assessment. The 29-day period within which parents may make representations is part of the six weeks.

7:69 *Decision not to make a statutory assessment:* if the LEA decides it is not necessary to carry out a statutory assessment they **must** write to the parents and explain the reasons; they should also set out the provision that they consider would meet the child's needs appropriately. The decision not to make a statutory assessment may be a severe disappointment to the child's parents and may also be unwelcome to the child's school. Regardless of whether the initiative for a possible assessment came from the LEA or a request from the parents or school, the LEA should write to the school, as well as the child's parents, giving full reasons for their decision.

7:70 The LEA should endeavour to ensure that the parents fully understand the school-based provision and their monitoring and review arrangements. In some cases, it may be helpful for the LEA's Named Officer to meet the parents to explain the position in detail. The LEA may consider it appropriate for the child's head teacher or SENCO to be present at such a meeting. A meeting of this kind will be particularly useful where it is clear that there is disagreement between the parents and the school about the child's progress and attainments at school, the appropriateness of school-based provision or about the need for a statutory assessment.

7:71 Where parents have formally requested a statutory assessment under section 328 or 329, or where their child's school or setting has made a request under section 329(A), the parents may appeal to the SEN Tribunal against a decision not to make an assessment.

LEAs must inform parents of the right to appeal and the time limits for appeal, the availability of disagreement resolution services and the fact that these do not affect the parent's right of appeal.

Time limits for making assessments

7:72 It is in the interests of all concerned that statutory assessments are carried out in a timely manner. It is important that each part of the process is conducted with all reasonable speed. The LEA may decide, having proposed to make an assessment, that they need not make that assessment, or having assessed the child, that they need not issue a proposed statement. Parents should be informed as quickly as possible of such decisions and of the appropriate alternative arrangements that will be made. LEAs **must** inform parents of the right of appeal to the SEN Tribunal at all appropriate stages of the statutory process.

7:73 Regulations set out time limits in which the various parts of the process of making statutory assessments and statements must normally be conducted. The cumulative effect of these time limits is that the period from the receipt of a request for a statutory assessment or the issue of a notice to parents under section 323(1) or section 329A(3) to the issue of the final copy of the statement should normally be no more than 26 weeks. A flow chart can be found at 8:134.

Making the assessment

7:74 After deciding to make a statutory assessment the LEA **must** seek parental, educational, medical, psychological and social services advice. They must also seek any other advice they consider appropriate[53] and, where reasonable, should consult those whom the parents have named. They should do so immediately and should ask all concerned to respond within six weeks.

7:75 At this point parents **must** be informed that, as part of the process of putting together all the relevant advice, their child may be called for an examination or assessment. If their child is to be examined or assessed, parents **must** also be informed of their right to be present with their child at any interview, test, medical or other assessment which is being conducted and should be told of the time, place and purpose of appointments. They **must** also be told of the name of an LEA officer from whom they can obtain further information, and that they have the right to submit information to the LEA if they want to. Parents should be told that, whilst it is their right to be present, in certain circumstances it may be counterproductive: for instance, where a classroom observation is carried out as part of the assessment, a child will behave differently if their parents are present, which would negate the purpose of the observation.

7:76 The health services and social services departments **must** normally respond within six weeks of the date of receiving the request for advice. The LEA will have previously notified the designated medical officer and the designated social services officer of the possibility of an assessment.

---

53 If a child is currently the subject of public law proceedings it would be advisable for the LEA to involve the Children's Guardian (formerly known as the guardian ad litem) in the assessment process.

7:77 The health services and social services departments are not obliged to respond within six weeks if they have had no relevant knowledge of the child concerned prior to the LEA informing them that they were considering whether to assess, or prior to the LEA notifying the health and social services that they have received a request for an assessment. In those circumstances, however, the health service and social services departments should make every effort to respond promptly.

Requests for advice

7:78 The LEA must now proceed to seek the advice required as part of the process of statutory assessment. The LEA must always give copies of any representations made by or evidence provided by the child's parents, under section 323(1)(d) or section 329A(3)(d) to those from whom advice is sought.

7:79 LEAs should make clear that the Regulations[54] require that the advice **must** relate to the educational, medical, psychological, or other features that appear relevant to a child's current and future educational needs. The advice **must** also set out how those features could affect the child's educational needs and the provision that is considered appropriate in the light of those features. Those giving advice may comment on the amount of provision they consider appropriate. Thus LEAs should not have blanket policies that prevent those giving advice from commenting on the amount of provision they consider a child requires.

7:80 However, the advice provided by all professionals should **not** be influenced by consideration of the name of the school at which the child might eventually be placed. Specific schools must not be suggested. Placement will be determined by the LEA at a later stage and in the light of any preference stated by or representations made by the parents. But discussions between advisers and parents about the child's needs may include consideration of various options, including the scope for mainstream education for the child and the type of school in which the child's needs might best be met, for example mainstream, special or residential. But such discussions should not commit the LEA, nor pre-empt the parents' statement of a preference, any representations they might make or the LEA's eventual decision.

7:81 LEA requests for advice should be accompanied by notification of the date by which the advice must be submitted.

7:82 For the purpose of making a statutory assessment, the LEA **must** seek written:

A. Parental advice

B. Educational advice

C. Medical advice

D. Psychological advice

E. Social services advice

---

54 The Education (Special Educational Needs) (England) (Consolidation) Regulations 2001

F. Any other advice (such as the ascertainable wishes of the child) which the LEA or any other body from whom advice is sought, consider desirable. In particular, advice from Service Children's Education (SCE) (see Glossary) must be sought where the child's parent is a serving member of the armed forces.

7:83 In the light of educational advice received from the school or early education setting, the LEA should consider whether they should seek separate advice from a teacher or professional from a support service who has been working with the child and the school or setting before the request for statutory assessment.

7:84 If it appears to the LEA that the child has sensory difficulties, the LEA **must** obtain educational advice from a teacher qualified to teach children who are visually or hearing impaired as well as from the school or setting.

Views of the child

7:85 *LEAs should also seek to ascertain the views of children and young people as part of the assessment*. They will be able to contribute valuable information about themselves and the ways in which they might like their needs to be met. A child's views about their needs and aspirations should, wherever possible, be recorded as part of the statutory assessment process. The LEA may consider providing a pupil report form for this purpose. Pupils who are able to do so could submit their views themselves on such a form. Where children or young people need help, special arrangements for gathering the child's views could include asking parents, educational psychologists, class teachers or form tutors and other adults who know the child well. Suggested guidelines for completing advice and suggestions for consulting children and young people are provided in the SEN Toolkit.

Next steps

7:86 Having received all the advice, the LEA **must** decide whether it needs to make a statement or amend an existing statement. It **must** make that decision within ten weeks of serving the notice under section 323(4) or 329A(7).

7:87 If the LEA decides that a statement or amended statement is necessary, it **must** draft a proposed statement or proposed amended statement and send a copy to the child's parents within two weeks. The advice received as part of the assessment should be attached. It is also good practice to send a copy of the draft to those who gave advice; it would then be possible to amend any misconceptions that have arisen in interpreting the advice, prior to finalising the statement.

7:88 If the LEA decides that a statement or an amended statement is not necessary, it **must** notify the parents and give reasons, and should also notify the school of that decision, giving the reasons, and preferably provide a note in lieu of the statement, also within two weeks. The period from the service of the notice under section 323(4) or 329A(7) to the issue of a proposed statement or a note in lieu of a statement should therefore normally be no more than 12 weeks.

7:89 The LEA should receive all the necessary advice within six weeks of the issue of the notice under section 323(4) or 329A(7), although the guidance sets out a maximum time span of ten weeks. The LEA must therefore decide whether to make a statement by the end of the ten weeks; and send parents a proposed statement or the written reasons why it will not make a statement, preferably in the form of a note in lieu, within a further two weeks. Further guidance on writing a note in lieu is to be found at paragraph 8.15.

7:90 The critical point is that parents must normally receive written notification of the outcome of the assessment within 12 weeks of the start of the statutory assessment. Where the LEA decides not to assess, parents **must** be informed of their right to appeal to the SEN Tribunal, the time limits for lodging an appeal, the availability of parent partnership and disagreement resolution services and that using disagreement resolution will not affect the parent's right of appeal.

Exceptions to the time limits

7:91 In describing the role of LEAs, the health services and social services in making a statutory assessment, this chapter has highlighted the time limits that these bodies must normally meet. There will, however, be circumstances in which it is not reasonable to expect the bodies concerned to meet those time scales and the normal time limits do not therefore apply. It is good practice for parents to be told if the exceptions apply, so that they understand the reasons for any delays.

7:92 The Education (Special Educational Needs) (England) (Consolidation) Regulations 2001 appended to this Code at Annex A set out the exceptions to:

- the six-week time limit within which LEAs must tell parents whether they will or will not make a statutory assessment
- the ten-week time limit within which LEAs must make an assessment
- the six-week time limit within which the health services and social services departments must provide information.

7:93 LEAs should always strive to ensure that any delay arising from the exceptions is kept to a minimum. As soon as the conditions that have led to an exception no longer apply, the LEA should endeavour to complete the process as quickly as possible. Any remaining components of the process must, of course, be completed within their prescribed periods, regardless of whether exceptions have delayed earlier components.

Requests for further statutory assessments

7:94 Under section 328 of the Education Act 1996, the parents of a child with a statement may request a new assessment of that child under section 323 of the Act. The LEA **must** comply with such a request, so long as:

- no such assessment has been made within the previous six months; and
- the LEA concludes that it is necessary to make a further assessment.

7:95 Under section 329A of the Education Act 1996 the child's school or setting may also request a new assessment of the child. The LEA **must** comply with such a request so long as:

- no such assessment has been made within the previous six months; and
- the LEA concludes that it is necessary to make a further assessment.

7:96 The LEA must follow the procedures set out at 7.16. The LEA should consider all such requests carefully. In particular, they should consider whether there have been changes that have impacted significantly on the child's special educational needs. If the request for a further assessment originates from an annual review, much of the necessary information on which to base their decision will already be available to the LEA.

7:97 If the LEA concludes that a further assessment is not necessary, it **must** write to the parents telling them of the decision and of their right to appeal to the SEN Tribunal, and the time limits for appeal, the availability of disagreement resolution procedures and that those procedures will not affect the parent's right to appeal. The LEA **must** always give parents full reasons for its decision. The LEA may wish to arrange a meeting between the parents and the school. If the request was made by the school or setting, the LEA **must** also give them notice of their decision and their reasons for it.

7:98 If the LEA decides that a further assessment is necessary, the procedures and time limits set out in this chapter apply. The resultant statement will supersede the previous statement.

8 Statements of Special Educational Needs

> **Where, in the light of a section 323 assessment, it is necessary for the LEA to determine the special educational provision which the child's learning difficulty calls for, the LEA shall make and maintain a statement of his or her special educational needs.**
>
> See Section 324(1), Education Act 1996

Introduction

8:1 Once all the advice requested for the statutory assessment has been received, as described in Chapter Seven, the LEA must decide whether to draw up a statement. The LEA may decide that the degree of the child's learning difficulty and the nature of the provision necessary to meet the child's special educational needs is such as to require the LEA to determine the child's special educational provision through a statement.

8:2 The LEA will make this decision when it considers that the special educational provision necessary to meet the child's needs cannot reasonably be provided within the resources normally available to mainstream schools and early education settings[55] in the area.

8:3 Maintained schools, other than special schools, should have within their delegated budget some funding that reflects the additional needs of pupils with special educational needs. They receive this through a funding formula that reflects the incidence of SEN measured in various ways. The budget statements that LEAs are required to produce under section 52 of the School Standards and Framework Act 1998 must show each school's notional budget for SEN.

8:4 LEAs are required under the Special Educational Needs (Provision of Information by Local Education Authorities) (England) Regulations 2001 to publish from April 2002, details of the kinds of support arrangements maintained schools in their area might normally provide from their budgets under *School Action* and *School Action Plus*. They are also required to publish their own plans for providing appropriate SEN support – particularly under *School Action Plus*.

8:5 Where extra resources are required to enable a school to make the provision specified in statements, the LEA can provide those resources directly from central provision, devolve them to schools on an earmarked basis or delegate them. Funds for pupils with statements in both mainstream and special schools have been delegated in a number of local education authorities with clear benefits in terms of more stable staffing arrangements, prompt and flexible responses to newly identified needs, better training and improvements in the skills of those working with children with special educational needs.

8:6 However resources are provided, schools and LEAs have specific duties in relation to children with special educational needs which funding for SEN should support. Community, foundation and voluntary school governing bodies are required under section 317 of the Education Act 1996 to use their best endeavours to see that pupils with special educational needs receive the help their learning difficulties call for. They are

55 In this chapter schools also refers to early education settings, except in respect of funding arrangements.

accountable through their reports to parents for how resources are allocated to and amongst pupils with special educational needs and the effectiveness of their provision for SEN. LEAs have a duty under section 324 of the Education Act 1996 to arrange the special educational provision in a child's statement. LEAs may provide the facility in their funding arrangements to intervene where a pupil is not receiving the provision in their statement and make the arrangements themselves, charging the costs to the school's budget.

8:7 In the light of their statutory duties, LEAs and schools should work together to establish sound arrangements for monitoring and accountability to ensure that resources are used to raise the achievement of pupils with SEN. These arrangements should promote greater transparency and should be based on a clear statement that indicates the respective responsibilities of LEAs and governing bodies and explains how these responsibilities will be supported through the LEA's school funding arrangements. They should focus on the effectiveness of provision made for pupils with SEN and look to ensure that children make progress and achieve well, provision specified in statements is made, and the input of LEA and other support services is effective.

Criteria for deciding to draw up a statement

8:8 As with the evidence for deciding whether a statutory assessment is necessary, the guidance set out below provides a framework within which it is important that schools, LEAs and other agencies involved develop the detail of local interpretation.

8:9 It is helpful for LEAs to set up moderating groups to support transparency in decision-making. Such groups can ensure consistent decisions are made about whether to make statements. Through sampling and retrospective comparison, moderating groups can also help LEA practice become more robust and clearly understood by schools, early education settings and parents.

8:10 In deciding whether to draw up a statement the LEA should consider all the information gathered during the statutory assessment and relate it to that presented by the school at the time of any request for assessment.

8:11 LEAs may therefore wish to consider the following:

a the child's learning difficulties

- does the information on the child's learning difficulties provided in the advice for the statutory assessment broadly accord with the original evidence presented by the school?
- if not, are there aspects of the child's learning difficulties which the school may have overlooked and which, with the benefit of advice, equipment or other provision, the school could effectively address through *School Action* or *School Action Plus*?

b the child's special educational provision

- do the proposals for the child's special educational provision arising from any of the assessment advice indicate that the special educational provision being made by the school, including teaching strategies or other approaches, is appropriate to the child's learning difficulties?

- if not, are there approaches which, with the benefit of advice, equipment or other provision, the school could effectively adopt within its own resources through *School Action* or *School Action Plus*?

Consideration of the provision that may need to be made

8:12 If the statutory assessment confirms that the assessment and provision made by the school or early education setting is appropriate but the child is nonetheless not progressing, or not progressing sufficiently well, the LEA should consider what further provision may be needed and whether that provision can be made within the school's or setting's resources or whether a statement is necessary.

8:13 The following are examples of possible approaches:

- If the LEA concludes that, for example, the child's learning difficulties call for:
  - occasional or irregular advice to the school from an external specialist
  - occasional or irregular support with personal care
  - access to a particular piece of equipment such as a portable word-processing device, an electronic keyboard or a tape-recorder, or
  - minor building alterations such as improving the acoustic environment[56]

  the LEA may feel that the school could reasonably be expected to make such provision from within its own resources through *School Action Plus*. If so, they will then need to set out their reasons for reaching this conclusion clearly in a note in lieu (described in more detail below).

- If the LEA conclude that, for example, the child's learning difficulties call for:
  - regular and frequent direct teaching by a specialist teacher
  - daily individual support from a learning support assistant
  - a significant piece of equipment such as a closed circuit television or a computer or CD-ROM device with appropriate ancillaries and software
  - the regular involvement of non-educational agencies

  the LEA may conclude that the school could not reasonably be expected to make such provision within its own resources and that the nature of the provision suggests that the LEA should formally identify in a statement the child's needs, the full range of provision to be made and the review arrangements that will apply. The LEA's conclusions will, of course, depend on the precise circumstances of each case, taking into account arrangements for funding schools in the area.

- Where the LEA conclude that a change of placement may be indicated for the child, even if such a change involves moving from a mainstream school to a specialist resource at the same school or another mainstream school, they should consider drawing up a statement.

- Where the LEA conclude that a day or residential special school placement might be necessary, they should draw up a statement.

---

56 Responsibility between the LEA and the school for particular building works will depend on the scope of the formula capital allocation to schools in the particular LEA.

8:14 The decision as to whether to make a statement should be determined by the child's identifiable special educational needs in the context of arrangements for funding schools in the area. LEAs should, of course, arrange for the provision specified in a child's statement to be made in a cost-effective manner, but that provision must be consistent with the child's assessed needs. The efficient use of resources must be taken into account when an LEA is considering the placement of a child with a statement, once the parents have had an opportunity to express a preference – see from 8:58–69.

Decision not to issue a statement: a note in lieu

8:15 Within two weeks of completing the statutory assessment the LEA must decide whether or not they will make a statement. They may conclude that the child's special educational needs can be met from within the school's own resources, with or without the intervention of a professional service from outside the school – that is special educational provision can be made through *School Action* or *School Action Plus*. Where an LEA decides not to make a statement they **must** write to the parents telling them of that decision and the reasons for it no later than two weeks after completion of the assessment. The LEA **must** also tell the parents of their right to appeal to the SEN Tribunal against the decision and set out the time limits for appeal, the availability of parent partnership and disagreement resolution services, and the fact that the parent's right of appeal cannot be affected by any disagreement resolution procedure.

8:16 The decision not to issue a statement may be disappointing to parents and be seen as a denial of additional resources for their child. The LEA should ensure that the parents (and the school) are aware of the resources available within all maintained schools to meet special educational needs; that the parents fully understand school-based provision for SEN; and understand too that there are monitoring and review arrangements in maintained schools which will ensure that their child's needs are met by the school, with external support if necessary, in an appropriate way.

8:17 The statutory assessment will have contributed significantly to the school's, parents' and the LEA's knowledge of the child. The LEA should therefore consider issuing a note in lieu of a statement. In such a note the LEA should set out the reasons for their conclusions, with supporting evidence from the statutory assessment of the child. All advice collected as part of the statutory assessment should be sent to the parents and, subject to their agreement, to the child's school and any other professionals who have given advice during the assessment process. This procedure will put to good use the information that emerges from the child's statutory assessment. Those working with the child in school to augment their strategies for meeting the child's special educational needs can use the information. As good practice LEAs may wish to consider arranging for the parents to meet with the LEA Named Officer and the head teacher or SENCO of the child's school, in order to ensure that all parties understand the reasons for the LEA's decision, the note in lieu and the provision to be made.

8:18 In some cases, the LEA may be able to decide very quickly that it is not necessary to make a statement: parents should be informed immediately through the issue of a written notice under section 325(1) or 329A(8). The LEA **must** always give their reasons. But the writing of a comprehensive and useful note in lieu will very often require as much thought and time as the drafting of a proposed statement. Indeed, the decision whether to make a statement or to issue a note in lieu may only become clear when the LEA officer marshals all the information and sets out the child's educational and non-educational needs and the provision required to meet those needs.

8:19 It may be appropriate for the format of a note in lieu to broadly follow the statutory format of the statement, although it will always be essential to make clear the different legal status of the two documents.

8:20 While the layout of any note in lieu is a matter for the LEA concerned, it is good practice for the first part to describe the child's special educational needs, based on the supporting evidence attached in the form of all the advice gathered during the assessment. The second part of the note should set out the LEA's reasons for deciding not to make a statement and offer guidance as to the special educational provision that might appropriately be made for the child from school resources, with specialist advice if necessary, but without being determined by the LEA. The third part might then, again reflecting the advice received and appended and agreement between the LEA and the agencies concerned, describe any non-educational needs and appropriate provision.

8:21 The statutory assessment process ends when the LEA decides whether or not they will make a statement. That decision must normally be taken within ten weeks of the issue of a notice under section 323(4) or 329A(7). The statutory time limits within which the LEA must either inform parents that they will not make a statement or issue to parents a proposed statement are then the same: normally, no more than two weeks after making their decision.

8:22 So, normally no more than 12 weeks after the issue of a notice under section 323(4) or 329A(7) that they will make a statutory assessment, the LEA must either:

a issue a notice under section 325(1) that they will not make a statement and explain their reasons (whether in the form of a note in lieu or otherwise), or

b issue a proposed statement, together with a written notice under Schedule 27, paragraph 2.

Assessment and emergency placements

8:23 In exceptional cases it may be necessary to make an emergency placement for a child, for example where:

a the child's medical circumstances have changed suddenly, causing a rapid and serious deterioration in the child's health or development

b the parents, school, relevant professionals and the LEA agree that a sudden and serious deterioration in the child's behaviour make the child's current placement untenable or unsafe

c where a child arriving unexpectedly in the LEA exhibits such significant learning difficulties as would normally warrant a statement; the LEA should consult the parents and those immediately concerned, including the previous LEA, about the most appropriate placement

d where a young person returns home from a secure unit or young offender institution.

8:24 An emergency placement should only be made when the LEA, parents, school and relevant professionals are all agreed that the child's needs are such that action must be taken immediately and an emergency placement is the best way forward.

8:25 When an emergency placement is made, the LEA should immediately initiate a statutory assessment or reassessment. It is likely that the assessment will conclude that a statement should be made, or amendments made to an existing statement. If the child has been placed and will remain in a special school, a statement should always be made. The circumstances in which a child without a statement can be placed in a special school are discussed at 7:30 – 33.

8:26 If, however, the assessment concludes that a statement is not necessary, the child's emergency placement should be reconsidered. Decisions about how the child's needs should be best met in the longer term should not be prejudiced by the nature of the emergency placement. If a child without a statement has been placed in a special school for an assessment but it is decided that no statement is necessary, the child can only remain in the school for 10 school days after the LEA has notified the parent that they do not intend to make a statement.

8:27 Statements drawn up or amended following an emergency placement should include detailed objectives with clearly specified review arrangements to monitor the efficacy of the provision made for the child. Whilst the LEA has a duty to review the statement on an annual basis, they may wish to use their powers to review more frequently and to ask for interim reports on the child's progress.

8:28 Where a social services department makes an emergency placement out of their own budget for a child with a statement of SEN, they should immediately inform the LEA, especially where the placement is in an independent school.

Writing the Statement

Where an LEA, having made an assessment of a child, decide to make a statement, they shall serve a copy of a proposed statement and a written notice on the child's parent within two weeks of the date on which the assessment was completed.

See Schedule 27, Education Act 1996 and the Education (Special Educational Needs) (England) (Consolidation) Regulations 2001

8:29 The notice must be in the form prescribed in Schedule 1 to the Regulations. The statement of special educational needs must follow the format and contain the information prescribed by the Regulations (see Schedule 2 to the Regulations):

Part 1 ***Introduction:*** **The child's name and address and date of birth. The child's home language and religion. The names and address (es) of the child's parents.**

Part 2 ***Special Educational Needs*** **(learning difficulties): Details of each and every one of the child's special educational needs as identified by the LEA during statutory assessment and of the advice received and attached as appendices to the statement.**

Part 3 *Special Educational Provision:* The special educational provision that the LEA consider necessary to meet the child's special educational needs.

a. the *objectives* that the special educational provision should aim to meet.

b. the *special educational provision* which the LEA consider appropriate to meet the needs set out in Part 2 and to meet the objectives.

c. the arrangements to be made for monitoring progress in meeting those objectives, particularly for setting short-term targets for the child's progress and for reviewing his or her progress on a regular basis.

Part 4 *Placement:* The type and name of school where the special educational provision set out in Part 3 is to be made or the LEA's arrangements for provision to be made otherwise than in school.

Part 5 *Non-Educational Needs:* All relevant non-educational needs of the child as agreed between the health services, social services or other agencies and the LEA.

Part 6 *Non-Educational Provision:* Details of relevant non-educational provision required to meet the non-educational needs of the child as agreed between the health services and/or social services and the LEA, including the agreed arrangements for its provision.

Signature and date

8:30 All the advice obtained and taken into consideration during the assessment process must be attached as appendices to the statement:

The advice appended to the statement **must** include:

A Parental evidence[57]

B Educational advice

C Medical advice

D Psychological advice

E Social services advice

F Any other advice, such as the views of the child, which the LEA or any other body from whom advice is sought consider desirable. In particular, where the child's parent is a serving member of the armed forces, advice from Service Children's Education (SCE).

---

57 Parental evidence will include parental representations presented to the LEA when considering the need for an assessment, and parental views and evidence submitted as part of the assessment and, when the statement is finalised, any parental representations made in response to the proposed statement.

8:31 LEAs should draft clear, unambiguous statements. Where diagnostic or technical terms are necessary or helpful, for example in referring to specific disabilities, their meaning should be explained in terms that parents and other non-professionals will readily understand. LEAs should take particular care to ensure that the text is placed in the correct part, so as to correspond with the form set out in Schedule 2 to the Education (Special Educational Needs) (England) Regulations 2001. Further detailed advice is provided in the SEN Toolkit.

Part 2: Special educational needs (learning difficulties)

8:32 Part 2 of the statement should describe **all** the child's learning difficulties identified during the statutory assessment. It should also include a description of the child's current functioning – what the child can and cannot do. The description in Part 2 should draw on and may refer to the professional advice attached in the appendices. Where the LEA adopt that advice in their description of the child's learning difficulties, they should say that they have done so. But merely stating that they are adopting the advice in the appendices is not sufficient. The advice received may contain conflicting opinions or opinions open to interpretation, which the LEA must resolve, giving reasons for the conclusions they have reached. All advice must be considered and appended to the statement. Part 2 should be set out in a fashion which can relate directly to the description of provision set out in Part 3 (b).

Part 3: Special educational provision

8:33 Once a child's special educational needs have been assessed and set out in full in part 2, the LEA must specify, in Part 3, the special educational provision to meet those needs. The key objective in specifying provision is to help the child to learn and develop.

8:34 Part 3 of the statement is divided into three sub-sections:

a **the first sub-section** should set out the main objectives which the provision aims to meet. These objectives should directly relate to the needs set out in Part 2 and should be described in terms that will allow the LEA and the school to monitor and review the child's progress over time. They should generally be of a longer-term nature than the more specific, short-term targets in the child's Individual Education Plan.

b **the second sub-section** should specify all of the special educational provision the LEA consider appropriate for **all** the learning difficulties in Part 2, even where some of the provision will be made by direct intervention on the part of the authority, some will be made by the child's school from within its own resources, and some may be made by the health authority. It is the LEA that is responsible for arranging the provision in the statement, irrespective of who actually delivers it, unless the LEA is satisfied that the child's parents have themselves made suitable arrangements.

8:35 The Education (Special Educational Needs) (England) (Consolidation) Regulations 2001 say that a statement **must** specify:

(a) any appropriate facilities and equipment, staffing arrangements and curriculum

(b) any appropriate modifications to the application of the National Curriculum

(c) any appropriate exclusions from the application of the National Curriculum, in detail, and the provision which it is proposed to substitute for any such exclusions in order to maintain a balanced and broadly based curriculum; and

(d) where residential accommodation is appropriate, that fact.

8:36 A statement should specify clearly the provision necessary to meet the needs of the child. It should detail appropriate provision to meet each identified need. It will be helpful to the child's parents and teachers if the provision in this sub-section is set out in the same order as the description of needs in Part 2.

8:37 LEAs must make decisions about which actions and provision are appropriate for which pupils on an individual basis. This can only be done by a careful assessment of the pupils' difficulties and consideration of the educational setting in which they may be educated. Provision should normally be quantified (e.g. in terms of hours of provision, staffing arrangements) although there will be cases where some flexibility should be retained in order to meet the changing special educational needs of the child concerned. It will always be necessary for LEAs to monitor, with the school or other setting, the child's progress towards identified outcomes, however provision is described. LEAs must not, in any circumstances, have blanket policies not to quantify provision.

8:38 LEAs should also set out, in accordance with section 364 of the Education Act 1996, any disapplications or modifications of the provisions of the National Curriculum (in terms of attainment targets, programmes of study and assessment arrangements) which they consider necessary to meet the child's special educational needs, together with details as to how a broad and balanced curriculum is to be maintained. It is not necessary to modify National Curriculum provisions to enable a child to study at a lower level than applies to most of the pupils working within the same key stage. Where pupils are educated at home by their parents there is no requirement to deliver the National Curriculum. Where pupils are at the foundation stage this section should set out how the special educational provision will enable the child to access the curriculum with reference to the early learning goals.

8:39 For pupils whose assessment is close to their preparation for GCSEs or vocational examinations, the LEA should indicate any special examination provision recommended to enable the pupil to have full access to the examination and demonstrate their attainment. In some cases, approval may be needed in advance from Awarding Bodies. This is rarely a complex process and is handled by the centre where the pupil takes their examinations, usually their school.[58]

58 A pupil does not require a statement in order to benefit from any concessions that an Examination Group might grant to a pupil with special educational needs.

c **the third sub-section** should describe the arrangements to be made for setting shorter-term educational and developmental targets for the child. The targets themselves should not be part of the statement but should form an integral part of their IEP. By their nature such targets will require regular review and revision while the longer-term objectives in sub-section 1 will not. The child's school should devise the first IEP, in consultation with their parents and, where appropriate the child, within two months of placement at a different school, or immediately the statement is finalised if the child remains in the same school. The child's achievements, in the light of the IEP, should be reviewed at least twice a year by the school, and fully considered at the first annual review of the statement when further targets can be set.

8:40 This sub-section should also identify any special arrangements for the annual review of the statement and recognise the need for the school to monitor and evaluate the child's progress during the course of the year. LEAs must review a child's statement at least once a year. The review should consider the child's progress towards the objectives in sub section 1 and in relation to the shorter-term objectives and targets set out by the school in the child's Individual Education Plan (IEP). It should also consider whether any changes are needed to the provision with reference to the child's progress.

8:41 *All the information in Part 3 should be written so as to be easily understood by all those involved in the child's education, including their parents.*

Part 4: Placement

8:42 In the final statement, Part 4 will set out the type of school and any particular school which the LEA consider appropriate for the child, or the LEA's arrangements for the provision for education otherwise than at school which the LEA consider appropriate. But this Part **must** be left blank when the proposed statement is issued, so that the LEA do not pre-empt consideration of any preference for a maintained school which the parents may state, or any representation the parents may make in favour of a non-maintained special or independent school (see Glossary).

Part 5: Non-educational needs

8:43 Part 5 should set out any non-educational needs of the child which the LEA either propose to meet or are satisfied will be met, by arrangement or otherwise, by the health services, social services department or some other body.

Part 6: Non-educational provision

8:44 Part 6 should set out the non-educational provision which is required to meet the needs identified in Part 5 and which the LEA either propose to make available or are satisfied will be provided by the social services department commissioned by the health authority in discussion with the Primary Care Group or Primary Care Trust for the area, or by other providers. The designated officer for social services should work with the LEA to confirm social services provision and the medical officer for special educational needs should liaise as necessary to ensure that the health service contribution has been confirmed.

8:45 Part 6 should also state the objectives to be achieved by such non-educational provision and should set out such arrangements as have been agreed by the LEA and the providing body for its delivery.

8:46 When describing a child's educational and non-educational needs and provision, the LEA should ensure that the needs are clearly and accurately described and that there is full agreement on the nature of the provision necessary to meet those needs, consulting the relevant responsible professionals as necessary.

8:47 LEAs should explain to parents that whilst Parts 2, 3 and 4 of the statement are legally binding on the LEA, Parts 5 and 6 are not and that there is no right of appeal to the SEN Tribunal about these sections.

8:48 Further suggestions on writing statements can be found in the SEN Toolkit.

Speech and language therapy

8:49 Case law has established that speech and language therapy can be regarded as either educational or non-educational provision, or both, depending upon the health or developmental history of each child. It could therefore appear in either Part 3 or Part 6 of the statement or in both. However, since communication is so fundamental in learning and progression, addressing speech and language impairment should normally be recorded as educational provision unless there are exceptional reasons for not doing so.[59]

8:50 Prime responsibility for the provision of speech and language therapy services to children rests with the NHS. This applies generally and also to any specification of such services in a statement of special educational needs, whether in Part 3 as educational provision or in Part 6 as non-educational provision, or in both parts. Health authorities are responsible for purchasing therapy services through the contracts they make with providers of health care (NHS Trusts). The NHS provides a professionally managed speech and language therapy service covering pre-school, school-age and adult age groups, which has close links with the other child health services.

8:51 Where the NHS does not provide speech and language therapy for a child whose statement specifies such therapy as educational provision, ultimate responsibility for ensuring that the provision is made rests with the LEA, unless the child's parents have made appropriate alternative arrangements. Schools, LEAs and the NHS should cooperate closely in meeting the needs of children with communication difficulties.

8:52 It is important that the nature and extent of provision required for individual children should be examined very carefully and that full consideration is given as to how such provision can best be delivered. In some cases, for example, children may need regular and continuing help from a speech therapist, either individually or in a group. In other cases, it may be appropriate for staff at the child's school to deliver a regular and discrete programme of intervention under the guidance and supervision of a speech and language therapist.

8:53 For some children a language programme that is an integral part of the whole school day is more appropriate. Such language programmes will be delivered by school staff but may require regular monitoring and evaluation by a speech and language therapist. It is good practice for education professionals who have received sufficient and appropriate professional development in the field of speech and language difficulties to support and assist the work of speech and language therapists in educational settings. Collaborative

---

59 This reflects a recommendation of the DH/DfEE working group on the provision of speech and language therapy services to children with special educational needs. DfEE document 0319/2000.

practice is essential for successful intervention with children and young people with speech and language difficulties. The operational flexibilities introduced under the Health Act 1999 for health services and local authorities will help to promote greater collaboration.[60]

The proposed statement

8:54 The LEA must draw up a proposed statement, completing all Parts except Part 4. The proposed statement **must** not contain any details relating to where the proposed special educational provision should be made. The LEA **must** send the proposed statement and copies of the advice that has been submitted during the assessment to the child's parents; copies of the proposed statement should also be sent to all those who submitted advice.

8:55 At the same time, the LEA **must** send the parents a notice which sets out the procedures to be followed, including setting out the arrangements for the choice of school, the parents' right to make representations about the content of the statement, their right to appeal to the SEN Tribunal against the contents of the final statement and the time limits for appeal. The notice must correspond substantially with that set out in Part A of Schedule 1 to the Regulations.

8:56 When making a statement, LEAs should remember the needs of parents and children whose first language is not English. Where children have different linguistic and cultural backgrounds, LEAs should seek advice from bilingual support staff, teachers of English as an additional language, interpreters and translators and other local sources of help as appropriate, to ensure that such parents and children are involved in all aspects of the process.

Time limits

8:57 On receipt of the proposed statement, parents have a right to state a preference for the maintained school their child should attend and to make representations to, and hold meetings with, the LEA. It must also be explained to parents that they have the right to raise any other issues relating to the body of the statement. The LEA must normally issue the final statement within eight weeks of the issue of the proposed statement. Exceptions to the eight-week time limit are set out in the Education (Special Educational Needs) (England) (Consolidation) Regulations 2001 appended at Annex A.

60 DH (with DfEE and DETR) Circular HSC2000/DH/LAC(2000)9: Implementation of Health Act Partnership Arrangements. April 2000.

Naming a school

Parents may express a preference for the maintained school (but not a PRU or hospital special school) they wish their child to attend, or make representations for a placement in any other school. LEAs must comply with a parental preference unless the school is unsuitable to the child's age, ability, aptitude or special educational needs, or the placement would be incompatible with the efficient education of the other children with whom the child would be educated, or with the efficient use of resources. LEAs must consider parental representations and arrange any meeting(s) with LEA advisers or officers the parents seek, before issuing the final statement.

See Schedule 27, Education Act 1996

Unless a parent indicates that they do not want their child educated in a mainstream school (whether by expressing a preference or making a representation for a particular school or otherwise) an LEA must ensure that a child is educated in a mainstream school unless that is incompatible with the efficient education of other children.

See Section 316, Education Act 1996

8:58 An LEA that believes that the education of a particular child in the mainstream would be incompatible with the efficient education of others must consider whether there are any reasonable steps they could take to prevent the child's inclusion from having that effect. In relation to a particular maintained school they must consider the reasonable steps that they or the governing body could take.

8:59 If an LEA decides that a particular maintained school might be able to make the special educational provision specified in a statement the governing body of that school can only argue against a place on the grounds that the child's education there would be incompatible with the efficient education of others. They must also consider whether there are any reasonable steps they (or the LEA) could take to prevent inclusion from having that effect. Additional practical guidance on the sorts of steps LEAs and maintained schools need to consider taking is provided in a separate circular on the statutory framework for inclusion.[61]

8:60 Parents may express a preference for any maintained school they wish their child to attend, or make representations for a placement in any other school. LEAs **must** comply with a parental preference in accordance with the provisions of Schedule 27 of the Education Act 1996. LEAs **must** consider parental representations and arrange any meeting(s) with LEA officers or advisers parents seek, before issuing the final statement. When considering parental representations for a place at a school or institution which is not a maintained school, LEAs must establish that the school or institution proposed can make the special educational provision necessary to meet the child's special educational

61 DfES 'Inclusive Schooling – Children with Special Educational Needs'. September 2001.

needs, and the provisions of section 9 of the Education Act 1996: that is, they must have regard to the parent's wishes, so far as that is compatible with the efficient instruction and training of the child and the avoidance of unreasonable public expenditure.

8:61 The LEA must explain to parents the arrangements for expressing a preference for a particular school under paragraph 3 of Schedule 27 and the LEA's duty to comply with that preference in all but a few cases. Paragraph 4 of the same Schedule gives parents the right to make representations, which the LEA must consider, about the content of the statement; and the right to request meetings to discuss any aspect of the content of the proposed statement, including the advice obtained during the statutory assessment. Parents should be informed that the parent partnership service is able to provide information about schools, explain the way the law operates and provide support for meetings with the LEA. Parents should also be informed about the availability of disagreement resolution services.

8:62 Where an LEA proposes to issue a statement or amend part 4 of an existing statement they **must** name the maintained school – mainstream or special – that is preferred by the parents, providing that:

- the school is suitable for the child's age, ability and aptitude and the special educational needs set out in part 2 of the statement
- the child's attendance is not incompatible with the efficient education of other children in the school, and
- the placement is an efficient use of the LEA's resources.

8:63 The LEA **must** consult the school preferred by the parent, and where the school is in another LEA's area, that LEA as well. They **must** provide, as part of the consultation, either a copy of the proposed statement and appendices or, where they are proposing to amend part 4 of an existing statement, either the proposed amended statement or the amendment notice together with a copy of the existing statement, and in either case, the appendices.

8:64 Where the parent's choice of a particular school cannot be met, the LEA should identify a mainstream school and consult them. Again the proposed statement or proposed amended statement or existing statement and amendment notice and appendices must be sent to the school and the LEA concerned if the school is not maintained by the placing LEA. However, the LEA **must** name that school unless it is incompatible with the provision of efficient education for other children and there are no reasonable steps that the LEA or school or another Authority could take to prevent the incompatibility.

8:65 The LEA should consider very carefully a preference stated by parents for a denominational mainstream maintained school and representations made by parents for a denominational non-maintained special school or independent school. Denominational considerations cannot override the requirements of section 316 of the Education Act 1996.

8:66 If City Technology Colleges, City Colleges for the Technology of the Arts or City Academies are named in a statement no consent for the placement of a child by the Secretary of State is required, so long as the pupil falls within the terms generally approved for the school.

8:67 Schedule 27 of the Education Act 1996 determines whether a parent's preference for a particular maintained school is met. Parents may, of course, express a preference for a maintained special school. If they do so, the LEA no longer have a duty under section 316A to secure a mainstream education for the child. The LEA must comply with a parental preference for a particular maintained special school so long as the conditions in Schedule 27 apply.

8:68 The LEA should inform parents that all maintained schools must publish information on their policies on special educational needs. Parents should be supported in making choices. Ways of helping parents are discussed in Chapter Two.

8:69 When LEAs send parents a copy of the proposed statement, they **must** tell the parents that they have the right to make representations to the LEA in favour of a non-maintained school and that, if they wish to make such representations, they should do so within 15 days of receiving the proposed statement. If the LEA does not agree to the parents' representations, they should inform the parents of their decision before naming any other school in the final statement. Parents will then have the opportunity to express a preference for a particular maintained school under Schedule 27 if they wish to do so.

Residential Placements

The LEA must inform the SSD in the area where the child's family resides or the SSD in the area of the residential school.

See Section 85, Children Act 1989

Where a child is looked after and the SSD propose to place the child in an educational setting they shall, as far as is reasonably practicable, consult the appropriate LEA before doing so.

See Section 28, Children Act 1989

8:70 If it is agreed that a residential school should be named in the statement, the LEA and parent should also agree the arrangements for the child's contact with their family and for any special help, such as transport, which may be needed to maintain home/school contact.

8:71 Whenever a child is placed in a residential school with the intention that it will be for longer than three months, the LEA **must** inform either the social services department where the child's family lives or the department in the area of the residential school. It is good practice to inform both SSDs.

8:72 LEAs may wish to work with social service colleagues and consider placement policies that can be consistent across the local authority. Social services departments will, so far as reasonably practicable and consistent with the child's welfare, seek to secure that residential placements are near the child's home.

8:73 Where SSDs make an emergency placement out of their own budget for a child with a statement of SEN, they should immediately inform the LEA, especially where the placement is in an independent school.

8:74 In general LEAs are likely to consider that there is a need for residential provision where there is multi-agency agreement that:

- the child has severe or multiple special educational needs that cannot be met in local day provision
- the child has severe or multiple special educational needs that require a consistent programme both during and after school hours that cannot be provided by parents with support from other agencies
- the child is looked after by the local authority and has complex social and learning needs, and placement is joint-funded with the social services department
- the child has complex medical needs as well as learning needs that cannot be managed in local day provision and the placement is joint-funded with the health authority.

8:75 If these conditions apply, a multi-agency plan should be put into place that enables tri-partite funding.

8:76 The LEA and the child's parents may conclude that the child should be placed in an independent school that is not approved by the Secretary of State under section 347. In such cases, the LEA must seek the Secretary of State's consent to the placement and should do so before naming the school in the final copy of the statement. The Secretary of State aims to make a decision within 15 working days of the date on which a request for consent was sent. Should the Secretary of State take more than three weeks, the LEA is not bound by the eight-week time limit governing the issue of the final statement. Nor will the time limit apply if the Secretary of State declines to give consent to a proposed placement and a request is made for the Secretary of State's consent to a placement at another independent school which is not approved under section 347.

8:77 Where the LEA decide that the final statement will not name the parents' first choice of school, the LEA should explain that decision in writing to the parents, and **must** also inform the parents of their right of appeal to the SEN Tribunal and the time limits for lodging an appeal, the availability of parent partnership and disagreement resolution services, and the fact that the parent's right of appeal cannot be affected by any disagreement resolution procedure.

8:78 Visits by parents to the school proposed by the LEA, with an opportunity to discuss their child's special needs with the head teacher, SENCO or any specialist teaching staff, may be helpful. Parents' concerns and disappointments should be taken seriously, and every effort should be made to provide any additional information and advice or to arrange any further visits which will help them reach an informed decision about their child's future.

8:79 A detailed explanation of the rules that determine the basis on which payments for out-of-authority placements may be made between LEAs in respect of the education of children with statements of special educational needs who are also looked after by the local authority are set out in DfEE/DH Guidance on the Education of Children and Young People in Public Care published in May 2000.

Consultation before naming a maintained school in a statement

> **A local education authority shall, before specifying the name of any maintained school in a statement, consult the governing body of the school, and if the school is maintained by another local education authority, that authority.**
>
> **The LEA must serve a copy of the proposed statement or amended statement, or of the existing statement and the amendment notice to the school(s) whom they are consulting, and if the school is maintained by another local education authority, that authority.**
>
> See Schedule 27, Education Act 1996

8:80 The LEA **must** consult the governing body of a school before naming it in a statement. If another authority maintains the school, the LEA **must** also consult that authority. The LEA should expect schools and other LEAs to respond within 15 working days, unless the time period falls within a school holiday that is longer than two weeks. The LEA should consider carefully any representations from governing bodies and other LEAs.

8:81 If the consultation is the result of a parental preference for a particular school, the LEA should consider any concerns the governing body may have about meeting the child's special educational needs or about how the child's attendance might impact on the education of other children at the school, or the efficient use of resources. However, the final decision as to whether to name the school falls to the LEA.

8:82 When the consultation is not as a result of a parental preference the LEA should consider any concerns the governing body may have that the child's attendance might be incompatible with the efficient education of other children at the school and whether the governing body or the LEA can take reasonable steps to prevent that incompatibility. However the final decision as to whether to name the school falls to the LEA.

8:83 The LEA have a duty to name the parents' preferred maintained school in a statement so long as the conditions in Schedule 27 (set out in paragraph 8.62) are met. For example, the LEA should not name a maintained school in a statement if the school is selective and the child does not meet the criteria for selection. The governing body of the school cannot refuse to admit a child solely because they have special educational needs.

8:84 If the LEA, after representations from the parents, decide to name an independent or non-maintained special school, they will, of course, as part of the process of agreeing the placement, consult the school.

8:85 The LEA should also consider carefully whether the admission of the child to a maintained mainstream school would take the school over the number fixed as the number of intended admissions for the year, which must not be less than the 'standard number' or 'approved admissions number', in other words, whether the school is already nominally full. Admitting children over this number might be incompatible with the provision of efficient education or the efficient use of resources. In some schools an additional child in a class would be incompatible with the efficient education of others as there might not be enough physical space, especially if all the children require particular aids that take up a lot of space. LEAs must also comply with the class size legislation in infant classes (see paragraphs 1:33 – 38).

Children placed by social services departments or the Courts

8:98 It is good practice for local authorities in their role as corporate parent to ensure that the social services departments work with LEAs, so that any educational provision they make meets the child's needs as appropriately as is possible in their particular circumstances.

8:99 Where a child is 'looked after' by the local authority, and the child's education is arranged by social services, the LEA should consider whether the local authority, as the child's parent, has made suitable provision under section 324(5)(a). If so, the LEA may refrain from arranging the provision specified in the statement. Section 324(4A) of the Education Act 1996 does not require the name of a school to be specified in part 4 of the statement but the LEA **must**, in such cases, name the type of provision.

8:100 Where a child is 'looked after' by the local authority and placed in a community home with education or other children's home that provides education, or with an independent fostering agency providing education, then the LEA may conclude that suitable arrangements have been made and the LEA is relieved of their duty to arrange the provision specified in the statement.

8:101 In such situations Part 4 should state the type of school the LEA consider appropriate but go on to say that: *"parents have made their own arrangements under section 7 of the Education Act 1996."*

8:102 LEAs should always ensure that they are involved in any plans to change the child's placement so that appropriate special educational provision can be arranged as necessary once the child leaves their current placement.

8:103 Where a young person with a statement is detained under a court order (for example in secure accommodation) or an order of recall by the Secretary of State, the LEA is no longer responsible for them and is under no duty to maintain the statement (see section 562 of the Education Act 1996).

8:104 Although there is no statutory duty to meet the special educational needs of these young people, LEAs may provide them with educational facilities and should ensure that the institutions receive information about their inmates' special educational needs including a copy of any statement and the last annual review report. The institutions should endeavour to make appropriate educational provision. As with children who are 'looked after', the LEA should be involved in the young person's exit plan.

Parental representations about the proposed statement

8:105 If parents have been fully consulted throughout the process they are more likely to consider that the proposed statement presents a positive and accurate appraisal of their child's special educational needs and that the provision proposed represents an appropriate response to those needs. The LEA should, however, using the Notice to Parents Part A of Schedule 1 of the Education (Special Educational Needs) (England) (Consolidation) Regulations 2001, inform parents that:

(a) they may within 15 days make representations to the LEA, and require that a meeting be arranged with an officer of the LEA to discuss the contents of the statement

(b) within 15 days of meeting the officer, the parents may make further representations or, if they disagree with any part of the assessment, require further meetings to be arranged with appropriate people within the LEA to discuss the advice given

(c) within a final 15 days from the last meeting the parents can make further comments to the LEA.

8:106 Every effort should be made to ensure that parents are happy with the proposed statement and that they understand the background to the proposals made for their child and consider that their wishes and feelings have been given full and sensitive consideration. Similar effort should be made to ensure that, so far as possible, the child's views are reflected in the proposed statement and that the child understands the reasons for the proposals.

8:107 At any meetings arising from the proposed statement, LEA officers should give parents sufficient time and information in order to discuss their anxieties with the Named LEA Officer, and seek as far as possible to come to a mutual agreement. Some parents may find assessment very stressful and need additional personal support. LEAs should inform parents that friends or relatives, or members of the parent partnership service (see Chapter Two) may accompany them. The LEA may wish to refer parents to professionals in health or other services for clarification of any relevant aspect of the provision proposed which is giving cause for concern.

The final statement

8:108 The LEA **must** send a copy of the final statement to the child's parents and give written notice of their rights of appeal to the Tribunal and the time limits for lodging an appeal, the availability of parent partnership and disagreement resolution services, and the fact that the parent's right of appeal cannot be affected by any disagreement resolution procedure. Parents may appeal against the description in the statement of the child's special educational needs, the special educational provision in the statement, and the school named, or if no school is named, that fact.

8:109 When changes are suggested to the proposed statement and agreed by the LEA and the parents, the final statement should be issued immediately. LEAs **must** arrange the special educational provision, and may arrange any non-educational provision specified in the statement, from the date on which the statement is made. Every effort should be made to ensure that parents understand the significance of any changes and the nature of the provision that is proposed to meet the child's special educational needs. Where, despite opportunities to discuss the situation with an officer of the LEA and any relevant professionals, the parents are unwilling to accept other changes to the proposed statement or the LEA refuses the parents' suggestions for changes to the proposed statement, the LEA may nonetheless proceed to issue the final statement. The LEA **must**, however, inform the parents of their right to appeal to the SEN Tribunal with regard to the provision specified in the statement, including the named school, and the procedures to be followed if they wish to do so.

8:110 Recourse to the Tribunal may be stressful for parents and time-consuming for the LEA concerned. To minimise appeals to the Tribunal, LEAs should ensure that parents have the fullest possible access to information and support during the statutory assessment process and that they are fully involved in contributing to their child's statement. Partnership with parents is fully discussed in Chapter Two.

Keeping, disclosure and transfer of statements

8:111 A statement must not be disclosed without the consent of the child's parents or, where the child is over eighteen, except for statutory purposes or in the interests of the child. Statutory purposes include disclosure to the SEN Tribunal when parents appeal, and to the Secretary of State if parents make a complaint to him under the 1996 Act; disclosure on the order of any court or for the purpose of any criminal proceedings; disclosure for the purposes of investigations of maladministration under the Local Government Act 1974; disclosure to enable any authority to perform duties resulting from the Disabled Persons (Services, Consultation and Representation) Act 1986, or from the Children Act 1989 relating to safeguarding and promoting the welfare of children; and disclosure to OFSTED inspection teams as part of their inspections of schools and LEAs.

8:112 The interests of the child include the provision of information to the child's school and teachers. It is important that teachers working closely with the child should have full knowledge of the child's statement, as should Connexions Personal Advisers (PAs). LEAs may also give access to the statement to persons engaged in research on special educational needs on the condition that the researchers do not publish anything derived from, or contained in, the statement which would identify the child or parents concerned. School governing bodies should have access to a child's statement commensurate with their duties towards pupils with special educational needs and should always bear in mind the need to maintain confidentiality about the child in question. Disclosure in the interests of the child also includes disclosure to any agencies other than the LEA who may be referred to in the statement as making educational or non-educational provision.

8:113 When the responsibility for a child with special educational needs changes from the LEA maintaining the statement (the old authority) to another LEA (the new authority), the old authority must transfer the statement to the new authority. They may also transfer any opinion they have received under the Disabled Persons (Services, Consultation and Representation) Act 1986 that the child is disabled. Upon the transfer of the statement, the new authority becomes responsible for maintaining the statement and for providing the special educational provision specified in the statement.

8:114 The duty to maintain the child at the school specified in Part 4 of the statement therefore also transfers to the new authority. The new authority may place the child temporarily at a school other than that specified in Part 4 where appropriate and sensible to do so – for example, where the distance between the child's new home and the school would be too great – prior to the statement being amended in accordance with the statutory procedures. Otherwise, the new LEA may not decline to pay the fees or otherwise maintain the child at an independent or non-maintained special school or a boarding school named in a statement unless and until they have formally amended the statement.

8:115 The new authority may, on the transfer of the statement, bring forward the arrangements for the review of the statement, and may conduct a new assessment regardless of when the previous assessment took place. The new authority **must** tell the parents, within six weeks of the date of transfer, when they will review the statement and whether they propose to make an assessment under section 323. The old authority and the child's school should alert parents to the educational implications of their proposed move and both the old authority and the new authority should be ready to discuss those implications with parents. Where a child with a statement moves to Northern Ireland or Scotland, the LEA should send a copy of the child's statement to the new authority or board and where a child moves to Wales, the statement **must** be transferred.

Maintenance of a statement

8:116 When a statement is made, the LEA should tell the 'responsible person' in a maintained school – see paragraph 1:19 – and the head teacher in all other schools and in early education settings. They must then ensure that the child's special educational needs are made known to all those who will teach them. Schools should ensure that teachers monitor and informally review the child's progress during the course of the year. Teachers should use both the normal curriculum and pastoral monitoring arrangements for all pupils as well writing IEPs, as appropriate. It is most important that, if a child's special educational needs change, a review is held as soon as possible to ensure that the provision specified in the statement is still appropriate.

Ceasing to maintain the statement

8:117 There should be no assumption that, once the LEA has made a statement, they should maintain that statement until they are no longer responsible for the young person. Statements should be maintained only when necessary. But a decision to cease to maintain a statement should be made only after careful consideration by the LEA of all the circumstances and after close consultation with parents.

8:118 The LEA may cease to maintain a statement for a child only if they believe that it is no longer necessary to maintain it. The LEA should consider the results of the recent annual reviews, whether the objectives of the statement have been achieved, and whether the child's needs could be met in future within the resources of mainstream schools within the area without the need for continuing LEA oversight. The LEA should always, therefore, consider whether, notwithstanding the achievement of some, or even all, of the objectives in the statement, the child's progress will be halted or reversed if the special educational provision specified in the statement or modified provision which justified the maintenance of a statement were not made.

8:119 The LEA may consider whether the following apply when considering if it is necessary to maintain a statement:

- a have the objectives of the statement have been met
- b can the child's needs be met in future within the resources of a mainstream school
- c do the child's special educational needs no longer significantly impede access to the National Curriculum
- d does the child no longer require daily adult supervision or substantial adaptation of teaching materials to access the curriculum fully
- e can the child cope with everyday social interaction at school
- f has the child no significant self-help difficulties that require more provision than is normally available within the school.

8:120 Once an LEA make a decision to cease to maintain a statement, they **must** write to the child's parents to give notice of their decision, and explain the parents' right of appeal to the SEN Tribunal and the time limits for lodging the appeal, the availability of parent partnership and disagreement resolution services, and the fact that the parent's right of appeal cannot be affected by any disagreement resolution procedure. The LEA must always explain the reasons for their decision and also ensure that parents have copies of any evidence that led to that decision. It is good practice to offer a meeting to explain the rationale for the decision and to discuss the provision the child will receive once the statement has ceased. Such a meeting should be held before the statement and its provisions actually cease. Provision **must** be maintained if parents lodge an appeal to the SEN Tribunal until after the Tribunal makes a decision.

8:121 A statement will generally remain in force until and unless the LEA ceases to maintain it. A statement will lapse automatically when a young person moves into further or higher education. Therefore, if the young person, the parents, the LEA and the further education institution are all in agreement about the young person's transfer, there is no need to formally cease the statement since the young person will cease to be a pupil for whom the LEA is responsible after leaving school, and so the statement will lapse.

8:122 A young person may leave school at age 16 plus to seek employment or training; again, there is no need to formally cease to maintain the statement since the young person would cease to be a pupil for whom the LEA is responsible once they leave school. By contrast, where there is agreement all-round that the pupil should stay at school post-16, and the LEA or other LEAs, have appropriate school provision, the LEA should normally continue to maintain the statement.

8:123 Where parents want their child to remain at school post 16, but the LEA considers that the young person's special educational needs would be better met in a further education institution, the LEA cannot know whether the child still requires a statement until it has contacted the FE institution in question and confirmed that it is both able to meet the young person's needs and has offered a place. The LEA should satisfy itself on both counts before taking formal steps to cease to maintain the young person's statement. At that time, the LEA **must** also notify the parents of their right of appeal to the Tribunal and the time limits for lodging the appeal, the availability of parent partnership and disagreement resolution services, and the fact that the parent's right of appeal cannot be affected by any disagreement resolution procedure. It is not sufficient for LEAs to have a general expectation that an FE institution should be able to meet a young person's needs.

8:124 Where the young person's present school does not cater for children aged 16 plus, the LEA should consider whether to amend the statement to name another school or cease the statement if an appropriate FE course is identified. The LEA should formally propose to amend the statement to name the alternative school or formally propose to cease the statement. In both cases the LEA must also notify the parents of their right to appeal to the Tribunal and the time limits for lodging the appeal.

Amending an existing statement

8:125 The LEA can only amend a statement in compliance with an order from the SEN Tribunal, as directed by the Secretary of State, or in accordance with Schedule 27.

8:126 Where the LEA propose to amend a statement following an annual review or at any other time, whether to change the name of the school in Part 4 or for any other reason, they **must** write to the child's parents informing them of that proposal and of the parents' right to make representations about the statement and the amendments within 15 days of the receipt of that proposal and to request a meeting with an officer of the LEA.

8:127 For amendments following a re-assessment, the procedure is the same as when making a new statement as set out earlier in this chapter.

8:128 For amendments following a review, other than after a reassessment, LEAs must send the parents an amendment notice that sets out the details of their proposed amendments. The amendment notice should be appended to the Notice to Parents set out at Part B of Schedule 1 at Annex A. They must explain the reasons for the proposal and ensure that the parents have copies of any evidence that prompted the proposal. Where a proposal to amend the statement arises from the annual review, the parents should have already received copies of the review report and the school's recommendations.

8:129 The LEA must consider any representations made by the parents before deciding whether and how to amend the statement. If the authority concludes that an amendment should be made, they must make that amendment within eight weeks of sending the amendment notice to the parents. If the LEA decides not to go ahead with the amendment, they should write to the parents explaining why, again within eight weeks of the original letter setting out the proposal to make an amendment.

8:130 When a child transfers from one school to another, either because they have moved to a different address but remain in the same authority or because of a phase change of school (for example from a primary to a secondary school), Part 4 of the statement will always need amending. Information and recommendations from an annual review meeting may also indicate the need for alterations to an existing statement. Where the proposal involves amending Part 4 of the statement the parents have the rights to express a preference or make representations described in paragraph 8:58.

8:131 When the statement is amended a new document must be issued which clearly states that it is an Amended Final Statement and the date on which it was amended, as well as the date of the original statement. Additional advice, such as the minutes of an annual review meeting and accompanying reports, that contributed to the decision to amend the statement, should be appended to the amended statement in the same way as the advice received during the statutory assessment. The amended statement should also make clear which parts of the statement have been amended, so that parents and professionals can clearly see and understand the changes.

8:132 When a child is moving to a new school, particularly at phase transfer, the statement should be amended to name in Part 4 both the current placement and the new placement, stating an appropriate start date for the latter. This will make sure that parents, children and the receiving school can plan well in advance of transfer, and entitle parents to appeal to the SEN Tribunal in good time if they disagree with the named school. At phase transfers, except from early education settings to the primary phase, the statement must be amended no later than 15th February in the year of transfer. The amended statement should specify the current school attended by the child (if any) and the new school, indicating the date on which the child will move there.

8:133 When the amended statement is issued parents **must** be informed of their right of appeal to the Tribunal against Parts 2, 3 and 4 of the statement and the time limits within which they should appeal, the availability of parent partnership and disagreement resolution services, and the fact that the parent's right of appeal cannot be affected by any disagreement resolution procedure.

Summary

8:134 The time limit for making assessments and statements are as follows:

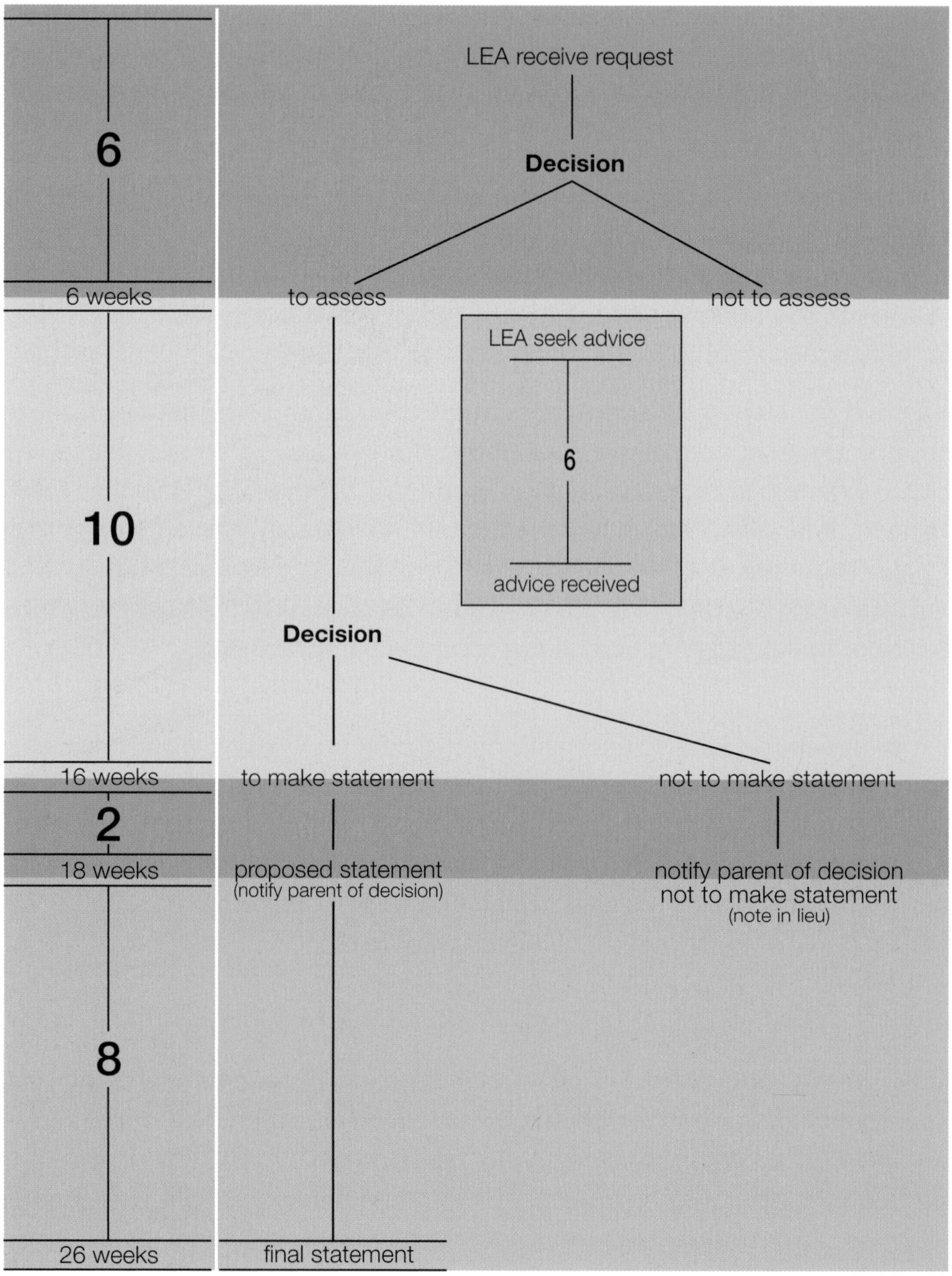

9 Annual Review

Introduction

9:1 All statements (other than those for children under two) must be reviewed at least annually. The annual review of a pupil's statement ensures that once a year the parents, the pupil, the LEA, the school[63], and all the professionals involved, consider both the progress the pupil has made over the previous 12 months and whether any amendments need to be made to the description of the pupil's needs or to the special educational provision specified in the statement. It is a way of monitoring and evaluating the continued effectiveness and appropriateness of the statement. LEAs must ensure that such a review is carried out within 12 months of either making the statement or of the previous review.

9:2 When a statement is amended following an annual review, the date of the next annual review should continue to be determined according to the date on which the statement was made or reviewed rather than the date on which it was amended. When a second or subsequent statutory assessment results in a new statement then the review should be within 12 months of the date of the new statement.

9:3 Although LEAs have the power to arrange a review of a statement at any time during the year, LEAs should aim to secure the agreement of the school and the child's parents before exercising that power. The timing of annual reviews should reflect the circumstances of the child and the action that may flow from the review, for example a move to secondary school. Timing should also reflect the circumstances of the child's school. Particularly in the case of special schools it may not be reasonable to review all statements at the same time. LEAs should seek to agree a reasonable spread of annual review dates with the school. Parents should always be informed.

9:4 The purpose of an annual review is to integrate a variety of perspectives on a child's progress, to ensure that they are achieving the desired outcomes and, if necessary, to amend the statement to reflect newly identified needs and provision. In some cases, the LEA will conclude that the statement's objectives have been achieved and that they should cease to maintain the statement. The annual review should focus on what the child has achieved as well as on any difficulties that need to be resolved. The annual review held in year 9 is particularly significant in preparing for the pupil's transition to the further education sector, work-based training, higher education and adult life.

9:5 While statements **must** be reviewed annually, schools and, as appropriate, the LEA should, during the course of the year monitor the child's progress towards the targets set out shortly after the statement was first made or at the last annual review. The IEP will normally be the vehicle for this process, alongside the usual school arrangements for monitoring the progress of all pupils.

9:6 Where children are 'looked after' by the local authority or are 'in need' consideration should be given to holding the SEN review and a 'looked after' or 'child in need' review at the same time. It will rarely be advisable for all the same people to attend the whole review but such joint arrangements are likely to contribute to effective collaboration.

---

63 In this chapter 'schools' also refers to early education settings.

Purpose of the Annual Review

9:7 The annual review should aim:

i to assess the child's progress towards meeting the objectives specified in the statement and to collate and record information that the school and other professionals can use in planning their support for the child

ii in the case of the first annual review, to assess the child's progress towards meeting the targets agreed and recorded in the IEP following the making of the statement; and in the case of all other reviews to assess progress towards the targets in the IEP set at the previous review

iii to review the special provision made for the child, including the appropriateness of any special equipment provided, in the context of the National Curriculum and associated assessment and reporting arrangements. Where appropriate, the school should consider providing a profile of the child's current levels of attainment in basic literacy, numeracy and life skills, and a summary of progress achieved in other areas of the curriculum, including the National Curriculum.[64] Where the statement involves a modification or disapplication of the National Curriculum, the school should indicate what special arrangements have been made for the child

iv to consider the continuing appropriateness of the statement in the light of the child's performance during the previous year, and any additional special educational needs which may have become apparent in that time, and thus to consider whether to cease to maintain the statement or whether to make any amendments, including any further modifications or disapplication of the National Curriculum, and

v if the statement is to be maintained, to set new targets for the coming year: progress towards those targets can be considered at the next review.

9:8 The child's circumstances may sometimes change during the year. They may have received education, for example, in a hospital school or in a pupil referral unit or through home tuition. Continuous assessment during the past year may have identified or confirmed a significant medical or social problem or learning difficulty that will require different or continuing support and intervention. The nature and outcomes of such provision should be addressed in the annual review and reports should be obtained from all those who have been involved in the child's educational progress during the preceding year.

The annual review for children at school

9:9 This section applies to all annual reviews except the review in year 9, which are described in detail at 9.45. The procedures to be followed are set out in Regulations and apply to all maintained schools[65] where a child with a statement is on roll.

---

64 Schools may, where appropriate, use the information gathered as part of the National Curriculum Assessment, Recording and Reporting procedures. Such information should not be used if it is considerably out of date at the time of the annual review meeting.

65 For the purpose of an annual review 'schools' refers to all schools, including maintained nursery schools.

9:10 The LEA **must** write to all head teachers no less than two weeks before the start of each term with a list of all pupils on roll at their school who will require an annual review that term. The head teacher **must** provide the LEA with a report following each annual review meeting before the end of that term, or 10 school days after the meeting takes place if that is any earlier. LEAs **must** provide similar amalgamated lists to the health authority (designated medical officer) and to the social services department, indicating the schools attended by the children identified. These lists should include **all** children with annual reviews in the forthcoming term, including those not educated in a school. These lists could also be copied to the LEA Educational Psychology Service and other LEA specialist support services.

9:11 Such early information will help professionals plan attendance at those reviews that they consider necessary.

Seeking written advice

9:12 The head teacher initiates the review process upon receipt of the termly list of annual reviews from the LEA. The head teacher can delegate to a qualified teacher at the school any or all of the duties and functions given to them in the Regulations. When such duties and functions are delegated, the head teacher should ensure that the teacher is aware of this Code and the Regulations, and that all parties involved in the review know the name of the teacher in question. The head teacher should also ensure that the designated teacher is aware of all relevant representatives of the health services, social services department, the Connexions Service where relevant and any individual professionals who should be invited to the review.

9:13 In preparing for the review meeting, the head teacher must request written advice from:

- the child's parents
- anyone specified by the authority
- and anyone else the head teacher considers appropriate.

The head teacher must also:

- circulate a copy of all advice received to all those invited to the review meeting at least two weeks before the date of the meeting, inviting additional comments, including comments from those unable to attend the review meeting.

9:14 The written advice will be used as the basis for the discussion at the review meeting and sent, with the report of the meeting and the head teacher's recommendations, to the LEA for their consideration. The advice should relate to:

- the child's progress towards meeting the objectives in the statement and any short-term targets established to help meet the objectives; the application of the National Curriculum; the progress the child has made in their behaviour and attitude to learning; the continued appropriateness of the statement; any Transition Plan (see 9.51); any amendments to the statement; or whether the statement should cease to be maintained.

9:15 Health authorities and social services departments are required by section 322(1) of the Act to respond to the head teacher's request for written advice (made on behalf of the LEA), unless the exceptions in section 321(2) and (3) apply. Other people from whom the head teacher requests written advice under Regulation 21(4) should also respond, although they are not under a statutory duty to do so. Head teachers must seek advice in accordance with Regulation 21(4). They are not required to seek advice on every one of the above points from **all** the persons they ask for advice, except for parents. Instead, head teachers can ask for specific advice from specific persons, or can ask for advice generally. The evidence received, and comments on that evidence, together with an account of the review meeting, form the basis of the review report.

The annual review meeting

9:16 Before producing the review report, the head teacher **must** convene a meeting. The head teacher **must** invite:

- the child's parents, (if the child is looked after by the local authority, under a care order, the child's social worker and the residential care worker or foster parents, should be invited as appropriate)
- a relevant teacher, who may be the child's class teacher or form/year tutor, the SENCO, or some other person responsible for the provision of education for the child, the choice resting with the head teacher
- a representative of the placing LEA
- any person who the LEA considers appropriate and specify in a notice
- any other person the head teacher considers appropriate.

9:17 Copies of all the advice received must be circulated at least two weeks before the meeting.

9:18 Parents should be encouraged to contribute their views to the annual review process, to attend the review meeting, and to contribute to discussions about any proposals for new targets for the child's progress. Parents may need support in attending reviews and help in writing advice, especially for a first review. Ways in which parents might be helped with this are referred to in Chapter Two. Where a parent does not respond to invitations to contribute in writing to the review, or to attend a review meeting, this should be recorded in the review report together with any reasons given.

9:19 Wherever possible, pupils should also be actively involved in the review process, attending all or part of the review meeting. They should be encouraged to give their views on their progress during the previous year; discuss any difficulties encountered; and share their hopes and aspirations for the future. Ways of helping the pupil to participate are discussed in Chapter Three.

9:20 Where appropriate, the LEA should tell the head teacher that representatives of the health services or social services department or other professionals closely involved with the child must be invited to contribute to the review and attend the meeting. The head teacher may also invite such representatives and professionals as they see fit, even if not asked to do so by the LEA. In some cases the professionals may themselves suggest that it could be appropriate for them to attend, or consider it necessary to provide a report on their involvement with the child over the past year.

9:21 It is unlikely that all relevant professionals will be able to attend all review meetings. It may therefore be helpful when inviting them to indicate the priority attached to their attendance. Liaison between the respective parties, over time and well in advance of the meeting, should help professionals decide whether it is appropriate to attend and also give them adequate prior notice. Schools should explain to parents that professionals will not always be able to attend all review meetings and that, if after the review meeting, parents wish to further discuss matters of concern in the professionals' reports, they should first approach the Named LEA Officer. This should be explained to the parents at the review meeting.

9:22 Where a child is placed outside the area of the LEA responsible for the statement, a representative of the placing LEA should where possible attend the review meeting. Parents should be strongly encouraged to attend. In particular circumstances LEAs may consider it appropriate to help parents with travel arrangements.

9:23 When a child with special educational needs or their family has English as an additional language, the timescale for planning the annual review should take into account the need to:

- translate any relevant documentation into the family's mother tongue
- ensure that interpreters are available to the child and family both in the preparatory stages to the review meeting and at the review meeting itself
- ensure that any professionals from the child's community have similar interpretation and translation facilities in order that they may contribute as fully as possible to the review process
- ensure that, if possible, a bilingual support teacher or teacher of English as an additional language is available to the child and family.

9:24 Where a child or their family have a communication difficulty because of a sensory or physical impairment, similar attention should be given to ensuring that information is available to them and to representation at the review meeting through interpreters. Where alternative communication systems are used, it would be good practice to make sure that the timing of the meeting takes into account the need to provide sufficient time for translation. Where a child or family has a visual impairment, similar attention should be given to the provision of all relevant information in Braille, large print or on tape as appropriate.

Children looked after by the local authority

9:25 Where the child with a statement is subject to a care order, the local authority designated by the order will share parental responsibilities with the child's birth parents. Such a child might be looked after by the local authority in a residential or foster placement, or might live at home. The extent of the contribution to be made by the child's parents, the residential care worker or foster parents and the social worker should be determined by the head teacher in consultation with the social services department. If both the parents and the residential care worker or foster parents will be attending a review meeting, head teachers should consider involving the social worker in preparing parents or carers for the review and providing support before and after the review itself. Where the local authority accommodates the child with a statement the child's parents retain parental responsibility for that child.

9:26 The head teacher should also consult the social services department if a child with a statement is currently subject to care proceedings. It may be advisable to invite the Children's guardian (see Glossary) to the review.

9:27 Where a child is subject to a care order, an education supervision order, or is accommodated by the local authority, the local authority social services department must include information on the arrangements for the education of the child within the Child Care Plan, as required under the Arrangements for Placement of Children (General) Regulations 1991 made under the Children Act 1989. The social services department must review the Child Care Plan and involve the child or young person in that process. The Child Care Plan must incorporate a Personal Education Plan that sets out the educational arrangements for the child and should include information from the statement, the annual review and IEPs. LEAs and social services departments may therefore wish to link the annual review of the statement with a review of the Child Care Plan in order to provide a holistic approach to meeting the child's needs.[66]

Conduct of the review meeting

9:28 The review meeting will normally take place in the child's school and should be chaired by the head teacher or the teacher to whom responsibility for the school-based elements of the review has been delegated. Further advice on annual reviews is included in the SEN Toolkit.

9:29 Those present at the meeting should, in the light of the issues raised in the reports as set out at 9:14, consider:

- does the statement remain appropriate?
- are any amendments to the statement required?
- should the LEA continue to maintain the statement, or should the LEA be recommended to cease to maintain the statement, and the child's needs be met appropriately through *School Action Plus*?
- any new targets to be set to meet the objectives set out in the statement
- whether any additions or amendments should be made to an existing Transition Plan.

9:30 A review meeting may make recommendations on any of the matters listed above. Amendments to a statement are likely to be recommended if:

- significant new evidence has emerged which is not recorded on the statement
- significant needs recorded on the statement are no longer present

66 More detailed advice can be found in DfEE/DH Guidance on the Education of Children in Public Care. May 2000.

- the provision should be amended to meet the child's changing needs and the targets specified at the review meeting, or
- the child should change schools, either at the point of transfer between school phases, for example infant to junior or primary to secondary, or when a child's needs would more appropriately be met in a different school, for example by inclusion in the mainstream.

9:31 The review meeting and the review report may also recommend that the LEA should cease to maintain the statement. If all those present cannot agree to the recommendations, the head teacher should ensure that this disagreement is recorded, together with the reasons for it.

Submitting the report

9:32 Following the annual review meeting the head teacher **must** prepare a report, and submit it to the LEA no later than 10 school days after the annual review meeting or the end of that school term, whichever is the earlier. The report should summarise the outcome of the review meeting, setting out the head teacher's assessment of the main issues discussed at the meeting; and the head teacher's recommendations about any educational targets for the coming year; and any other steps that ought to be taken including whether the statement should be amended or maintained. The head teacher should always give reasons for the recommendations. The head teacher must send a copy of the report to all concerned in the review, including the parents and any relevant professionals.

9:33 The review report should be written as quickly as possible. The head teacher should make sure that the recommendations are clear and that any relevant professional reports are appended to the review report so that the LEA is able to review the statement and make decisions without any unnecessary delay. LEAs may find it helpful to offer guidance as to the form that reports should follow, or provide a common format for review reports for all schools in their area.

The role of the LEA after receiving the review report

9:34 The LEA concludes the review process by considering the report of the review meeting and the recommendations prepared by the head teacher. The LEA must then review the statement, in the light of the report and recommendations and any other information they consider relevant. The LEA must decide whether to accept the head teacher's recommendations. In particular the LEA must decide whether to amend or cease to maintain the statement. Within one week of making a decision, the LEA must send a copy of its decision on these matters to the head teacher, the child's parents and anyone else they think appropriate.

9:35 Where the decision is to amend the statement, the LEA should start the process of amendment without delay.

9:47 The annual review of the statement must consider all the same issues as at all other reviews, and the report to the LEA should be in the same format. LEAs must also complete the review process in the same way as for all other annual reviews and within the same timescale.

9:48 The LEA **must** send the Connexions Service a list of all pupils in their area who will require a year 9 review no later than two weeks before the start of the school year. The list **must** include all pupils whether or not they are educated in a school and indicate any schools that the children specified attend. This information will help Connexions Services to plan attendance at year 9 reviews.

9:49 The head teacher together with the Connexions Service should facilitate the transfer of relevant information to ensure that young people receive any necessary specialist help or support during their continuing education and vocational or occupational training after leaving school. For young people with specific disabilities, the role of social services departments will be of particular importance and local authorities have specific duties relating to other legislation. Further detailed information can be found in the SEN Toolkit.

9:50 The annual review procedure described above applies with the following additions:

- **the head teacher must invite the Connexions Service to provide written advice and invite them to the review meeting, to enable all options for continuing education, careers and occupational training to be given serious consideration**
- **a representative of the Connexions Service is obliged, by the conditions of grant, to attend the review**
- **the head teacher should ensure that other providers, such as health authorities and trusts, are aware of the particular procedures to be followed in year 9**
- **the head teacher must invite the social services department to attend the review so that any parallel assessments under the Disabled Persons (Services, Consultation and Representations) Act 1986; the NHS and Community Care Act 1990; and the Chronically Sick and Disabled Persons Act 1970 can contribute to and draw information from the review process**
- **the head teacher must ensure that a Transition Plan is drawn up. This should be done in consultation with the Connexions Service.**

The Transition Plan

9:51 The annual review in year 9 and any subsequent annual reviews until the young person leaves school **must** include the drawing up and subsequent review of a Transition Plan. The **Transition Plan** should draw together information from a range of individuals within and beyond school in order to plan coherently for the young person's transition to adult life. Transition Plans when first drawn up in year 9 are not simply about post-school arrangements, they should also plan for on-going school provision, under the statement of SEN as overseen by the LEA.

9:52 All those involved in the process should adhere to the principles that underpin the nature of transition and transition planning and the requirements of the young people and their families. Transition planning should be:

- participative
- holistic
- supportive
- evolving
- inclusive
- collaborative.

9:53 The Connexions Service is responsible for overseeing the delivery of the Transition Plan and the Connexions Personal Adviser (PA) should co-ordinate its delivery. Further detailed advice on the principles and processes of transition planning are set out in the SEN Toolkit. The Connexions Framework for Assessment Planning, Implementation and Review also contains information on transition planning and is likely to be the first port of call for PAs (see Glossary).

9:54 In order to ensure coherence for the young person, there should not be a separate Transition Plan and Connexions action plan. Where the young person has been involved with a PA previously and therefore already has an action plan, the Transition Plan should build on, update and expand this earlier plan. The action plan could, if the young person agrees, be circulated with the reports prior to the annual review meeting in year 9.

Student involvement in decision-making during transition

9:55 The views of young people themselves should be sought and recorded wherever possible in any assessment, reassessment or review from year 9 onwards. PAs, student counsellors, advocates or advisers, teachers and other school staff, social workers or peer support may be needed to support the young person in the transition process. Chapter Three of this Code and the SEN Toolkit consider in detail the ways in which young people can be helped to participate fully in this process.

The role of the Connexions Service

9:56 The Connexions Service will have a particular role to play in ensuring the participation and progression of young people with SEN aged 13 – 19. PAs should ensure that they are aware of all young people with SEN in year 8. A representative of the Connexions Service, in most cases this is likely to be a PA, **must** be invited to the year 9 annual review meeting and, as a condition of grant, **must** attend, whether or not the young person is in school. The attendance of the PA is critical to the process. PAs should be invited to all subsequent annual reviews, and are expected to attend where appropriate.

9:57 Year 9 review meetings are the start of a process for longer-term decision-making. Vocational guidance provided by the school or the PA should include information on key stage 4 and post-16 options and take fully into account the wishes and feelings of the young person concerned. The Connexions Service should assist the young person and their parents to identify the most appropriate post-16 provision, provide counselling and support, and have continuing oversight of, and information on, the young person's choice of provision. These processes will need to be carried out in partnership with the LEA's SEN officers and those professionals who know the young person well.

Involvement of social services departments

9:58 LEAs **must** seek information from social services departments under section 5 of the Disabled Persons (Services, Consultation and Representation) Act 1986, as to whether a young person with a statement under Part IV of the Education Act 1996 is disabled (and so may require services from the local authority when leaving school).

9:59 Multi-agency input at year 9 is important for all young people with SEN. Under the Children Act 1989 social services departments may arrange multi-disciplinary assessments and must establish Children's Service Plans which may include the provision of further education for children in need (likely to include those with significant special needs). Social services departments should ensure that a social worker attends the year 9 annual review meeting and contributes to the formation of the Transition Plan where a young person is subject to a care order, accommodated by the local authority or is a 'child in need'.

Involvement of health services

9:60 Health professionals involved in the management and care of the young person should provide advice towards transition plans in writing and, wherever possible, should attend the annual review meeting in year 9. They should advise on the services that are likely to be required and should discuss arrangements for transfer to adult health care services with the young person, their parents and their GP. They should facilitate any referrals and transfers of records, which may be necessary, subject to the informed consent of the young person and parents, and should liaise with the Connexions Service as appropriate.

Annual reviews from year 10

9:61 The school remains responsible for convening annual review meetings until such time as the pupil leaves school. Some pupils with statements of special educational needs will remain in school after the age of 16. LEAs remain responsible for such pupils until they are 19. There will be occasions where the natural completion of an academic year or completion of a particular course would take a pupil with a statement beyond their 19th birthday. The Learning and Skills Council, when it becomes responsible for the funding of sixth form provision, will, as a condition of funding, require LEAs in those situations to maintain statements until the end of the academic year in which their 19th birthday falls.

9:62 Whatever the intended future destination of the young person, the annual review has an additional significance as the young person approaches the age of 16. The Connexions Service should be invited to and should attend the review meeting in year 11 in order to ensure that the Transition Plan is updated appropriately. In the young person's final year of school, the Connexions Service has a separate responsibility, under section 140 of the Learning and Skills Act 2000, for ensuring that an assessment of their needs on leaving school is undertaken and the provision identified. Every effort should be made to link this final annual review of the statement and to consider the Transition Plan together with this assessment so that a holistic approach is maintained. Where post 16 provision has already been identified it is good practice for the head teacher to invite a representative from the provision to the review meeting.

Transfer of information

9:63 The Connexions Service should seek the agreement of students and parents to the transfer of information (including statements) from school to the continuing education sector or other provision, and explain the importance of such information and the desirability of the transfer.

9:64 The Connexions Service should ensure that where a young person has a statement of special educational needs, a copy of the statement together with a copy of the most recent annual review, and the Transition Plan, is passed to the social services department and any post 16 provision that the young person will be attending. Where a decision might need to be taken about the placement of a student in a specialist college, a copy of the Transition Plan should be sent to the local Learning and Skills Council.

Students without statements but with special educational needs

9:65 In some instances, a student approaching the age of 16 may have special educational needs which do not call for a statement, but which are likely to require some support if they go on to further education or training. To ensure that these students are able to make decisions, and to facilitate their successful transition, it is important that they have appropriate help and guidance. This might include the provision of school/college link courses or work placements and should involve the different local agencies concerned.

9:66 The Connexions Service provides support for all young people aged 13 – 19. It has a particular focus on supporting disadvantaged young people or those likely to underachieve, including those with SEN but without statements. The Connexions Service should provide schools with information which will help these students make successful transitions to post-school education, training or work, including details of local and national voluntary organizations. Schools should consult as appropriate with the Connexions Service and other services to ensure that detailed information is transferred to further education providers with the young person's consent.

9:67 As a condition of grant, the Connexions Service has a responsibility to ensure that all young people who may have difficulty in transferring to further education or training after they have completed their compulsory schooling, including those with SEN but without a statement, have a needs and provision assessment. When undertaken for young people with SEN but without statements these assessments may be recorded as having been carried out under Section 140 of the Learning and Skills Act (see 9.62).

Children subject to a care order or accommodated by a local authority

9:68 Under the provisions of the Children (Leaving Care) Act 2001 every eligible young person looked after by a local authority on their 16th birthday, including those with SEN, will have a pathway plan. This plan will build on the Care and Personal Education Plans, mapping out a pathway to independence, including education, training and employment. The local authority will also be required to appoint a personal adviser who will normally act as the Connexions PA for each of these young people. The adviser must work with the young person and others to devise the pathway plan and ensure its implementation. The pathway plan should cover all the areas that are relevant to enabling a care leaver to make a successful transition to adulthood. As such, the pathway plan fulfils the same function as the Transition Plan and Connexions personal action plan. It is therefore good practice that they should be the same document so avoiding unnecessary duplication for the young person.

9:69 It is important that the PA ensures that the young person is fully aware of the local authority's responsibilities towards them and to agree with the social services department, other agencies and the young person the services to be delivered. Where a young person has been looked after in a foster care or residential placement or attended a residential school outside their own local authority area, the PA for the responsible authority together with the LEA should seek to ensure liaison between all relevant LEAs and social services departments. The responsible authority is the local authority that is looking after the young person or, in the case of a young person who has left care, the authority that last looked after them.

10 Working in partnership with Other Agencies

Introduction

10:1 Meeting the special educational needs of individual children requires flexible working on the part of statutory agencies. They need to communicate and agree policies and protocols that ensure that there is a 'seamless' service. Working supportively and in partnership with parents and the children and young people themselves will ensure that everyone involved understands the responses of the professionals concerned, and lead to a better quality of provision.

10:2. Maintained schools **must** publish information that includes the school's arrangements for working in partnership with LEA support services, health and social services, the Connexions Service and any relevant local and national voluntary organizations. Teachers have a great deal of expertise in identifying and meeting the needs of their pupils. External support services can however play an important part in helping schools identify, assess and make provision for pupils with special educational needs.

Principles of inter-agency working for children with SEN

10:3 All services for children with SEN should focus on identifying and addressing the needs of children and enabling them to improve their situation through:

- early identification
- continual engagement with the child and parents
- focused intervention
- dissemination of effective approaches and techniques.

10:4 The objective should be to provide integrated, high quality, holistic support focused on the needs of the child. Such provision should be based on a shared perspective and should build wherever possible on mutual understanding and agreement. Services should adopt a flexible child-centred approach to service delivery to ensure that the changing needs and priorities of the child and their parents[70] can be met at any given time.

10:5 All agencies should recognise the need for effective collaboration of services involved with the child and with parents. Consultative responsibilities and effective communication systems at management and practitioner levels should be clearly identified. Developments in organisational structures and working practices should reflect this principle. Joint planning arrangements should:

- take account of good practice
- ensure consultation with all relevant services
- agree priorities
- publicise decisions to parents and professionals
- regularly review policies and objectives.

---

70 'Parent' is used throughout the text to refer to all those with parental responsibility.

LEA support services

10:6 LEA support services can provide advice to teachers (e.g. on teaching techniques and strategies, classroom management, and curriculum materials); support for curriculum development; direct teaching or practical support for class teachers; part-time specialist help, or access to learning support assistance.

10:7 Such services include specialist teachers of pupils with hearing, visual, and speech and language impairments, teachers providing more general learning and behaviour support services, counsellors, educational psychologists, and advisers or teachers with knowledge of information technology for children with special educational needs. Curriculum support and advisory services can also be a resource for advice on specific subject-related teaching techniques and strategies and curriculum materials.

10:8 The educational psychologist can be a very important resource for the school. The psychologist's knowledge of the school and its context is key. Through regular consultation with schools educational psychology services can provide help in clarifying problems and devising problem solving strategies; in carrying out specialised assessments, including techniques in managing behaviour, and evaluating individual pupil progress. In addition to working with individual children, the educational psychologist can work with groups of pupils or teachers and learning support assistants at the classroom or whole school level, for example assisting schools with the development of SEN and behaviour policies, helping to develop knowledge and skills for school staff and assisting with projects to raise achievement and promote inclusion.

10:9 The LEA may offer a range of services through the Education Welfare Service. This service works closely with schools, parents and children to try to resolve attendance issues for all children. This may involve arranging home and school visits to discuss the situation. They will try to find out the reason why a child is not attending school, and take steps to try to get the child back into school. There will, of course, be times when the child should not return to maintained mainstream schooling, whether or not they have identified special educational needs. In such cases the LEA might arrange an alternative provision that helps pupils who have problems with settling in school.

10:10 Education Welfare Services may undertake other functions on behalf of the LEA. These can range from checking on child employment legislation, to dealing with the education provision of those children who have been excluded from school, or working with the school when a child is at serious risk of disaffection or exclusion, and in some cases, exercising responsibility for child protection issues. Education welfare officers may also offer support and counselling to help children who are not in school. They may also talk to other Local Authority Departments and agencies, like social services, local Housing Departments and Health, and the Education Psychology Service about the needs of a particular child.

10:11 Schools should work in close partnership with the providers of all these services. The SENCO, in particular, should be aware of the LEA's policy for the provision of support services and how the school can gain access to them. LEAs should provide full information to all schools in their area about the range of services locally available and how they can be secured. Whether or not funding for particular support services is delegated to schools, it may be helpful for schools and LEAs to draw up service level agreements for such services, specifying the scope, quality and duration of the service to be provided. When schools enter into contracts with private or voluntary sector providers, they should satisfy themselves of the qualifications and experience of the specialists involved, that the service represents good value for money and carry out appropriate police checks.

10:12 The SENCO and class teachers need to be very clear why they need external assistance. If there is an identifiable lack of expertise within the range that can be offered by the staff in a mainstream school, then the school should consider seeking external advice. Even when outside specialists are involved the SENCO still has prime responsibility for coordinating the special educational provision made for the child and for any decisions taken over this.

10:13 It is most likely that schools will consult specialists when they take action on behalf of a child through *School Action Plus*. But the involvement of specialists need not be limited to children receiving provision through *School Action Plus*. Outside specialists can play an important part in the very early identification of special educational needs and in advising schools on effective provision designed to prevent the development of more significant needs. They can act as consultants and be a source for in-service advice on learning and behaviour management strategies for all teachers.

The Connexions Service

10:14 The Connexions Service has a responsibility to work with all young people between the ages of 13 and 19. The LEA must have in place arrangements for working in partnership with Connexions to ensure the needs of these young people are fully served.

10:15 The Connexions Service provides guidance and support to young people through their teenage years and into adult life. The Service is delivered primarily through a network of Personal Advisers linking in with specialist support services, including services for young people with SEN. The Personal Advisers are supported by a comprehensive and coherent service delivery structure as a wide range of local organisations work together within Connexions Partnerships.

10:16 The Service is for all 13 to 19 year olds in England, giving particular priority to those young people at greatest risk of not making a successful transition to adulthood. The Service will have a particular role to play in ensuring the participation and progression of young people with SEN. The service has a key role in the transition process for young people with SEN from year 9 onwards. Exceptionally, a person with complex learning difficulties or disabilities may need continued enhanced guidance beyond the age of 19. The level of support should be agreed and reviewed jointly by the Connexions Service and the local Learning and Skills Council and agreement reached as to who will be responsible for the provision of information, advice and guidance.

10:17 An awareness of the local management, structure and services available through the Connexions Service will help schools to address the needs of young people with SEN. PAs located within schools will work directly with a range of young people, including those with SEN. The specific role to be undertaken by the PAs with regard to transition planning for young people with SEN is outlined in Chapter Nine.

Learning and Skills Councils

10:18 The Learning and Skills Council (LSC) is responsible for the development, planning, funding and management of all post-16 education and training (except higher education) and Work Based Training for Young People. Its 47 local arms in England are responsible for raising standards and securing provision to match local learning and skills needs. In meeting its responsibilities the Council must have regard to the needs of people with learning difficulties and it has a statutory duty to take account of the assessments of people with learning difficulties and disabilities that are arranged by the Connexions Service. Planning to ensure that young people with learning difficulties and disabilities have access to high quality learning is one of the Council's key objectives and the local Learning and Skills Councils monitor the arrangements that are in place in their areas to meet the needs of these young people. The LSC at the local level and the Connexions Service need to work closely together, drawing in post-16 providers and schools and LEAs as necessary, to ensure that the appropriate support and funding arrangements are in place for the provision set out in Transition Plans.

Health Services

Health Authorities and LEAs must comply with a request from a social services department for assistance in providing services for *children in need*, so long as the request is compatible with their duties and does not unduly prejudice the discharge of any of their functions.

See Section 27, Children Act 1989

Health authorities, subject to the reasonableness of the request in the light of the resources available to them, must comply with a request for help from an LEA in connection with children with special educational needs, unless they consider that the help is not necessary for the exercise of the LEA's functions.

See Section 322, Education Act 1996

10:19 Schools' first point of contact with health services will usually be through the local school health services, or similar, which deliver health advisory and support services to schools. These health professionals will usually be able to advise the school but, if a problem is confirmed, should also tell the medical officer designated to work with children with special educational needs that the school has sought advice about a child. Health professionals such as speech and language therapists, occupational therapists and physiotherapists, as well as doctors and the school nurse, also provide advice and support for children with special educational needs.

10:20 Early education settings should seek advice from their local Early Years Development and Childcare Partnership about partnership arrangements in place with other agencies.

10:21 Health Authorities and Trusts **must** give parents the names of voluntary organisations that might be of assistance when they consider that a child under five may have special educational needs.[71] Under the Children Act 1989, local authority social services departments must produce written information on the range of services they provide in their area for children 'in need', and may include details of information provided by others and take reasonable steps to ensure that such information reaches those who might require it.

10:22 When schools are concerned about the educational progress of a child they should, with the informed consent and involvement of the child's parents, consult the school health service or child's general practitioner about whether a medical condition may be contributing to the child's difficulties in school. Where the child's difficulties are sufficient to make it likely that they will be the subject of statutory assessment, the health professional consulted should, with parental consent, notify and provide relevant medical information to the medical officer designated by the Health Authority to work with the LEA on behalf of children with SEN and to lead the Health Authority's contribution to the statutory assessment process.

10:23 The Health Authority (HA) should agree with Primary Care Groups and Trusts how the local health authority contribution to statutory assessment and to meeting the medical needs of children with special educational needs will be discharged. Primary Care Trusts or Community Trusts may employ the staff from whom the HA will need to designate a medical officer for special educational needs.

10:24 The designated medical officer for special educational needs will need to have a strategic and operational role in co-ordinating activity across HAs, NHS Trusts, Primary Care Groups and GPs.

10:25 At the strategic level, the designated medical officer should check that the Health Authority have arrangements for ensuring that the Trusts and GPs providing child health services:

- **inform LEAs of children who they think may have special educational needs**
- **provide medical advice to LEAs for the assessment of children within the statutory time limits**
- **consider, with LEAs and with regard to available resources, the health services' contribution to the non-educational provision to be specified in a statement.**

10:26 At the operational level, the designated medical officer should:

- **ensure that all schools have a contact (usually the school health service) for seeking medical advice on children who may have special educational needs**
- **provide a resource to other health service staff – for example, GPs and therapists – who require assistance in preparing reports on the medical history and health needs of children for schools and LEAs**
- **co-ordinate the health services' advice for a statutory assessment and, frequently, participate in multi-agency meetings on assessments and making statements**

---

71 Section 332, Education Act 1996.

- **co-ordinate the provision to be made by the health services for a child with special educational needs when, as may be the case with therapy and nursing services, either a HA or Primary Care Group may be responsible for the purchasing of these services**
- **consider how the powers in the Health Act 1999, allowing pooling of budgets and integration of commissioning or providing functions between the NHS and Local Authorities, can best support services for children with SEN.**

Child and Adolescent Mental Health Services (CAMHS)

10:27 Children with SEN are more likely to have mental health problems than those without, emphasising the importance of close links between education services and CAMHS. Many children with mental health problems, but by no means all, may also be recognised as children with emotional and behavioural difficulties.

10:28 Children with mental health problems may receive help from a range of sources – from highly specialised health services through to those provided at primary care level, for example general practitioners. Some children and young people identified as having SEN may benefit from referral to CAMHS specialists for the assessment and treatment of mental health problems. CAMHS can also provide advice, support and consultation to family members, carers and workers from health, social care, educational and voluntary agencies. Joint initiatives in some schools between the NHS and education services focus on children's mental health exist. These can facilitate a co-operative relationship between specialist child mental health care and education including educational psychology services.

Social Services

> **Social services departments must comply with a request for help from an LEA in connection with children with special educational needs, unless they consider that the help is not necessary for the exercise of the LEA's functions and so long as the request is compatible with their duties and does not unduly prejudice the discharge of any their functions.**
>
> See Section 322, Education Act 1996

10:29 Social services departments should designate an officer or officers who are responsible for working with schools and LEAs on behalf of children with special educational needs and to whom schools and LEAs should refer for advice. If the designated officer has early information about a child, the social services department will be able to react quickly, and within the statutory time limits, to any later request from the LEA for advice in the making of a statutory assessment. Social services departments should ensure that all schools in the area know the name of, and how to contact, a designated social services officer who has responsibilities for special educational needs.

10:30 At the strategic level, the designated officer for social services should check that the social service department has arrangements to:

- **inform LEAs of children who they think may have special educational needs**

- **provide social services advice to LEAs for the assessment of children within the statutory time limits**
- **consider, with LEAs and with regard to available resources, the social services' contribution to the non-educational provision to be specified in a statement.**

10:31 At the operational level, the designated officer should:

- **ensure that all schools have a contact for seeking social work advice on children who may have special educational needs**
- **provide a resource to social workers who require assistance in preparing reports for SEN statutory assessment**
- **co-ordinate the social services services' advice for a statutory assessment**
- **participate in multi-agency meetings on assessments and making statements.**

Children in need

> **It is the general duty of every local authority:**
>
> - **to safeguard and promote the welfare of children within their area who are in need;**
>
> **and**
>
> - **so far as is consistent with that duty, to promote the upbringing of such children by their families, by providing a range and level of services appropriate to those children's needs.**
>
> See Section 17(1), Children Act 1989

10:32 Under section 17 of the Children Act 1989, the local authority social services department has a duty to safeguard and promote the welfare of children in their area who are 'in need'.

10:33 While a child with special educational needs will not necessarily be 'in need' as defined in the Children Act 1989, that Act allows an integrated approach to the educational, health and welfare needs of children with special educational needs who are 'in need.'

10:34 LEAs **must** co-operate with social services departments if a child is 'in need' and the LEA can assist (Section 27 of the Children Act 1989) or is suffering or at risk of suffering significant harm (Section 47 of the Children Act 1989), although this would not automatically mean a child had special education needs.

10:35 At the same time as the LEA is carrying out a statutory assessment under section 323 of the Education Act 1996, a Social Services Department may decide to undertake a child 'in need' assessment under section 17 of the Children Act 1989 to ascertain whether social services help may benefit the child or their family. This assessment will be undertaken in accordance with the DH et al 'Framework for the Assessment of Children in Need and their Families' (2000) to which teachers and other educational professionals will be expected to contribute.

10:36 In addition, Social Services Departments are required (under Schedule 1 of the Children Act 1989) to provide information on services for children in need and their families. This information should be available to schools. They should also make available to the LEA all relevant information of planning processes or data collection (such as the Register of Children with Disabilities, the Children's Services Plan or the Community Care Plan). Social services should also ensure that information is provided about direct payments under the Carers and Disabled Children Act 2000.

Looked after children

10:37 Every child who is 'looked after' by a local authority must have a Care Plan, whether they are accommodated or on a care order and regardless of placement. The Care Plan sets out the long-term objectives for the child and the arrangements for achieving those objectives. The overall Care Plan will incorporate the Personal Education Plan which must include information on the special educational arrangements made for the child and will involve parents, carers and the child in forward planning.

The Voluntary Sector

10:38 Voluntary agencies and groups have an important role to play in meeting the needs of pupils with special educational needs. They provide services and in some cases offer their own provision. It is essential that schools and local authorities seek to work actively in partnership with the voluntary sector to meet pupils' needs. LEAs and schools should demonstrate a willingness to work with and value the contribution they can make. Local authorities also need to help join up the different local partners in order to maximise the benefit this can have for pupils.

10:39 The DfES sponsors a network of eleven SEN Regional Partnerships. These bring together groups of local authorities and local health, social services, voluntary and private sector partners. The overall aim of the network is to secure greater consistency in the quality of the response to pupils with similar special educational needs.

Providing information

10:40 The LEA should give schools, social services departments, health authorities and local voluntary agencies full information on the LEA's statutory assessment arrangements and procedures. LEAs and social services departments and health authorities should agree the procedures to be followed when the LEA notify a social services department or health authority of their proposal to assess a child's special educational needs.

Annex A

The Education (Special Educational Needs) (England) (Consolidation) Regulations 2001

The Education (Special Educational Needs) (Provision of Information by Local Education Authorities) (England) Regulations 2001

The Education (Special Educational Needs) (Information)(England) Regulations 1999

STATUTORY INSTRUMENTS

2001 No. 3455

EDUCATION, ENGLAND

The Education (Special Educational Needs) (England) (Consolidation) Regulations 2001

Made......22 October 2001

Laid before Parliament......23 October 2001

Coming into force......1st January 2002

ARRANGEMENT OF REGULATIONS

PART I

GENERAL

PART II

ASSESSMENTS

Part B – Notice to Parent (amendment notices)

Schedule 2

Statement of Special Educational Needs

In exercise of the powers conferred on the Secretary of State by sections 316A(2), 322(4), 324(2), 325(2A) and (2B), 326A(4), 328(1), (3A) and (3B), 329(2A), 329A(9), 336A(1) and 569(1), (2), (4) and (5) of, and paragraphs 2, 3(1), (3) and (4) of Schedule 26, and paragraphs 2(3), 2B(3), 5(3), 6(3), 7(1) and (2), 8(3A) and (5), 11(2A) and (4) of Schedule 27 to, the Education Act 1996**(a)**, the Secretary of State for Education and Skills hereby makes the following Regulations:

PART I

GENERAL

Citation and commencement

1.-(1) These Regulations may be cited as the Education (Special Educational Needs) (England) (Consolidation) Regulations 2001.

(2) These Regulations shall come into force on 1st January 2002.

(3) These Regulations apply only in relation to England.

Interpretation

2.-(1) In these Regulations—

'the Act' means the Education Act 1996;

'annual review' means a review of a child's statement of educational needs carried out within 12 months of making the statement or the previous review under section 328(5)(b) of the Act;

'assessment' means an assessment of a child's educational needs under section 323 of the Act;

'authority' means a local education authority;

'Careers Service' means a body established to provide careers services under sections 8 to 10 of the Employment and Training Act 1973**(b)**;

(a) 1996 c.56. By virtue of the National Assembly for Wales (Transfer of Functions) Order 1999 (S.I. 1999/672), the powers conferred by sections 322(4), 324(2), 328(1), and 569, and by paragraphs 2(1) and (2) of Schedule 26 are exercisable by the Secretary of State only in relation to England. For the meaning of regulations see section 579(1) of the Act. Sections 316A(2), 325(2A) and 2(B), 326A(4), 328(3A) and (3B), 329A(9) and 336A(1) were inserted by the Special Educational Needs and Disability Act 2001 (c.10), section 1, paragraph 6 of Schedule 8, section 5, paragraph 7 of Schedule 8, section 8 and section 4 respectively.

(b) 1973 c.50; sections 8, 9 and 10 were substituted by the Trade Union Reform and Employment Rights Act 1993 (c.19), section 45.

'Connexions Service' means a person of any description with whom the Secretary of State has made an arrangement under section 114(2)(a) of the Learning and Skills Act 2000**(c)** and section 10(1) of the Employment and Training Act 1973 and any person to whom he has given a direction under section 114(2)(b) of the Learning and Skills Act 2000 and section 10(2) of the Employment and Training Act 1973;

'early education provider' means a provider of relevant nursery education except that it shall not include an authority in respect of a maintained nursery school;

'head of SEN' means the person responsible for co-ordinating the day-to-day provision of education for pupils with special educational needs;

'head teacher' includes any person to whom the duties or functions of a head teacher under these Regulations have been delegated by the head teacher in accordance with regulation 3;

'health authority' has the same meaning as in the National Health Service Act 1977**(d)**;

'parent partnership services' means the arrangements made by an authority under section 332A of the Act for the provision of advice and information about matters relating to special educational needs to parents of children with special educational needs;

'social services authority' means a local authority for the purposes of the Local Authority Social Services Act 1970**(e)** acting in the discharge of such functions as are referred to in section 1A of that Act;

'statement' means a statement of a child's special educational needs made under section 324 of the Act;

'target' means the knowledge, skills and understanding which a child is expected to have by the end of a particular period;

'tenth year of compulsory education' means the ninth school year after the school year in which a child reaches compulsory school age;

'transition plan' means a document which sets out the appropriate arrangements for a young person during the period beginning with the commencement of his tenth year of compulsory education and ending when aged 19 years, including arrangements for special educational provision and for any other necessary provision, for suitable employment and accommodation for leisure activities, and which will facilitate a satisfactory transition from childhood to adulthood;

'Tribunal' means the Special Educational Needs Tribunal having the jurisdiction conferred on it by section 333 of the Act;

'working day' means a day other than a Saturday, Sunday, Christmas Day, Good Friday or Bank Holiday within the meaning of the Banking and Financial Dealings Act 1971 **(f)**;

'the 1994 Regulations' means the Education (Special Educational Needs) Regulations

---

(c) 2000 c.21.
(d) 1977 c.49 amended by the Health Authorities Act 1995 (c.17) and the Health Act 1999 (c.32).
(e) 1970 c.42; section 1A was inserted by the Local Government Act 2000 (c.22), section 102(3).
(f) 1971 c.80.

1994(**g**).

(2) The expressions used in these Regulations set out in the first column of the table below have the meaning given by (or, as the case may be, are to be interpreted in accordance with) the provisions referred to in the second column of that table:

'compulsory school age'	section 8 of the Act;
'maintained school'	section 312 of the Act;
'parent'	section 576 of the Act;
'qualified teacher'	section 218 Education Reform Act 1988 (**h**);
'relevant nursery education'	section 509A(5) of the Act;
'responsible body'	section 329A(13) of the Act;
'school day'	section 579(1) of the Act;
'school year'	section 579(1) of the Act;
'special school'	section 337 of the Act;
'young offender institution'	section 43 of the Prison Act 1952(**i**).

(3) In these Regulations any reference to the health authority or the social services authority is, in relation to a particular child, a reference to the health authority or social services authority in whose area that child lives.

(4) Where a thing is required to be done under these Regulations—

(a) within a period after an action is taken, the day on which that action was taken shall not be counted in the calculation of that period, and

(b) within a period and the last day of that period is not a working day, the period shall be extended to include the following working day.

(5) Unless the context otherwise requires references in these Regulations—

(a) to a section are references to a section of the Act;

(b) to a Schedule are references to a Schedule of the Act;

(c) to a regulation are references to a regulation in these Regulations;

(d) to a paragraph are references to a paragraph in the regulation concerned.

Delegation of functions

3. Where a head teacher has any functions or duties under these Regulations he may delegate those functions or duties-

---

(**g**) S.I. 1994/1047.
(**h**) 1988 c.40.
(**i**) 1952 c.52.

(a) generally to a member of the staff of the school who is a qualified teacher, or

(b) in a particular case to a member of the staff of the school who teaches the child in question.

Notices

4. Any notice required to be given by these Regulations shall be given in writing.

Service of documents

5.-(1) Where any provision in Part IV of the Act or in these Regulations authorises or requires any document to be served or sent to a person or any notice to be given to a person the document may be served or sent or the notice may be given by properly addressing, pre-paying and posting a letter containing the document or notice.

(2) For the purposes of this regulation, the proper address of a person is –

(a) in the case of the child's parent, his last known address;

(b) in the case of a head teacher or other member of the staff of a school, the school's address, or

(c) in the case of any other person, the last known address of the place where he carries on his business, profession or other employment.

(3) Where first class post is used, the document or notice shall be treated as served, sent or given on the second working day after the date of posting, unless the contrary is shown.

(4) Where second class post is used, the document or notice shall be treated as served, sent or given on the fourth working day after the date of posting, unless the contrary is shown.

(5) The date of posting shall be presumed, unless the contrary is shown, to be the date shown in the post-mark on the envelope in which the document is contained.

PART II

ASSESSMENTS

Notices relating to assessment

6.-(1) Paragraph (2) applies where –

(a) under section 323(1) or 329A(3) an authority serve notice on a child's parent that they are considering whether to make an assessment, or

(b) no notice has been given in relation to a particular assessment under section 323(1) or 329A(3), and under section 323(4) or 329A(7) an authority give notice to a child's parent of their decision to make an assessment.

(2) Where this paragraph applies an authority shall send copies of the relevant notice-

(a) to the social services authority; and

(b) to the health authority; and

(c) if the child is registered at a school, to the head teacher of that school; or

(d) if the child receives education from an early education provider, to the head of SEN in relation to that provider.

(3) Where a copy of a notice is sent under paragraph (2) an endorsement on the copy or a notice accompanying that copy shall inform the recipient what help the authority are likely to request.

(4) Where -

(a) under section 328(2) or 329(1) a child's parent asks an authority to arrange for an assessment, and

(b) no assessment has been made for that child within the period of six months ending with the date on which the request is made,

the authority shall give notice to the persons referred to in paragraph (2)(a) to (d) that the request has been made and inform them what help the authority are likely to request.

(5) Where -

(a) under section 329A(1) a responsible body asks an authority to arrange for an assessment, and

(b) no assessment has been made for that child within the period of six months ending with the date on which the request is made,

the authority shall give notice to the persons referred to in paragraphs (2)(a) to (d) that the request has been made and inform them what help the authority are likely to request.

(6) Where the head teacher at a school or head of SEN in relation to an early education provider is the responsible body referred to at paragraph (5)(a) the authority may-

(a) choose not to serve a notice on the head teacher or head of SEN under paragraph (5)(b), and

(b) endorse the notice served on the responsible body under section 329A(7) or serve a further notice accompanying that notice informing the head teacher of the school or the head of SEN in relation to the early education provider of the help the authority are likely to request.

Advice to be sought

7.-(1) For the purpose of making an assessment an authority shall seek –

(a) advice from the child's parent;

(b) educational advice as provided for in regulation 8;

(c) medical advice from the health authority as provided for in regulation 9;

(d) psychological advice as provided for in regulation 10;

(e) advice from the social services authority, and

(f) any other advice which the authority consider appropriate for the purpose of arriving at a satisfactory assessment.

(2) The advice referred to in paragraph (1) shall be written advice relating to -

(a) the educational, medical, psychological or other features of the case (according to the nature of the advice sought) which appear to be relevant to the child's educational needs (including his likely future needs);

(b) how those features could affect the child's educational needs, and

(c) the provision which is appropriate for the child in light of those features of the child's case, whether by way of special educational provision or non-educational provision, but not relating to any matter which is required to be specified in a statement by virtue of section 324(4)(b).

(3) A person from whom the advice referred to in paragraph (1) is sought may in connection therewith consult such persons as it appears to him expedient to consult; and he shall consult such persons, if any, as are specified in the particular case by the authority as persons who have relevant knowledge of, or information relating to, the child.

(4) When seeking the advice referred to in paragraphs (1)(b) to (f) an authority shall provide the person from whom it is sought with copies of -

(a) any representations made by the parent, and

(b) any evidence submitted by, or at the request of, the parent

under section 323(1)(d) or section 329A(3)(d) as the case may be.

(5) The authority need not seek the advice referred to in paragraph (1)(b), (c), (d), (e) or (f) if -

(a) the authority have obtained advice under paragraph (1)(b), (c), (d), (e) or (f) respectively within the preceding 12 months, and

(b) the authority, the person from whom the advice was obtained and the child's parent are satisfied that the existing advice is sufficient for the purpose of arriving at a satisfactory assessment.

Educational Advice

8.-(1) The educational advice referred to in regulation 7(1)(b) shall, subject to paragraphs (2) to (5), be sought -

(a) from the head teacher of any school which the child is currently attending;

(b) if advice cannot be obtained from a head teacher of a school which the child is currently attending (because the child is not attending a school or otherwise) then from a person who the authority are satisfied has experience of teaching children with special educational needs or knowledge of the differing provision which may be called for in different cases to meet those needs;

(c) if the child is not currently attending a school and if advice obtained under sub-paragraph (b) is not advice from such a person, from a person responsible for educational provision for him, and

(d) if any parent of the child is a serving member of Her Majesty's armed forces, from Service Children's Education.

(2) Subject to paragraph (3), the advice sought as provided in paragraphs (1)(a) to (c) shall not be sought from any person who is not a qualified teacher.

(3) If the advice sought as provided in paragraph (1)(c) is to be obtained in respect of a child receiving education from an early education provider and there is no person responsible for that child's educational provision who is a qualified teacher, advice shall be sought from a person responsible for his educational provision who is not a qualified teacher.

(4) The advice sought from a head teacher as provided in paragraph (1)(a) shall, if the head teacher has not himself taught the child within the preceding 18 months, be advice given after consultation with a teacher who has so taught the child.

(5) The advice sought from a head teacher as provided in paragraph (1)(a) shall include advice relating to the steps which have been taken by the school to identify and assess the special educational needs of the child and to make provision for the purpose of meeting those needs.

(6) The advice sought under paragraph (1)(b) or (1)(c) in relation to a child receiving education from an early education provider shall include advice relating to the steps which have been taken by the provider to identify and assess the special educational needs of the child and to make provision for meeting those needs.

(7) Where it appears to the authority, in consequence of medical advice or otherwise, that the child in question is -

(a) hearing impaired;

(b) visually impaired; or

(c) both hearing impaired and visually impaired,

and any such person from whom advice is sought as provided in paragraph (1) is not qualified to teach pupils who are so impaired then the advice sought shall be advice given after consultation with a person who is so qualified.

(8) For the purposes of paragraph (7) a person shall be considered to be qualified to teach pupils who are hearing impaired or visually impaired or who are both hearing impaired and visually impaired if he is qualified to be employed at a school as a teacher of a class for pupils who are so

impaired otherwise than to give instruction in a craft, trade, or domestic subject.

(9) Paragraphs (4) and (7) are without prejudice to regulation 7(3).

Medical advice

9. The advice referred to in regulation 7(1)(c) shall be sought from the health authority, who shall obtain the advice from a fully registered medical practitioner.

Psychological advice

10.- (1) The psychological advice referred to in regulation 7(1)(d) shall be sought from a person—

(a) regularly employed by the authority as an educational psychologist, or

(b) engaged by the authority as an educational psychologist in the case in question.

(2) The advice sought from a person as provided in paragraph (1) shall, if that person has reason to believe that another psychologist has relevant knowledge of, or information relating to, the child, be advice given after consultation with that other psychologist.

(3) Paragraph (2) is without prejudice to regulation 7(3).

Matters to be taken into account in making an assessment

11. When making an assessment an authority shall take into consideration-

(a) any representations made by the child's parent under section 323(1)(d) or section 329A(3)(d);

(b) any evidence submitted by, or at the request of, the child's parent under section 323(1)(d) or section 329A(3)(d), and

(c) the advice obtained under regulation 7.

Time limits and prescribed information

12.- (l) Where under section 323(1) an authority serve a notice on a child's parent informing him that they are considering whether to make an assessment they shall within 6 weeks of the date of service of that notice give notice to the child's parent of -

(a) their decision to make an assessment, and of their reasons for making that decision, or

(b) their decision not to assess the educational needs of the child and of their reasons for making that decision, and in either case the availability to the parent of advice and information on matters related to his child's special educational needs from the parent partnership service.

(2) Where under sections 328(2) or 329(1) a parent asks the authority to arrange for an assessment to be made they shall within 6 weeks of the date of receipt of the request give notice to the child's parent-

(a) of-

(i) their decision to make an assessment;

(ii) their reasons for making that decision, and

(iii) the availability to the parent of advice and information on matters related to his child's special educational needs from the parent partnership service;

(b) of-

(i) their determination not to comply with the parent's request;

(ii) their reasons for making that determination;

(iii) the availability to the parent of advice and information on matters related to his child's special educational needs from the parent partnership service;

(iv) the availability to the parent of arrangements for the prevention and resolution of disagreements between parents and authorities made by the authority under section 332B(1);

(v) the parent's right to appeal to the Tribunal against the determination not to make an assessment;

(vi) the time limit within which an appeal must be made to the Tribunal, and

(vii) the fact that the arrangements made under section 332B(1) cannot affect the parent's right to appeal to the Tribunal and that a parent may appeal to the Tribunal and enter into the arrangements made under section 332B(1).

(3) Where section 329A applies an authority shall, within 6 weeks of the date of receipt of a request from a responsible body that an assessment of a child be made, give notice to that body –

(a) of their decision to make an assessment, and of their reasons for making that decision, or

(b) of their decision not to assess the educational needs of the child, and of their reasons for making that decision.

(4) Where section 329A applies an authority shall, within 6 weeks of the date of receipt of a request from a responsible body that an assessment of a child be made, give notice to the child's parent -

(a) of-

(i) their decision to make an assessment;

(ii) their reasons for making that decision, and

(iii) the availability to the parent of advice and information about matters related to his child's special educational needs from the parent partnership service, or

(b) of -

(i) their decision not to assess the educational needs of the child;

(ii) their reasons for making that decision;

(iii) the availability to the parent of advice and information on matters related to his child's special educational needs from the parent partnership service;

(iv) the availability to the parent of arrangements for the prevention and resolution of disputes between parents and authorities made by the authority under section 332B(1);

(v) the parent's right to appeal to the Tribunal against the decision not to make an assessment;

(vi) the time limit within which an appeal must be made to the Tribunal, and

(vii) the fact that the arrangements made under section 332B(1) cannot affect the parent's right to appeal to the Tribunal and that the parent may appeal to the Tribunal and enter into the arrangements made under section 332B(1).

(5) An authority need not comply with the time limits referred to in paragraphs (1) to (4) if it is impractical to do so because-

(a) the authority have requested advice from the head teacher of a school during a period beginning 1 week before any date on which that school was closed for a continuous period of not less than 4 weeks from that date and ending 1 week before the date on which it re-opens;

(b) the authority have requested advice from the head of SEN in relation to or other person responsible for a child's education at an early education provider during a period beginning 1 week before any date on which that early education provider was closed for a continuous period of not less than 4 weeks from that date and ending 1 week before the date on which it re-opens;

(c) exceptional personal circumstances affect the child or his parent during the 6 week period referred to in paragraphs (1) to (4), or

(d) the child or his parent are absent from the area of the authority for a continuous period of not less than 4 weeks during the 6 weeks period referred to in paragraphs (1) to (4).

(6) Subject to paragraph (7), where under sections 323(4) or 329A(7) an authority have given notice to the child's parent of their decision to make an assessment they shall complete that assessment within 10 weeks of the date on which such notice was given.

(7) An authority need not comply with the time limit referred to in paragraph (6) if it is impractical to do so because-

(a) in exceptional cases after receiving the advice sought under regulation 7 it is necessary for the authority to seek further advice;

(b) the child's parent has indicated to the authority that he wishes to provide advice to the authority after the expiry of 6 weeks from the date on which a request for such advice under regulation 7(1)(a) was received, and the authority have agreed to consider such advice before completing the assessment;

(c) the authority have requested advice from the head teacher of a school under regulation 7(1)(b) during a period beginning 1 week before any date on which that school was closed for a continuous period of not less than 4 weeks from that date and ending 1 week before the date on which it re-opens;

(d) the authority have requested advice from the head of SEN in relation to or other person responsible for a child's education at an early education provider under regulation 7(1)(b) during a period beginning 1 week before any date on which that early education provider was closed for a continuous period of not less than 4 weeks from that date and ending 1 week before the date on which it re-opens;

(e) the authority have requested advice from a health authority or a social services authority under regulation 7(1)(c) or (e) respectively and the health authority or the social services authority have not complied with that request within 6 weeks from the date on which it was made;

(f) exceptional personal circumstances affect the child or his parent during the 10 week period referred to in paragraph (6);

(g) the child or his parent are absent from the area of the authority for a continuous period of not less than 4 weeks during the 10 week period referred to in paragraph (6); or

(h) the child fails to keep an appointment for an examination or a test during the 10 week period referred to in paragraph (6).

(8) Subject to paragraphs (9), (10) and (11), where an authority have requested advice from a health authority or a social services authority under regulation 7(1)(c) or (e) respectively the health authority or social services authority shall comply with that request within 6 weeks of the date on which they receive it.

(9) A health authority or a social services authority need not comply with the time limit referred to in paragraph (8) if it is impractical to do so because-

(a) exceptional personal circumstances affect the child or his parent during the 6 week period referred to in paragraph (8);

(b) the child or his parent are absent from the area of the authority for a continuous period of not less than 4 weeks during the 6 week period referred to in paragraph (8), or

(c) the child fails to keep an appointment for an examination or a test made by the health authority or the social services authority respectively during the 6 week period referred to in paragraph (8).

(10) A health authority need not comply with the time limit referred to in paragraph (8) if they have not before the date on which a copy of a notice has been served on them in accordance with regulation 6(2), 6(4) or 6(5) produced or maintained any information or records relevant to the assessment of the child.

(11) A social services authority need not comply with the request referred to in paragraph (8) if they have not before the date on which a copy of a notice has been served on them in accordance with regulation 6(2), 6(4) or 6(5) produced or maintained any information or records relevant to the assessment of the child.

Children without statements in special schools

13. If a child without a statement has been admitted to a special school for the purposes of an assessment, as provided for in section 316A(2), he may remain at that school -

(a) until the expiry of ten school days after the authority serve a notice under section 325 informing the child's parent that they do not propose to make a statement, or

(b) until a statement is made(j).

PART III

(j) Once a statement has been made for a child that statement will determine whether he will be educated in a special school or elsewhere.

STATEMENTS

Notices accompanying a proposed statement or proposed amended statement

14. The notice which shall be served by an authority on a parent pursuant to paragraph 2B(2) of Schedule 27 to accompany –

(a) a copy of a proposed statement (served under paragraph 2(1) of Schedule 27), or

(b) a copy of a proposed amended statement (served under paragraph 2A(2) of Schedule 27)

shall contain the information as specified in Part A of Schedule 1 to these Regulations.

Notice accompanying an amendment notice

15. The notice which shall be served by an authority on a parent pursuant to paragraph 2B(2) of Schedule 27 to accompany an amendment notice (served under paragraph 2A(4) of Schedule 27) shall contain the information as specified in Part B of Schedule 1 to these Regulations.

Statement of special educational needs

16. A statement shall -

(a) be in a form substantially corresponding to that set out in Schedule 2 to these Regulations;

(b) contain the information therein specified;

(c) be dated and authenticated by the signature of a duly authorised officer of the authority concerned;

(d) set out whether it is the first statement made by the authority for the child or a subsequent statement;

(e) indicate on the front page if it is-

(i) amended pursuant to an annual review and the date of any such annual review;

(ii) amended pursuant to a review other than an annual review, and the date of any such review;

(iii) amended pursuant to an order of the Tribunal, and the date of any such order, or

(iv) amended pursuant to a direction of the Secretary of State, and the date of any such direction.

Time limits and prescribed information

17.- (l) Where an authority have made an assessment of a child for whom no statement is maintained they shall within 2 weeks of the date on which the assessment was completed either-

(a) serve a copy of a proposed statement and a notice on the child's parent under paragraphs 2(1) and 2B(2) of Schedule 27 respectively, or

(b) give notice to the child's parent-

(i) under section 325(1) that they have decided not to make a statement;

(ii) of their reasons for that decision;

(iii) of the parent's right of appeal against that decision to the Tribunal, and

(iv) of the time limit within which an appeal to the Tribunal must be made.

(2) Where an authority have made an assessment of a child for whom a statement is maintained they shall within 2 weeks of the date on which the assessment was completed-

(a) serve on the child's parent a copy of a proposed amended statement and a notice under paragraphs 2A(2) and 2B(2) of Schedule 27 respectively, or

(b) give notice to the child's parent-

(i) under paragraph 11 (2) of Schedule 27 that they have determined to cease to maintain the statement;

(ii) of the parent's right of appeal against that determination to the Tribunal, and

(iii) of the time limit within which an appeal to the Tribunal must be made, or

(c) serve on the child's parent a notice-

(i) which informs him that they have determined not to amend the statement;

(ii) which informs him of their reasons for that determination;

(iii) which is accompanied by copies of the professional advice obtained during the assessment;

(iv) which informs him that under section 326(1)(c) he may appeal to the Tribunal against the description in the statement of the authority's assessment of the child's special educational needs, the special educational provision specified in the statement (including the name of a school so specified) or, if no school is named in the statement, that fact, and

(v) which informs him of the time limit within which an appeal to the Tribunal must be made.

(3) Subject to paragraph (4), where an authority have served a copy of a proposed statement or proposed amended statement on the child's parent under paragraphs 2(1) or 2A(2) of Schedule 27 the authority shall within 8 weeks of the date on which the proposed statement or proposed amended statement was served, serve a copy of the completed statement or completed amended statement and a written notice on the child's parent under paragraphs 6(1) and 6(2) respectively of Schedule 27.

(4) The authority need not comply with the time limit referred to in paragraph (3) if it is impractical to do so because-

(a) exceptional personal circumstances affect the child or his parent during the 8 week period referred to in paragraph (3);

(b) the child or his parent are absent from the area of the authority for a continuous period of not less than 4 weeks during the 8 week period referred to in paragraph (3);

(c) the child's parent indicates that he wishes to make representations to the authority about the content of the statement under paragraph 4(1) of Schedule 27 after the expiry of the 15 day period for making such representations provided for in paragraph 4(4) of that Schedule;

(d) a meeting between the child's parent and an officer of the authority has been held pursuant to paragraph 4(1) of Schedule 27 and the child's parent under paragraph 4(2) of that Schedule has either required that another such meeting be arranged or has required a meeting with the appropriate person be arranged, or

(e) the authority have sent a written request to the Secretary of State seeking his consent under section 347(5) to the child being educated at an independent school which is not approved by him and such consent has not been received by the authority within 2 weeks of the date on which the request was sent.

(5) Where under paragraph 8(1) of Schedule 27 the child's parent asks the authority to substitute for the name of a school or institution specified in a statement the name of another school specified by him and where the conditions referred to in paragraph 8(1)(b) of Schedule 27 have been satisfied the authority shall within 8 weeks of the date on which the request was received either-

(a) comply with the request, or

(b) give notice to the child's parent under paragraph 8(3) of Schedule 27 that they have determined not to comply with the request, their reasons for that decision, and of his right to appeal against that determination to the Tribunal.

(6) Where under paragraph 2A(4) of Schedule 27 an authority serve an amendment notice on the child's parent informing him of their proposal to amend a statement they shall amend the statement before the expiry of 8 weeks from the date on which the notice was served.

(7) The authority need not comply with the time limit in paragraph (6) where -

(a) the amendment notice contained an amendment about the type or name of a school or institution or the provision made for the child concerned under arrangements made under section 319, and

(b) it is impractical to do so because any of the circumstances referred to in paragraph (4)(a) to (e) apply in relation to the 8 week period referred to in paragraph 6.

(8) Where under paragraph 11(1) of Schedule 27 an authority give notice to the child's parent that they have determined to cease to maintain a statement, the authority shall not cease to maintain the statement before the expiry of the prescribed period during which the parent may appeal to the Tribunal against the determination**(k)**.

(9) Any notice given in accordance with this regulation shall inform the parent on whom it is served of –

(a) the availability to the parent of arrangements for the prevention and resolution of disagreements between parents and authorities made by the authority under section 332B, and

(b) the fact that the arrangements made under section 332B cannot affect any right the parent has to appeal to the Tribunal and that the parent may appeal to the Tribunal and take up the arrangements made under section 332B.

Reviews of statements

18.-(1) Not less than two weeks before the first day of every school term an authority shall serve a notice on the head teacher of every school listing those pupils with statements registered at that school -

(a) for whom the authority is responsible, and

(b) whose annual reviews fall to be carried out before the commencement of the

---

(k) The Special Educational Needs Tribunal Regulations 2001 (S.I. 2001/600) provide that an appeal must be made no later than the first working day after the expiry of two months from which the authority notify a parent of his right of appeal. Under paragraph 11(5) of Schedule 27 to the Act an authority may not cease to maintain a statement if a parent has appealed against the authority's determination to cease to maintain a statement and that appeal has not been determined by the Tribunal or withdrawn.

second term after the notice is given.

(2) In this regulation "school" means -

(a) a community, voluntary or foundation school, or a community or foundation special school;

(b) a maintained nursery school;

(c) a pupil referral unit;

(d) a school approved by the Secretary of State under section 342 or section 347, and

(e) a City Technology College, a City College for Technology and the Arts, or a City Academy,

at which a pupil for whom the authority is responsible is a registered pupil.

(3) The notice served in accordance with paragraph (1) shall-

(a) require the head teacher to submit a report to the authority in respect of each child mentioned in it which shall be prepared by the head teacher and reviewed by the authority in accordance with-

(i) paragraphs (4) to (15) of regulation 20 in respect of a child, other than a child in his tenth year of compulsory education, or

(ii) paragraphs (4) to (15) of regulation 21 in respect of a child in his tenth year of compulsory education, and

(b) specify for each child any person from whom the authority consider advice should be sought for the purpose of arriving at a satisfactory report.

(4) The report referred to in paragraph (3) shall be prepared by the head teacher -

(a) by the end of the term which follows service of the notice, or if earlier

(b) within ten school days of the review meeting referred to in regulation 20(6), or in the case of a child in his tenth year of compulsory education, regulation 21(6).

(5) Not less than two weeks before the first day of a school year an authority shall serve on the Connexions Service for their area, or where no Connexions Service has been established at that date, the Careers Service for their area, a notice-

(a) listing all the children with statements for whom the authority is responsible and who will be in their tenth year of compulsory education in that school year, and

(b) indicating the school attended by each of those children or the educational provision made in respect of them.

(6) Not less than two weeks before the first day of every school term an authority shall serve a notice on the health authority and on the social services authority-

(a) listing -

(i) those children with statements of special educational needs living in the area of the health authority or social services authority;

(ii) for whom the authority is responsible, and

(iii) whose annual reviews fall to be carried out before the commencement of the second term after the notice is given, and

(b) indicating the school attended by those children or the educational provision made in respect of them.

Phase transfers

19.-(1) This Regulation applies where-

(a) a statement is maintained for a child, and

(b) the child is within twelve calendar months of a transfer between phases of his schooling.

(2) In this Regulation a transfer between phases of schooling means a transfer from-

(a) primary school to middle school;

(b) primary school to secondary school;

(c) middle school to secondary school, or

(d) secondary school to an institution specified in section 2(2A) of the Act.

(3) Where this Regulation applies an authority must ensure that the child's statement is amended so that before 15th February in the calendar year of the child's transfer the statement names the school or other institution which the child will be attending following that transfer.

Review of statement of child attending school (other than a review in respect of a child in his tenth year of compulsory education)

20.- (1)This Regulation applies where-

(a) an authority carry out an annual review of a child's statement;

(b) the child concerned attends a school, and

(c) the child is not in his tenth year of compulsory education.

(2) Subject to paragraph (3) the authority shall by notice in writing require the head teacher of the child's school to submit a report to them under this Regulation by a specified date not less than two months from the date the notice is given.

(3) If the name of the child is included in the notice served under paragraph (1) of regulation 18 no further notice need be served on the head teacher in respect of that child under paragraph (2) of this regulation.

(4) The head teacher shall for the purpose of preparing the report referred to in paragraph (2) of this regulation or paragraph (3) of regulation 18 seek the advice referred to in paragraph (5) from-

(a) the child's parent (in relation to all the matters referred to in paragraph (5));

(b) any person whose advice the authority consider appropriate for the purpose of arriving at a satisfactory report and whom they specify in the notice referred to in paragraph (2) of this regulation or in paragraph (1) of regulation 18 in relation to the particular child (in relation to such of the matters referred to in paragraph (5) as the head teacher considers are within that person's knowledge or expertise), and

(c) any person whose advice the head teacher considers appropriate for the purpose of arriving at a satisfactory report (in relation to such of the matters referred to in paragraph (5) as the head teacher considers are within that person's knowledge or expertise).

(5) The advice referred to in paragraph (4) shall be written advice as to-

(a) the child's progress towards meeting the objectives specified in the statement;

(b) the child's progress towards attaining any targets established in furtherance of the objectives specified in the statement;

(c) where the school is a community, foundation or voluntary school or a community or foundation special school other than a special school established in a hospital, the application of the provisions of the National Curriculum to the child, and the progress made in relation to those provisions by the child since the statement was made or the last review under section 328;

(d) the application of any provisions substituted for the provisions of the National Curriculum in order to maintain a balanced and broadly based curriculum and the progress made in relation to those provisions by the child since the statement was made or the last review under section 328;

(e) the progress made by the child since the statement was made or the last review under section 328 in his behaviour and attitude to learning;

(f) where appropriate, and in any case where a transition plan exists, any matters which are the appropriate subject of such a plan;

(g) whether the statement continues to be appropriate;

(h) any amendments to the statement which would be appropriate, and

(i) whether the authority should cease to maintain the statement.

(6) The notice referred to in paragraph (2) of this regulation or paragraph (1) of regulation 18 shall require the head teacher to invite the following persons to attend a meeting in respect of each child specified in the report to be held on a date before the report referred to in that paragraph is to be submitted-

(a) the representative of the authority specified in the notice;

(b) the child's parent;

(c) a member or members of the staff of the school who teach the child or who are otherwise responsible for the provision of education for the child whose attendance the head teacher considers appropriate;

(d) any other person whose attendance the head teacher considers appropriate, and

(e) any person whose attendance the authority consider appropriate and who is specified in the notice.

(7) The head teacher shall not later than two weeks before the date on which a meeting referred to in paragraph (6) is to be held send to all the persons invited to that meeting and who have not informed the head teacher that they will not be attending it copies of the advice he has received pursuant to his request under paragraph (4) and by written notice accompanying the copies shall request the recipients to submit to him before or at the meeting written comments on that advice and any other advice which they think appropriate.

(8) The meeting referred to in paragraph (6) shall consider-

(a) the matters referred to in paragraph (5), and

(b) any significant changes in the child's circumstances since the date on which the statement was made or last reviewed.

(9) The meeting shall recommend-

(a) any steps which it concludes ought to be taken, including whether the authority should amend or cease to maintain the statement;

(b) any targets to be established in furtherance of the objectives specified in the statement which it concludes the child ought to meet during the period until the next review, and

(c) where a transition plan exists, the matters which it concludes ought to be included in that plan.

(10) If the meeting cannot agree the recommendations to be made under paragraph (9) the persons who attended the meeting shall make differing recommendations as appears necessary to each of them.

(11) The report to be submitted under paragraph (2) of this regulation or paragraph (3) of regulation 18 shall be completed after the meeting is held and shall include the head teacher's assessment of the matters referred to in paragraph (8) and his recommendations as to the matters referred to in paragraph (9), and shall refer to any difference between his assessment and recommendations and those of the meeting.

(12) When the head teacher submits his report to the authority under paragraph (2) of this regulation or paragraph (3) of regulation 18 he shall at the same time send copies to-

(a) the child's parent;

(b) any other person who submitted advice under paragraph (4) or paragraph (7);

(c) any other person to whom the authority consider it appropriate that a copy be sent and to whom they direct him to send a copy, and

(d) any other person to whom the head teacher considers it appropriate that a copy be sent.

(13) The authority shall review the statement under section 328 in light of the report and any other information or advice which they consider relevant, record in writing their decisions on the matters referred to in paragraphs 9(a) and (b) and, where a transition plan exists, shall make written recommendations for amendments to the plan as they consider appropriate

(14) The authority shall within one week of completing the review under section 328 send copies of their decisions and recommendations to-

(a) the child's parent;

(b) the head teacher, and

(c) any other person to whom the authority consider it appropriate that a copy be sent.

(15) The head teacher shall be responsible for ensuring that any necessary amendments to any transition plan are made.

(16) In this regulation the term "school" shall have the same meaning as it does in regulation 18.

Reviews of statements where child in his tenth year of compulsory education attends school

21.-(1) This regulation applies where-

(a) an authority carry out an annual review of a child's statement;

(b) the child concerned attends a school, and

(c) the review is the first review after the child has commenced his tenth year of compulsory education.

(2) Subject to paragraph (3) the authority shall by notice in writing require the head teacher of the child's school to submit a report to them under this regulation by a specified date not less than two months from the date when the notice is given.

(3) If the name of the child is included in the notice served under paragraph (1) of regulation 18 no further notice need be served on the head teacher in respect of that child under paragraph (2) of this regulation.

(4) The head teacher shall for the purposes of the report referred to in paragraph (2) of this regulation or paragraph (3) of regulation 18 seek the advice referred to in paragraph (5) from-

(a) the child's parent (in relation to all the matters referred to in paragraph (5));

(b) any person whose advice the authority consider appropriate for the purpose of arriving at a satisfactory report and whom they specify in the notice referred to in paragraph (2) or in paragraph (1) of regulation 18 in relation to a particular child (in relation to such of the matters referred to in paragraph (5) as the head teacher considers are within that person's knowledge or expertise);

(c) a representative of the Connexions service, or if no Connexions Service has been established at the date the advice is requested, a representative of the Careers Service (in relation to the matters referred to in sub-paragraph (5)(f) and such other matters referred to in paragraph (5) as the head teacher considers are within the representative's knowledge or expertise), and

(d) any person whose advice the head teacher considers appropriate for the purpose of arriving at a satisfactory report (in relation to such of the matters referred to in paragraph (5) as the head teacher considers are within that person's knowledge or expertise).

(5) The advice referred to in paragraph (4) shall be written advice as to-

(a) the child's progress towards meeting the objectives specified in the statement;

(b) the child's progress towards attaining any targets established in furtherance of the objectives specified in the statement;

(c) where the school is a community, foundation or voluntary school or a community or foundation special school other than a special school established in a hospital, the application of the provisions of the National Curriculum to the child, and the progress made in relation to those provisions by the child since the statement was made or the last review under section 328;

(d) the application of any provisions substituted for the provisions of the National Curriculum in order to maintain a balanced and broadly based curriculum and the progress made in relation to the provisions by the child since the statement was made or the last review under section 328;

(e) the progress made by the child since the statement was made or the last review under section 328 in his behaviour and attitude to learning;

(f) any matters which are the appropriate subject of a transition plan;

(g) whether the statement continues to be appropriate;

(h) any amendments to the statement which would be appropriate, and

(i) whether the authority should cease to maintain the statement.

(6) The notice referred to in paragraph (2) of this regulation or paragraph (1) of regulation 18 shall require the head teacher to invite the following persons to attend a meeting to be held on a date before the report referred to in that paragraph is required to be submitted-

(a) the child's parent;

(b) a member or members of the staff of the school who teach the child or who are otherwise responsible for the provision of education for the child whose attendance the head teacher considers appropriate;

(c) a representative of the social services authority;

(d) a representative of the Connexions service or, if no Connexions Service has been established at the date of the request, a representative of the Careers Service;

(e) any person whose attendance the head teacher considers appropriate;

(f) any person whose attendance the authority consider appropriate and who is specified in the notice, and

(g) a representative of the authority.

(7) The head teacher shall not later than two weeks before the date on which the meeting referred to in paragraph (6) is to be held serve on all the persons invited to attend that meeting and who have not informed the head teacher that they will not be attending it copies of the advice he has received pursuant to his request under paragraph (4) and shall by written notice request the recipients to submit to him before or at the meeting written comments on that advice and any other advice which they think appropriate.

(8) The meeting referred to in paragraph (6) shall consider-

(a) the matters referred to in paragraph (5), in all cases including the matters referred to in paragraph (5)(f), and

(b) any significant changes in the child's circumstances since the date on which the statement was made or last reviewed under section 328.

(9) The meeting shall recommend-

(a) any steps which it concludes ought to be taken, including whether the authority should amend or cease to amend the statement;

(b) any targets to be established in furtherance of the objectives specified in the statement which it concludes the child ought to meet during the period until the next review, and

(c) the matters which it concludes ought to be included in a transition plan.

(10) If the meeting cannot agree the recommendations to be made under paragraph (9) the persons who attended the meeting shall make differing recommendations as appears necessary to each of them.

(11) The report to be submitted under paragraph (2) of this regulation or paragraph (3) of regulation 18 shall be completed after the meeting is held, shall include the head teacher's assessment of the matters referred to in paragraph (8) and his recommendations as to the matters referred to in paragraph (9), and shall refer to any difference between his assessment and recommendations and those of the meeting.

(12) When the head teacher submits his report to the authority under paragraph (2) of this regulation or paragraph (3) of regulation 18 he shall at the same time send copies to-

(a) the child's parent;

(b) any other person to whom the authority considers it appropriate that a copy be sent and to whom they direct him to send a copy, and

(c) any other person to whom the head teacher considers it appropriate that a copy be sent.

(13) The authority shall review the statement under section 328 in light of the report and any other information or advice which they consider relevant and shall make written recommendations as to the matters referred to in paragraph 9(a), (b) and (c).

(14) The authority shall within one week of completing the review under section 328 send copies of the recommendations and the transition plan to-

(a) the child's parent;

(b) the head teacher, and

(c) any other person to whom they consider it appropriate to send a copy.

(15) The head teacher shall be responsible for ensuring that a transition plan is drawn up.

(16) In this regulation the term "school" shall have the same meaning as it does in regulation 18.

Review of statement where child does not attend school

22.-(1) This regulation applies where an authority carry out an annual review of a statement and the child concerned does not attend a school.

(2) The authority shall prepare a report addressing the matters referred to in regulation 20(5), including the matters referred to in regulation 20(5)(f) in any case where the review referred to in paragraph (1) is commenced after the child begins his tenth year of compulsory education, and for that purpose shall seek advice on those matters from the child's parent and on such of those matters from any other person whose advice they consider appropriate in the case in question for the purpose of arriving at a satisfactory report.

(3) The authority shall invite the following persons to attend a meeting to be held on a date before the review referred to in paragraph (1) is required to be completed-

(a) the child's parent;

(b) where the review referred to in paragraph (1) is the first review commenced after the child has begun his tenth year of compulsory education, a representative of the social services authority;

(c) where sub-paragraph (b) applies, a representative of the Connexions Service, or if no Connexions Service has been established at the date the invitation is made, a representative of the Careers Service, and

(d) any person or persons whose attendance the authority consider appropriate.

(4) The authority shall not later than two weeks before the date on which the meeting referred to in paragraph (3) is to be held send to all the persons invited to that meeting a copy of the report which they propose to make under paragraph (2) and by written notice accompanying the copies shall request the recipients to submit to the authority written comments on the report and any other advice which they think appropriate.

(5) A representative of the authority shall attend the meeting.

(6) The meeting shall consider the matters referred to in regulation 20(5), and in any case where the review is commenced after the child has begun his tenth year of compulsory education, the matters referred to in regulation 20(5)(f), and shall make recommendations in accordance with regulation 20(9), and in any case where the child has begun his tenth year of compulsory education, recommendations as to the matters which it concludes ought to be included in a transition plan.

(7) The report prepared by the authority under paragraph (2) shall be completed after the meeting referred to in paragraph (3) is held, shall contain the authority's assessment of the matters required to be considered by the meeting and their recommendations as to the matters required to be recommended by it, and shall refer to any difference between their assessment and recommendations and those of the meeting.

(8) The authority shall within one week of the date on which the meeting referred to in paragraph (3) was held send copies of the report completed under paragraph (7) to-

(a) the child's parent;

(b) any person to whom they consider it appropriate to send a copy.

(9) The authority shall review the statement under section 328 in light of the report and any other information or advice which it considers relevant, shall make written recommendations as to the matters referred to in regulation 20(9) and in any case where the review is the first review commenced after the child has commenced his tenth year of compulsory education prepare a transition plan, and in any case where a transition plan exists amend the plan as they consider appropriate.

(10) The authority shall within one week of completing the review under section 328 send copies of the recommendations and any transition plan referred to in paragraph (9) to the persons referred to in paragraph (8).

(11) In this regulation the term "school" shall have the same meaning as it does in regulation 18.

Transfer of statements

23.- (1) This regulation applies where a child in respect of whom a statement is maintained moves from the area of the authority which maintains the statement ('the old authority') into that of another ('the new authority').

(2) The old authority shall transfer the statement to the new authority.

(3) From the date of the transfer-

(a) the statement shall be treated for the purposes of the new authority's duties and functions under Part IV of the Act and these Regulations as if it had been made by the new authority on the date on which it was made by the old authority, and

(b) where the new authority make an assessment and the old authority have supplied the new authority with advice obtained in pursuance of a previous assessment regulation 7(5) shall apply as if the new authority had obtained the advice on the date on which the old authority obtained it.

(4) The new authority shall within 6 weeks of the date of the transfer serve a notice on the child's parent informing him-

(a) that the statement has been transferred;

(b) whether they propose to make an assessment, and

(c) when they propose to review the statement in accordance with paragraph (5).

(5) The new authority shall review the statement under section 328(5)(b) before the expiry of whichever of the following two periods expires later-

(a) the period of 12 months beginning with the making of the statement, or as the case may be, with the previous review, or

(b) the period of 3 months beginning with the date of the transfer.

(6) Where by virtue of the transfer the new authority come under a duty to arrange the child's attendance at a school specified in the statement but in light of the child's move that attendance is no

longer practicable the new authority may arrange for the child's attendance at another school appropriate for the child until such time as it is possible to amend the statement in accordance with the procedure set out in Schedule 27.

(7) In this regulation "the new authority" shall include a local education authority in Wales for the purposes of paragraphs (1) and (2) only.

(8) An authority to whom a statement is transferred from a local education authority in Wales shall treat the statement as having been transferred by an old authority for the purposes of paragraphs (3) to (6).

Restriction on disclosure of statements

24.- (l) Subject to the provisions of the Act and of these Regulations, a statement in respect of a child shall not be disclosed without the child's consent except-

(a) to persons to whom, in the opinion of the authority concerned, it is necessary to disclose the statement in the interests of the child;

(b) for the purposes of any appeal under the Act;

(c) for the purposes of educational research which, in the opinion of the authority, may advance the education of children with special educational needs, if, but only if, the person engaged in that research undertakes not to publish anything contained in, or derived from, a statement otherwise than in a form which does not identify any individual concerned including, in particular, the child concerned and his parent;

(d) on the order of any court or for the purposes of any criminal proceedings;

(e) for the purposes of any investigation under Part III of the Local Government Act 1974[l] (investigation of maladministration);

(f) to the Secretary of State when he requests such disclosure for the purposes of deciding whether to give directions or make an order under section 496, 497 or 497A;

(g) for the purposes of an assessment of the needs of the child with respect to the provision of any statutory services for him being carried out by officers of a social services authority by virtue of arrangements made under section 5(5) of the Disabled Persons (Services, Consultation and Representation) Act 1986[m];

---

[l] 1974 c.7.
[m] 1986 c.33; section 5 is amended by the Special Educational Needs and Disability Act 2001; paragraphs 16 to 18 of Schedule 8.

(h) for the purposes of a local authority in the performance of their duties under sections 22(3)(a), 85(4)(a), 86(3)(a) and 87(3) of the Children Act 1989[(n)];

(i) to Her Majesty's Chief Inspector of Schools, one of Her Majesty's Inspectors of Schools, or to a registered inspector or a member of an inspection team, who requests the right to inspect or take copies of a statement in accordance with section 2(8) or 3(3) of, or paragraph 7 of Schedule 3 to, the School Inspections Act 1996[(o)] respectively;

(j) to the Connexions Service for the purposes of writing or amending a transition plan, or

(k) to a Young Offender Institution for the purposes of the performance of its duties under rule 38 of the Young Offender Institution Rules 2000[(p)].

(2) A child may consent to the disclosure of a statement for the purposes of this regulation if his age and understanding are sufficient to allow him to understand the nature of that consent.

(3) If a child does not have sufficient age or understanding to allow him to consent to disclosure of his statement his parent may consent on his behalf.

(4) The arrangements for keeping such statement shall be such as to ensure, so far as is reasonably practicable, that unauthorised persons do not have access to them.

(5) In this regulation any reference to a statement includes a reference to any representations, evidence, advice or information which is set out in the appendices to a statement.

PART IV

COMPLIANCE WITH TRIBUNAL ORDERS

Compliance with Tribunal Orders

25.-(1) Subject to paragraph (4), if the Tribunal, following an appeal to it by a parent, makes an order requiring an authority to perform an action referred to in paragraph (2) the authority shall perform that action within the period specified in paragraph (2).

(2) In the case of an order-

(n) 1989 c.41; section 87(3) is prospectively amended by the Care Standards Act 2000 (c.14), section 105.
(o) 1996 c.57; section 28 is amended by the Education Act 1997 (c.44), section 42 and Schedule 6 and paragraph 7 of Schedule 3 is amended by the Education Act 1997, section 42 and Schedule 6, paragraph 12.
(p) S.I. 2000/3371.

(a) to make an assessment, the authority shall notify the child's parent that it will make an assessment under section 323(4) or 329A(7) as the case may be within 4 weeks;

(b) to make and maintain a statement, the authority shall make a statement within 5 weeks;

(c) remitting a case back to the authority under section 325(3)(c), the authority shall take the action referred to in regulation 17(1)(a) or 17(1)(b) within 2 weeks;

(d) to amend a statement, the authority shall serve an amendment notice on the child's parent under paragraph 2A of Schedule 27 within 5 weeks;

(e) to continue to maintain a statement, the authority shall continue to maintain the statement with immediate effect;

(f) to continue to maintain and to amend a statement, the authority shall continue to maintain the statement with immediate effect and shall serve an amendment notice on the child's parent under paragraph 2A of Schedule 27 within 5 weeks;

(g) to substitute the name of the school or other institution specified in a child's statement with the name of a school specified by a parent, the authority shall specify the school specified by the parent within 2 weeks, and

(h) dismissing an appeal against a determination to cease to maintain a statement, the authority shall cease to maintain that statement immediately or on a date proposed by the authority, whichever is the later.

(3) In each case the period shall begin on the day after the issue of the Order in question.

(4) The authority need not comply with the time limits referred to in paragraph (2) if it is impractical to do so because-

(a) exceptional personal circumstances affect the child or his parent during the relevant time period;

(b) the child or his parent are absent from the area of the authority for a continuous period of not less than 2 weeks during the relevant time period;

(c) the child's parent indicates that he wishes to make representations to the authority about the content of the statement under paragraph 4(1) of Schedule 27 after the expiry of the 15-day period for making such representations provided for in paragraph 4(4) of that Schedule;

(d) a meeting between the child's parent and an officer of the authority has been held pursuant to paragraph 4(1) of Schedule 27 and the child's parent under paragraph 4(2) of that Schedule either required that another such meeting be arranged or has required that a meeting with the appropriate person be arranged, or

(e) the authority have sent a written request to the Secretary of State seeking his consent under section 347(5) to the child being educated at an independent school which is not approved by him and such consent has not been received by the authority within 3 weeks of the day on which the request was sent.

Compliance with parents' requests when an authority concedes an appeal to the Tribunal

26.-(1) Subject to paragraph (3) if, under section 326A(2), an appeal to the Tribunal is treated as having been determined in favour of the parent making the appeal, the authority shall–

(a) in the case of an appeal under section 325, make a statement within 5 weeks;

(b) in the case of an appeal under section 328, 329 or 329A, the authority shall make an assessment within 4 weeks, and

(c) in the case of an appeal under paragraph 8(3) of Schedule 27 against a determination not to comply with the parent's request to substitute the name of a maintained school for the name of the school or institution specified in the statement, comply with that request within 2 weeks.

(2) In each case the period shall begin on the day after the authority notifies the Tribunal that they have determined that they will not, or will no longer, oppose the appeal.

(3) The authority need not comply with the time limits referred to in paragraph (1) if it is impractical to do so because-

(a) exceptional personal circumstances affect the child or his parent during the relevant time period;

(b) the child or his parent are absent from the area of the authority for a continuous period of not less than 2 weeks during the relevant time period;

(c) the child's parent indicates that he wishes to make representations to the authority about the content of the statement under paragraph 4(1) of Schedule 27 after the expiry of the 15 day period for making such representations provided for in paragraph 4(4) of that Schedule;

(d) a meeting between the child's parent and an officer of the authority has been held pursuant to paragraph 4(1) of Schedule 27 and the child's parent under paragraph 4(2) of that Schedule either required that another such meeting be arranged or has required that a meeting with the appropriate person be arranged, or

(e) the authority have sent a written request to the Secretary of State seeking his consent under section 347(5) to the child being educated at an independent school which is not approved by him and such consent has not been received by the authority within 3 weeks of the day on which the request was sent.

REVOCATION AND TRANSITIONAL PROVISIONS

Revocations

27. - (1) Subject to regulation 28, the 1994 Regulations are revoked.

(2) The Education (Special Educational Needs) (England) Regulations 2001[q], the Education (Special Educational Needs) (England) (Amendment) Regulations 2001[r], and the Education (Special Educational Needs) (England) (Amendment No 2) Regulations 2001[s], are hereby revoked.

Transitional provisions

28.- (1) Subject to the following provisions of this regulation references in these Regulations to anything done under these Regulations shall be read in relation to the times, circumstances or purposes in relation to which a corresponding provision of the 1994 Regulations had effect and so far as the nature of the reference permits as including a reference to that corresponding provision.

(2) Regulations 6 to 11 of the 1994 Regulations shall continue to apply in relation to any assessment where before 1st January 2002 in pursuance of section 323(4) the authority notify the parent that they have decided to make an assessment, and regulations 6 to 12 of these Regulations shall not apply in relation to any such assessment.

(3) Where regulations 6 to 11 of the 1994 Regulations continue to apply in relation to any assessment but the authority have not before 1st May 2002 -

(a) notified the parent of their decision that they are not required to determine the special educational provision of the child in accordance with section 325(1);

(b) served on the parent a copy of a proposed statement in accordance with paragraph 2 of Schedule 27, or

(c) served on the parent a copy of a proposed amended statement under paragraph 3 of Schedule 27,

regulations 6 to 12 of these Regulations shall apply in relation to the assessment from 1st May 2002 as if on that date the authority had given notice to the parent under section 323(4) of their decision to make an assessment.

(4) Where in accordance with paragraph (3) above regulations 6 to 12 of these Regulations apply in relation to an assessment the authority shall obtain advice in accordance with Part II, but advice obtained in accordance with the 1994 Regulations shall be considered to have been obtained under Part II of these Regulations if such advice is appropriate for the purpose of arriving at a satisfactory assessment under that Part.

(5) Where before 1st January 2002 in accordance with section 323(1) the authority have served notice on the child's parent that they propose to make an assessment but they have not before that date notified the parent under section 323(4) of the Act that they have decided to make the assessment or notified him under section 323(6) that they have decided not to make the assessment, regulation 11 of the 1994 Regulations shall continue to apply for the purpose of any such notification under section 323(4) or 323(6) only.

(6) Where before 1st January 2002 in accordance with section 328 or 329 a parent has asked the authority to arrange for an assessment to be made of his child's educational needs but the authority have not before that date notified the parent under section 323(4) that they have decided to make the assessment or notified him under section 328(3) or 329(2) that they have decided not to

---

(q) S.I. 2001/2216.
(r) S.I. 2001/2468.
(s) S.I. 2001/2612.

make the assessment, regulation 11 of the 1994 Regulations shall continue to apply for the purpose of any notification under section 323(4), 328(3) or 329(2) only.

(7) Regulations 13 and 14 of the 1994 Regulations shall continue to apply to the making of any statement where before 1st January 2002 the authority have served on the parent a copy of a proposed statement in accordance with paragraph 2 of Schedule 27.

(8) Regulation 14 of the 1994 Regulations shall continue to apply in relation to a proposal to amend or cease to maintain a statement where an authority serve a notice under paragraphs 10(1) or 11(2) of Schedule 27 before 1st January 2002.

(9) Regulation 15 of the 1994 Regulations shall continue to apply to a review of a statement in respect of which an authority serve a notice as required by regulation 15(2) of the 1994 Regulations before 1st January 2002.

(10) Regulation 16 of the 1994 Regulations shall continue to apply to a review of a statement in respect of which an authority serve a notice as required by regulation 16(2) of the 1994 Regulations before 1st January 2002.

(11) Regulation 17 of the 1994 Regulations shall continue to apply to a review in respect of which an authority in accordance with regulation 17(3) of the 1994 Regulations have before 1st January 2002 invited the attendance of the persons specified in that regulation to a meeting.

(12) The first occasion before which an authority must, under regulation 19 of these Regulations, ensure that a child's statement is amended, shall be 15th February 2003.

22nd October 2001

Secretary of State,

Department for Education and Skills

SCHEDULE 1

Regulation 14

Part A

Notice to parent

Name and address of authority

Date

Address of Parents

Dear *[here insert name of parents]*

I am pleased to enclose a copy of *[child's name (s)][proposed statement of special educational needs/proposed amended statement of special educational needs]*. We have attached to it copies of all the advice we were given during *[child's name]* assessment for the statement.

If you want to meet us to talk about the statement you need to tell us within 15 days of receiving this letter. This is not the final statement. You can ask for changes to be made to it. The rest of this letter tells you how you can do this.

As you will see the statement is in six parts:

Part 1 Introduction

Part 2 Special Educational Needs

Part 3 Special Educational Provision, including objectives and monitoring arrangements

Part 4 Placement

Part 5 Non-educational Needs

Part 6 Non-educational Provision

We have left part 4 blank so that you can tell us where you think *[child's name]* should be educated. You can tell us which maintained (Local Education Authority) school, including an LEA-maintained special school, you would like *[child's name]* to go to and tell us the reasons. To help you decide, a list of all the maintained *[primary/secondary]* schools in the area is attached.

[A list of all primary or secondary schools, depending on whether the child requires primary or secondary education must be attached to this letter].

If you suggest the name of a maintained school, including a maintained special school, we must name the school in part 4 of the statement unless-

a) the school is unsuitable to *[child's name]* age, ability or aptitude or to *[his/her]* special educational needs, or

b) the attendance of *[child's name]* at the school would be incompatible with the provision of efficient education for the children with whom *[he/she]* would be educated or the efficient use of resources

If you think that *[child's name]* should attend a non-maintained special school or an independent school you can suggest the name of a school and tell us why you think that school should be named in *[child's name]* statement. A list of non-maintained special schools and independent schools approved by the Secretary of State [*and if such a list is produced by the National Assembly of Wales]* and the National Assembly of Wales is attached to help you.

[Such lists of independent and non-maintained special schools as the Secretary of State and the National Assembly of Wales may issue from time to time must be attached to this letter]

If you want to tell us the name of a school you want *[child's name]* to go to you must do so within 15 days of getting this letter. However, if you attend a meeting with us to discuss this statement after getting this letter you will have another 15 days from that meeting to suggest a school. You can also tell us if you disagree with what the statement says. If you do disagree with the statement you must also tell us within 15 days of getting this letter, or 15 days from when you meet us to talk about the statement. If you still disagree with the statement, or any of the advice given during the assessment after you meet us, you can ask us for another meeting to discuss the advice you disagree with but you must ask us within 15 days of the first meeting. We will arrange for the person who gave the advice, or someone else they suggest, to attend this new meeting. We can arrange more than one meeting if necessary, if you disagree with more than one part of the advice.

Once all these stages are finished we will send you a final statement that will have part 4 completed.

If you have any concerns or questions about this process, or disagree with any part of the statement you may wish to get advice or support from the local parent partnership service. They can be contacted at *[contact address and telephone number].*

They can also put you in touch with the informal arrangements set up to help resolve or prevent any disagreements between you and the authority. Using either of these services does not prevent you from appealing to the Special Educational Needs Tribunal about Parts 2, 3 or 4 of the Statement at the same time; your rights are not affected and an appeal to the Tribunal can run at the same time as any disagreement resolution.

When you receive the final statement, if you disagree with parts 2, 3 or 4 you can appeal to the Special Educational Needs Tribunal. The Tribunal can hold a hearing to decide what should be in these parts of *[child's name]* statement. You have to appeal to the Tribunal within two months of getting the final statement. The address of the Tribunal is 50 Victoria Street, London, SWIH 0HW.

If you have any questions, now or at any time, about this process or about the statement itself, our case officer *[name]* can be contacted at *[address and telephone number].*

Please do not hesitate to get in touch.

Yours sincerely

[Signature of officer responsible]

PART B

Regulation 15

Name and address of authority

Date

Address of Parents

Dear *[here insert name of parents]*

As you know *[child's name]* has a statement of special educational needs dated *[here insert date of statement]*

We propose amending *[child's name]* statement *[insert reasons e.g. following an annual review]*. Details of the amendments are in the amendment notice attached.

If you disagree with the suggested changes and want to meet us to talk please tell us within 15 days.

(when amendment to part 4 is recommended)

We *[also]* want to amend part 4 of the statement *[explain reasons why e.g. so that a child can go to secondary school]*

You can tell us which maintained (LEA) school, including an LEA-maintained special school you would like *[child's name]* to get to and tell us the reasons. To help you decide, a list of all the maintained *[primary/secondary]* schools in the area is attached.

[A list of all primary or secondary schools, depending on whether the child requires primary or secondary education must be attached to this letter]

If you suggest the name of a maintained school, including a maintained special school, we must name the school in part 4 of the statement unless -

a) the school is unsuitable to *[child's name]* age, ability or aptitude or to *[his/her]* special educational needs, or

b) the attendance of *(insert child's name)* at the school would be incompatible with the provision of efficient education for the children with whom *[he/she]* would be educated or the efficient use of resources.

If you think that *[child's name]* should attend a non-maintained special school or an independent school you can suggest the name of a school and tell us why you think that school should be named in *[child's name]* statement. A list of non-maintained special schools and independent schools approved by the Secretary of State *[and if such a list is produced by the National Assembly for Wales]* and the National Assembly of Wales is attached to help you.

[Such lists of independent and non-maintained special schools as the Secretary of State and the National Assembly of Wales may issue from time to time must be attached to this letter]

If you want to tell us the name of a school you want *[child's name]* to go to you must do so within 15 days of getting this letter. However, if you attend a meeting with us to discuss the suggested changes to this statement after getting this letter you will have another 15 days from that meeting to name a school. You can also tell us if you disagree with the changes to the statement that we are suggesting. If you do disagree with the suggested changes you must also tell us within 15 days of getting this letter.

Once all these stages are finished we will send you an amended final statement. If you have any concerns or disagree with any part of the amended final statement you may wish to get advice or support from the local parent partnership service. They can be contacted *[here insert contact address and telephone number]*. They can also put you in touch with the informal arrangements set up to help resolve or prevent any disagreements between you and the authority. Using either of these services does not prevent you from appealing to the Special Educational Needs Tribunal about Parts 2, 3 or 4 of the Statement at the same time; your rights are not affected and an appeal to the Tribunal can run at the same time as any disagreement resolution.

When you receive the amended final statement, if you disagree with parts 2, 3 or 4 of the statement you can appeal to the Special Educational Needs Tribunal. The Tribunal can hold a hearing to decide what should be in these parts of *[child's name]* statement. You have to appeal to the Tribunal within two months of getting the final statement. The address of the Tribunal is 50 Victoria Street, London, SW1H 0HW.

If you have any questions, now or at any time, about this process or about the statement itself, our case officer *[name]* can be contacted at *[address and telephone number]*. Please do not hesitate to get in touch.

Yours sincerely

[Signature of officer responsible]

SCHEDULE 2

Regulation 16

Set out name of Authority

STATEMENT OF SPECIAL EDUCATIONAL NEEDS

PART 1: INTRODUCTION

1. In accordance with Section 324 of the Education Act 1996 ('the Act'), and the Education (Special Educational Needs) (England) (Consolidation) Regulations 2001, the following statement is made on [***here set out date***] by [***here set out name of authority***] ('the education authority') in respect of [***here set out name of child***] whose particulars are set out below.

Child

Surname:	Other Names:
Home Address:	
	Sex:
Date of Birth:	Religion:
	Home Language:

Child's Parent or person responsible

Surname:	Other Names:
Home Address:	Relationship to Child:
Telephone Number:	

2. When assessing the child's educational needs under Section 323 of the Education Act 1996 the authority took into consideration, in accordance with Regulation 11 of the Regulations, the evidence and advice set out in the Appendices A to F to this statement.

Name of parent:	Parental Advice	Dated:
Name of head teacher /head of SEN or other person responsible:	Educational Advice	Dated:
Name of Doctor:	Medical Advice	Dated:
Name of Educational Psychologist:	Psychological Advice	Dated:
Name of Social Worker:	Advice for Social Services Authority	Dated:
Name of persons providing other advice:	Advice from others	Dated:

(In making this statement the authority have taken into account the additional representations, evidence and advice set out in Appendix G to this statement).

PART 2: SPECIAL EDUCATIONAL NEEDS

[*Here set out child's special educational needs, in terms of the child's learning difficulties which call for special educational provision, as assessed by the authority.*]

PART 3: SPECIAL EDUCATIONAL PROVISION

Objectives

[*Here specify the objectives which the special educational provision for the child should aim to meet.*]

Educational provision to meet needs and objectives

[Here specify the special educational provision which the authority consider appropriate to meet the needs specified in Part 2 and to meet the objectives Specified in this Part, and in particular specify -

(a) any appropriate facilities and equipment, staffing arrangements and curriculum,

(b) any appropriate modifications to the application of the National Curriculum,

(c) any appropriate exclusions from the application of the National Curriculum, in detail, and the provision which it is proposed to substitute for any such exclusions in order to maintain a balanced and broadly based curriculum; and

(d) where residential accommodation is appropriate, that fact].

Monitoring

[Here specify the arrangements to be made for-

(a) regularly monitoring progress in meeting objectives specified in this Part,

(b) establishing targets in furtherance of those objectives,

(c) regularly monitoring the targets referred to in (b),

(d) regularly monitoring the appropriateness of any modifications to the application of the National Curriculum and

(e) regularly monitoring the appropriateness of any provision substituted for exclusions from the application of the National Curriculum.

[Here also specify any special arrangements for reviewing this statement.]

PART 4: PLACEMENT

[Here specify]

(a) the type of school which the authority consider appropriate for the child and if the authority are required to specify the name of a school for which the parent has expressed a preference, the name of that school, or, where the authority are otherwise required to specify the name of a school or institution, the name of the school/or institution which they consider would be appropriate for the child and should be specified; or

(b) any provision for his education otherwise than at a school which the authority make under section 319 of the Education Act 1996 and consider it appropriate to specify.]

PART 5: NON-EDUCATIONAL NEEDS

[*Here specify the non-educational needs of the child for which the authority consider provision is appropriate if the child is to properly benefit from the special educational provision specified in Part* 3.]

PART 6: NON-EDUCATIONAL PROVISION

[*Here specify any non-education provision which the authority propose to make available or which they are satisfied will be made available by a health authority, a social services authority or some other body, including the arrangements for its provision. Also specify the objectives of the provision, and the arrangements for monitoring progress in meeting those objectives.*]

____________________ ______________________________

Date — A duly authorised officer of the authority

Appendix A: Parental Advice

[*Here set out*

(1) *any written representations made by the child's parent under section 323(1)(d) or 329A(3)(d) of or paragraph* 4(1) *of Schedule* 27 *to the Act and a summary which the parent has accepted as accurate of any oral representations so made or record that no such representations were made,*

(2) *any written evidence either submitted by the parent of the child under section 323(1)(d) or 329A(3)(d) of the Act or record that no such evidence was submitted; and*

(3) *the advice obtained under regulation 7(1)(a).*]

Appendix B: Educational Advice

[*Here set out the advice obtained under regulation 7(1)(b).*]

Appendix C: Medical Advice

[*Here set out the advice obtained under regulation 7(1)(c).*]

Appendix D: Psychological Advice

[*Here set out the advice obtained under regulation 7(1)(d).*]

Appendix E: Advice from the Social Services Authority

[*Here set out the advice obtained under regulation 7(1)(e).*]

Appendix F: Other Advice Obtained by the Authority

[*Here set out the advice obtained under regulation 7(1)(f).*]

Appendix G: Advice Obtained by the Authority since the last assessment of the child under section 323 of the Education Act 1996 was made

[*Here set out the advice about the child obtained by the authority since the last assessment of the child under section 323 of the Education Act 1996 was made*]

EXPLANATORY NOTES

(This note is not part of the Regulations)

These Regulations relate to the assessment of special educational needs and to statements of such needs under Part IV of the Education Act 1996. These Regulations re-enact with modifications the Education (Special Educational Needs) Regulations 1994, which are revoked for England (regulation 27).

These Regulations also consolidate the Education (Special Educational Needs) (England) Regulations 2001, the Education (Special Educational Needs) (England) (Amendment) Regulations 2001 and the Education (Special Educational Needs) (England) (Amendment No 2) Regulations 2001, all of which are revoked (regulation 27) prior to their coming into force.

The Regulations make provision for a head teacher to delegate his functions under them generally to a qualified teacher, or in a particular case to the staff member who teaches the child (regulation 3).

The Regulations also supplement the procedural framework for making an assessment and a statement contained in Part IV of the Education Act 1996 and Schedules 26 and 27 thereto. Detailed provision is made for the service of documents by post (regulation 4). The Regulations require copies of notices of a local education authority's proposal to make an assessment, their decision to make an assessment or notices of a parent's or responsible body's request for an assessment, to be served on the social services authority, the health authority and the head teacher of the child's school, or the head of SEN if a child is receiving relevant nursery education (regulation 6). Subject to exceptions, they require local education authorities to carry out various steps in making an assessment or a statement within prescribed time limits, including the provision of prescribed information (regulations 12 and 17 respectively).

The Regulations provide that local education authorities in making an assessment of a child's special educational needs must seek advice from the child's parent, educational advice, medical advice, psychological advice, advice from the social services authority and any other advice which they consider appropriate for the purpose of arriving at a satisfactory assessment (regulation 7). If such advice has been obtained on making a previous assessment within the last 12 months and certain persons are satisfied that it is sufficient, it is not necessary to obtain new advice (regulation 7(5)). Provision is made as to the persons from whom educational, medical and psychological advice must be sought (regulations 7 to 10). It is provided that in making an assessment an authority shall take into consideration representations from the parent, evidence submitted by the parent, and the advice which has been obtained (regulation 11).

Provision is made for a child without a statement admitted to a special school for the purpose of an assessment to remain there once the assessment is complete (regulation 13).

The Regulations prescribe the draft of a notice to be served on a parent with a draft statement of special educational needs or amended statement, or amendment notice (regulations 14 and 15 and Part A and B of Schedule 1 respectively). The form and content of a statement is also prescribed (regulation 16).

Detailed provision is made as to how an annual review of a statement by a local education authority under section 328 of the Education Act 1996 is to be carried out (regulations 18 to 22). Local education authorities are required to send composite lists of pupils requiring annual reviews to head teachers and health and social services in advance of each term and to the Connexions Service annually (regulation 18). Special provision for reviews is made where the review is the first review after a child has commenced his tenth year of compulsory education. Regulation 20 requires authorities to ensure that statements are amended by 15 February in the year of a child's transfer between phases of his schooling.

The Regulations provide for the transfer of a statement from one local education authority to another (regulation 23). The duties of the transferor are transferred to the transferee, and within 6 weeks of the transfer the transferee must serve a notice on the parent informing him of the transfer, whether they propose to make an assessment, and when they propose to review the statement (regulation 23(2), (3) and (4)). It is provided that where it would not be practicable to require the transferee to arrange for the child's attendance at a school specified in the statement they need not do so, but can arrange for attendance at another school until it is possible to amend the statement (regulation 23(6)).

There are restrictions on the disclosure of statements and steps are to be taken to avoid unauthorised persons having access to them (regulation 24).

Regulation 25 sets out time limits within which authorities must comply with orders made by the Special Educational Needs Tribunal, and regulation 26 sets out time limits within which authorities must take specified action following their concession of certain appeals to the Tribunal.

Provision is made for the transition from the regime imposed by the 1994 Regulations to the regime imposed by these Regulations (regulation 28). Broadly, any action taken under the 1994 Regulations can be completed under those Regulations. If an assessment has been commenced before 1st January 2002 the local education authority may continue to make the assessment under the 1994 Regulations. However if the assessment is not complete before 1st May 2002 these Regulations will apply to the assessment as if it had been commenced under them on that date (regulation 28(3)).

STATUTORY INSTRUMENTS

2001 No. 2218

EDUCATION, ENGLAND

The Special Educational Needs (Provision of Information by Local Education Authorities) (England) Regulations 2001

Made	16th June 2001
Laid before Parliament . .	19th June 2001
Coming into force . . .	1st September 2001

In exercise of the powers conferred on the Secretary of State by sections 29(5), and 569(4) and (5) of the Education Act 1996(**a**) the Secretary of State hereby makes the following Regulations:

Citation, commencement, interpretation and extent

1.(1) These Regulations may be cited as the Special Educational Needs (Provision of Information by Local Education Authorities)(England)Regulations 2001 and shall come into force on 1st September 2001.

(2) In these Regulations-

"health authority" has the same meaning as in the National Health Service Act 1977(**b**);

"social services authority" means a local authority for the purposes of the Local Authority Social Services Act 1970(**c**) acting in the discharge of such functions as are referred to in section 1A of that Act, and

"statement" means a statement of special educational needs made under section 324 of the Education Act 1996.

(3) These Regulations apply only in relation to England.

(4) Nothing in these Regulations applies in relation to-

(a) nursery schools, or

(a) 1996 c.56.
(b) 1977 c.49; amended by the Health Authorities Act 1995 (c.17) and the Health Act 1999 (c.32).
(c) 1970 c.42; section 1A was inserted by the Local Government Act 2000 (c.22), section 102(3).

(b) children under compulsory school age.

Publication of information

2. A local education authority shall-

(a) publish information about the matters set out in the Schedule to these Regulations in accordance with regulation 3(1), (2) and (3);

(b) keep that information under review, and

(c) where there is a significant change in any of that information, revise the information accordingly and publish the revised information in accordance with regulation 3(5).

Manner of publication of information

3.-(1) The local education authority shall publish the information referred to in regulation 2(a) by –

(a) providing a written copy of the information to any health authority or social services authority which in the opinion of the local education authority has an interest in that information;

(b) making the information available on a website which the authority maintain on the Internet, and

(c) providing a written copy of the information to any person on request.

(2) The information about the matters set out in paragraph 1 of the Schedule to these Regulations shall be published on or before 1st April 2002.

(3) The information about the matters set out in paragraphs 2 and 3 of the Schedule to these Regulations shall be published on or before 31st July 2002.

(4) Any information to be published pursuant to regulation 2(c) shall be published by the local education authority as soon as reasonably practicable after a revision has been made by -

(a) providing the revised information to a health authority or social services authority previously provided with information by the local education authority pursuant to regulation 3(1)(a);

(b) updating the website maintained by the authority on the Internet to display the revised information, and

(c) notifying the maintained schools in the authority's area of the revisions by post or by electronic communication.

(5) Information published in accordance with this regulation shall be published free of charge.

Estelle Morris

16th June 2001

Secretary of State,
Department for Education and Skills.

SCHEDULE

Regulation 2

INFORMATION TO BE PROVIDED BY LOCAL EDUCATION AUTHORITIES

1. An explanation of that element of special educational provision for children with special educational needs (but without statements) which the local education authority expect normally to be met from maintained schools' budget shares and that element of such provision that the authority expect normally to be met by the authority from funds which it holds centrally.

2. The broad aims of the local education authority's policy in respect of children with special educational needs together with information about the action the authority is taking to-

(a) promote high standards of education for children with special educational needs;

(b) encourage children with special educational needs to participate fully in their school and community and to take part in decisions about their education;

(c) encourage schools in their area to share their practice in making special educational provision for children with special educational needs, and

(d) work with other statutory and voluntary bodies to provide support for children with special educational needs.

3. The general arrangements made by the local education authority, including any plans, objectives and timescales, for-

(a) identifying children in their area with special educational needs;

(b) monitoring the admission of children with special educational needs (whether or not those children have a statement)to maintained schools in their area;

(c) organising the assessment of children's educational needs pursuant to section 323 of the Education Act 1996 in the local education authority's area including any local protocols for so doing;

(d) organising the making and maintaining of statements in their area including any local protocols for so doing;

(e) providing support to schools in their area with regard to making special educational provision for children with special educational needs;

(f) auditing, planning, monitoring and reviewing provision for children with special educational needs in their area, both generally and in relation to individual children;

(g) securing training, advice and support for staff working in their area with children with special educational needs, and

(h) reviewing and updating the arrangements referred to in sub-paragraphs (a) to (g).

EXPLANATORY NOTE

(This note is not part of the Regulations)

These Regulations place a duty on local education authorities to publish information about matters relating to the provision of education for children with special educational needs.

In particular they are required to publish an explanation of the that part of special educational provision that they expect maintained schools to fund from their budget shares, and that element that the authority expect to fund themselves.

They must also publish information about the broad aims of their policy on special educational needs, as well as specific action the authority is taking on special educational needs issues.

STATUTORY INSTRUMENTS

1999 No. 2506

EDUCATION, ENGLAND

The Education (Special Educational Needs) (Information) (England) Regulations 1999

Made - - - -	*2nd September 1999*
Laid before Parliament	*8th September 1999*
Coming into force	*1st October 1999*

In exercise of the powers conferred on the Secretary of State by sections 317(5) and 569(4) and (5) of the Education Act 1996(**a**) and sections 92(3) and (6) and 138(7) and (8) of the School Standards and Framework Act 1998(**b**), the Secretary of State for Education and Employment hereby makes the following Regulations.

Citation, commencement, extent and revocation

1.—(1) These Regulations may be cited as the Education (Special Educational Needs) (Information) (England) Regulations 1999 and shall come into force on 1st October 1999.

(2) These Regulations apply only in relation to England.

(3) The Education (Special Educational Needs) (Information) Regulations 1994(**c**) shall be revoked in relation to England.

Interpretation

2. In these Regulations—

"the 1996 Act" means the Education Act 1996;

"the 1998 Act" means the School Standards and Framework Act 1998;

"maintained school" means a community, foundation or voluntary school;

"maintained special school" means a community or foundation special school; and

"statement" means a statement of special educational needs within the meaning of section 324(1) of the 1996 Act.

Publication of information about special educational needs

3.—(1) The governing body of every maintained school shall publish information about the matters set out in Schedule 1.

(2) The governing body of every maintained special school, other than one established in a hospital, shall publish information about the matters set out in Schedule 2.

(3) The governing body of every maintained special school which is established in a hospital shall publish information about the matters set out in Schedule 3.

(**a**) 1996 c. 56. By virtue of S.I. 1999/672 the powers conferred by these sections are exercisable by the Secretary of State only in relation to England. Section 317(5) is amended by paragraph 74(6) of Schedule 30 to the School Standards and Framework Act 1998. For the meaning of "prescribed" and "regulations" see section 579(1).

(**b**) 1998 c. 31. By virtue of S.I. 1999/672 the powers conferred by these sections are exercisable by the Secretary of State only in relation to England. For the meaning of "prescribed" and "regulations" see section 142(1).

(**c**) S.I. 1994/1048.

Manner of publication of information

4.—(1) The information referred to in regulation 3 shall be published in a single document by making copies available free of charge–

(a) for distribution–

(i) to parents of pupils or prospective pupils, and

(ii) to the local education authority and District Health Authority for the area in which the school is situated,

who or which request a copy at the school or through the post; and

(b) for reference at the school.

(2) The first occasion on which copies of the document referred to in paragraph (1) above are made available in accordance with that paragraph shall be no later than 1st November 1999.

Publication of information—supplementary

5. Where the information referred to in regulation 3 is to be published by the local education authority with the agreement of the governing body pursuant to section 92(5) of the 1998 Act it shall be supplied to them by the governing body and shall be published without material alteration.

Jacqui Smith
Parliamentary Under Secretary of State,
Department for Education and Employment

2nd September 1999

SCHEDULE 1

Regulation 3(1)

INFORMATION FROM MAINTAINED SCHOOLS

Basic information about the school's special education provision

1. The objectives of the governing body in making provision for pupils with special educational needs, and a description of how the governing body's special educational needs policy will contribute towards meeting those objectives.

2. The name of the person who is responsible for co-ordinating the day to day provision of education for pupils with special educational needs at the school (whether or not the person is known as the SEN co-ordinator).

3. The arrangements which have been made for co-ordinating the provision of education for pupils with special educational needs at the school.

4. The admission arrangements for pupils with special educational needs who do not have a statement in so far as they differ from the arrangements for other pupils.

5. The kinds of provision for special educational needs in which the school specialises and any special units.

6. Facilities for pupils with special educational needs at the school including facilities which increase or assist access to the school by pupils who are disabled.

Information about the school's policies for the identification, assessment and provision for all pupils with special educational needs

7. How resources are allocated to and amongst pupils with special educational needs.

8. How pupils with special educational needs are identified and their needs determined and reviewed.

9. Arrangements for providing access by pupils with special educational needs to a balanced and broadly based curriculum (including the National Curriculum).

10. How pupils with special educational needs engage in the activities of the school together with pupils who do not have special educational needs.

11. How the governing body evaluate the success of the education which is provided at the school to pupils with special educational needs.

12. Any arrangements made by the governing body relating to the treatment of complaints from parents of pupils with special educational needs concerning the provision made at the school.

Information about the school's staffing policies and partnership with bodies beyond the school

13. Any arrangements made by the governing body relating to in-service training for staff in relation to special educational needs.

14. The use made of teachers and facilities from outside the school including links with support services for special educational needs.

15. The role played by the parents of pupils with special educational needs.

16. Any links with other schools, including special school, and the provision made for the transition of pupils with special educational needs between schools or between the school and the next stage of life or education.

17. Links with child health services, social services and educational welfare services and any voluntary organisations which work on behalf of children with special educational needs.

SCHEDULE 2

Regulation 3(2)

INFORMATION FROM MAINTAINED SPECIAL SCHOOLS

Basic information about the school's special educational provision

1. The objectives of the governing body in making provision for pupils with special educational needs, and a description of how the governing body's special educational needs policy will contribute towards meeting those objectives.

2. The kinds of special educational needs for which provision is made at the school.

3. Facilities for pupils at the school including facilities which increase or assist access to the school by pupils who are disabled.

Information about the school's policies for the assessment and provision for all pupils with special educational needs

4. How resources are allocated amongst pupils.

5. How the needs of pupils are identified and reviewed.

6. Arrangements for providing access by pupils to a balanced and broadly based curriculum (including the National Curriculum).

7. How the governing body evaluate the success of the education which is provided at the school to pupils.

8. Any arrangements made by the governing body relating to the treatment of complaints from parents of pupils concerning the provision made at the school.

Information about the school's staffing policies and partnership with bodies beyond the school

9. Any arrangements made by the governing body relating to in-service training for staff in relation to special educational needs.

10. The use made of teachers and facilities from outside the school including the links with support services for special educational needs.

11. The role played by parents of pupils.

12. Any links with other schools, and any arrangements for managing the transition of pupils between schools or between the school and the next stage of life or education.

13. Links with child health services, social services and educational welfare services and any voluntary organisations which work on behalf of children with special educational needs.

SCHEDULE 3

Regulation 3(3)

INFORMATION FROM SPECIAL SCHOOLS IN HOSPITALS

1. The name of the person who is responsible for co-ordinating the day to day provision of education for pupils with special educational needs at the school (whether or not the person is known as the SEN co-ordinator).

2. How pupils with special educational needs are identified and their needs determined and reviewed.

3. How resources are allocated to and amongst pupils with special educational needs.

4. How the educational progress of pupils with special educational needs is monitored.

5. How the contents of a pupil's statement are ascertained and made known to staff.

6. The arrangements for ensuring continuity of the educational provision set out in a pupil's statement differentiating where necessary between long stay and short stay patients.

7. Arrangements for providing access by pupils with special educational needs to a balanced and broadly based curriculum.

8. The use made of teachers and facilities from outside the school including links with support services for special educational needs.

EXPLANATORY NOTE

(This note is not part of the Regulations)

These Regulations, which come into force on 1st October 1999 and apply only to England, make provision for the publication of information about matters relating to the provision of education for pupils with special educational needs in their schools by the governing bodies of maintained schools.

The Regulations replace the Education (Special Educational Needs) (Information) Regulations 1994, which are revoked in relation to England.

The Regulations refer to the new categories of maintained schools in the School Standards and Framework Act 1998. They also remove the requirement to deal with the implementation of the school's SEN policy in the governors' annual report which is now dealt with by the Education (Governors' Annual Reports) (England) Regulations 1999 (S.I. 1999/2157). Otherwise there are no changes of any substance from the 1994 Regulations.

Glossary

These definitions relate to terms used in the Code. In the case of terms defined in legislation, the definitions given here are simplified and the full legal definitions can be found in the legislation referred to.

Annual review: the review of a statement of special educational needs which an LEA must make within 12 months of making the statement or, as the case may be, of the previous review.

British Educational Technology and Communications agency (BECTa): BECTa is a Government-funded agency that promotes information communications technology and its use to support the Government's efforts to raise standards in curriculum subjects, in the teaching of key skills, in institutional effectiveness, and in the development of lifelong learning. BECTa is responsible for developing the National Grid for Learning (NGfL). Further information on information technology for children with special educational needs may be obtained from BECTa at Milburn Hill Road, Science Park, Coventry, CV4 7JJ. Telephone: 0247 641 6994. Websites: *inclusion.ngfl.gov.uk* and *www.becta.org.uk*

Carer: for the purpose of this Code, a carer is a person named by a local authority to care for a child for whom the social services department has parental responsibility, i.e. a child who is the subject of a care order and who has been placed in a residential or foster placement. The carer may qualify as a parent for the purposes of the Education Acts because they have care of the child (see the definition of Parent below). If so, they will have a role to play in the consideration of a child's special educational needs.

Child protection register: in each area covered by a social services department, a central register must be maintained which lists all the children in the area who are considered to be suffering from, or are likely to suffer, significant harm and for which there is a child protection plan. This is not a register of children who have been abused but of children for whom there are currently unresolved child protection issues.

Children 'in need': a child is deemed to be 'in need' if:

- they are unlikely to achieve and maintain, or do not have the opportunity to achieve or maintain a reasonable standard of health or development without provision made by the local authority; or
- their health and development are likely to be significantly impaired, or further impaired, without provision made by the local authority; or
- they are disabled. (Section 17(10))Children Act 1989)

Children's Guardian: Children's guardians are appointed by the court under section 41 of the Children Act 1989 as part of care and related proceedings to safeguard the welfare of the child.

City Academies: CAs were introduced in 2000 as publicly funded independent schools with private or voluntary sector sponsors intended to replace existing secondary schools or provide new secondary school places in disadvantaged urban areas. The legal basis for City Academies is set out in sections 482, 483 and 483A of the Education Act 1996 (as amended by the Learning and Skills Act 2000).

City Technology Colleges: CTCs are independent all-ability, non fee-paying schools for pupils aged 11-18. Their purpose is to offer pupils of all abilities in urban areas across England the opportunity to study successfully a curriculum geared, with the help of private sector sponsors, towards the world of work. CTCs are also encouraged to innovate in the development, management and delivery of the curriculum.

Connexions Service: The service provides a single point of access for *all* 13 – 19 year olds to help them prepare for the transition to work and adult life.

Connexions Personal Advisers (PAs): provide a universal information, advice and guidance service for all young people 13 – 19 years when and where they need it – whether they are at school, in further education, in or out of work.

Disagreement Arrangements: All LEAs must provide arrangements to help prevent or resolve disagreements between parents, whose children have special educational needs, and the LEA or a school. They must include an independent element. They are designed to bring together the different parties in an informal way to seek to resolve the disagreement through discussion. Using these arrangements is voluntary and does not in any way affect a parents right to appeal to the SEN Tribunal.

Disapplication: removal or lifting of a programme of study, attainment target, assessment, or any other component of the National Curriculum, or any combination of these including entire subjects or the entire National Curriculum through relevant regulations. (See also **Modification**, below.)

Early education practitioners: all the adults who work with children in early education settings, whatever their qualifications.

Early education settings: providers in receipt of government funding to deliver early education including – maintained mainstream and special schools, maintained nursery schools, independent schools, non-maintained special schools, local authority daycare providers such as day nurseries and family centres, other registered daycare providers such as pre-schools, playgroups and private day nurseries, local authority Portage schemes and accredited childminders working as part of an approved National Childminding Association network.

Early learning goals: expectations in each of the six areas of learning for most children to reach by the end of the foundation stage.

Early Years Action: when the early education practitioner who works day-to-day with the child or the SENCO identify that a child has special educational needs together they provide interventions that are additional to or different from those provided as part of the setting's usual curriculum offer and strategies. An IEP will usually be devised.

Early Years Action Plus: when the early education practitioner who works day-to-day with the child and the SENCO are provided with advice or support from outside specialists, so that alternative interventions additional or different strategies to those provided for the child through *Early Years Action* can be put in place. A new IEP will usually be devised.

Early Years Development and Childcare Partnerships: Every LEA is required to establish an early years development partnership to work with them in reviewing the sufficiency of nursery education and preparing early years development plans.

Education supervision order: an order that LEAs, under section 36 of the Children Act 1989, can apply for a child of statutory school age who is not being properly educated to be put under the supervision of the LEA, with the intention of ensuring that he or she receives efficient full-time education suited to his or her age, aptitude, ability and any special educational needs, and that sufficient support, advice and guidance are provided to the parents.

Education Welfare Officer: person employed by an LEA to help parents and LEAs meet their respective statutory obligations in relation to school attendance. In some LEAs Education Welfare Officers are known as Education Social Workers.

Foundation stage: the foundation stage begins when children reach the age of three. Many children attend an early education setting soon after their third birthday. The foundation stage continues until the end of the reception year and is consistent with the National Curriculum. It prepares children for learning in year 1, when programmes of study for key stage 1 are taught.

Graduated approach: a model of action and intervention in schools and early education settings to help children who have special educational needs. The approach recognises that there is a continuum of special educational needs and that, where necessary, increasing specialist expertise should be brought to bear on the difficulties that a child may be experiencing.

Group Education Plan: where pupils in the same group, class or subject lesson have common targets and hence, common strategies a group learning plan can be drawn up rather than IEPs for each child.

Independent Parental Supporter: a person to whom all parents should have access, if they so wish. The Independent Parental Supporter must be someone who can support parents for example by attending meetings, encouraging parental participation, and helping the parent understand the SEN framework. Independent means someone independent of the decision making process that determines the type and level of support for a child with special educational needs. Independent Parental Supporters will often be someone from a voluntary organisation, a parent partnership service, another parent or a friend.

Independent school: a school that is not maintained by a local education authority and is registered under section 464 of the Education Act 1996. Section 347 of the Education Act 1996 sets out the conditions under which an independent school may be approved by the Secretary of State as being suitable for the admission of children with statements of special educational needs.

Individual Education Plan: The IEP is a planning, teaching and reviewing tool. It is a working document for all teaching staff recording key short-term targets and strategies for an individual pupil that are <u>different from</u> or <u>additional to</u> those in place for the rest of the group or class. The interventions will be provided Early Years Action, *Early Years Action Plus*, *School Action*, *School Action Plus* and statements of SEN.

Learning Mentors: school staff who work with teaching and pastoral staff to assess, identify and work with those pupils who need extra help to overcome barriers to learning inside and outside school. They are a single point of contact for accessing specialist support services, such as the Social Services, Youth Services, Education Welfare Services etc.

Learning support assistant (LSA): a widely used job title for an assistant providing in-school support for pupils with special educational needs and/or disabilities. An LSA will normally work with a particular pupil or pupils providing close support to the individual pupil and assistance to those responsible for teaching him/her. Some assistants specialising in SEN may also be known by titles other than LSA as these matters are decided locally. LSAs are one of a group of assistants coming within the broader DfES classification of "teaching assistant".

Maintained school: for the purposes of this Code, schools maintained by a local education authority – any community, foundation, voluntary schools, community special and foundation special schools.

Modification: amendment or alteration of a programme of study, attainment target, assessment or any other component of the National Curriculum in order to give the child access to that area of the Curriculum (see also **Disapplication** and National Curriculum **Inclusion statement**).

Named LEA Officer: the person from the LEA who liaises with parents over all the arrangements relating to statutory assessment and the making of a statement. LEAs must inform parents of the identity of the Named Officer when they issue a notice of a proposal to make a statutory assessment of a child.

National Curriculum: this sets out a clear, full and statutory entitlement to learning for all pupils, determining what should be taught and setting attainment targets for learning. It also determines how performance will be assessed and reported.

National Curriculum Inclusion Statement: A detailed overarching statement on Inclusion is included in the National Curriculum; it makes clear the principles schools must follow in their teaching right across the curriculum, to ensure that all pupils have the chance to succeed, whatever their individual needs and the potential barriers to their learning may be. It includes modification of the National Curriculum.

National Literacy and Numeracy Strategies: the literacy and numeracy strategies were introduced in September 1998 and 1999 respectively to raise standards of literacy and mathematics. Primary schools are now teaching a dedicated daily Literacy Hour and daily mathematics lesson.

The KS3 Strategy is being introduced to raise standards in all schools with KS3 pupils through new teaching and learning programmes for English, mathematics, ICT, science and in the Foundation subjects.

Note in lieu: a note that may be issued to the child's parents and school when, following a statutory assessment, the LEA decide not to make a statement. The note should describe the child's special educational needs, explain why the LEA does not think it necessary to make a statement and make recommendations about appropriate provision for the child. All the advice received during the assessment should be attached to the note sent to the parents and, with their consent, should also be sent to the child's school.

Non-maintained special school: schools in England approved by the Secretary of State under section 342 of the Education Act 1996 as special schools which are not maintained by the state but charge fees on a non-profit-making basis. Most non-maintained special schools are run by major charities or charitable trusts.

Occupational therapy: Occupational therapy is the use of purposeful activity and play to help a child attain maximum levels of functional performance, thus gaining self-esteem and independence. Motor, sensory, perceptual, social, emotional and self-care skills are assessed. Working with the child, parents and teachers, occupational therapists use therapeutic techniques (advising on equipment and environment adaptations where appropriate) to improve a child's ability to access the physical and learning curriculum.

OFSTED – Office for Standards in Education; a non-Ministerial government department established under the Education (Schools) Act 1992 to take responsibility for the inspection of all schools in England. Her Majesty's Inspectors (HMI) forms their professional arm.

Parent – under section 576 of the Education Act 1996 a parent includes any person who is not a parent of the child but has parental responsibility (see also Parental Responsibility), or who cares for him.

Parental responsibility: under section 2 of the Children Act 1989, parental responsibility falls upon:

- all mothers and fathers who were married to each other at the time of the child's birth (including those who have since separated or divorced);
- mothers who were not married to the father at the time of the child's birth; and
- fathers who were not married to the mother at the time of the child's birth, but who have obtained parental responsibility either by agreement with the child's mother or through a court order.

Under section 12 of the Children Act 1989 where a court makes a residence order in favour of any person who is not the parent or guardian of the child that person has parental responsibility for the child while the residence order remains in force.

Under section 33 (3) of the Children Act 1989, while a care order is in force with respect to a child, the social services department (SSD) designated by the order will have parental responsibility for that child, and will have the power (subject to certain provisions) to determine the extent to which a parent or guardian of the child may meet his or her parental responsibility for the child. The SSD cannot have parental responsibility for a child unless that child is the subject of a care order, except for very limited purposes where an emergency protection Order is in force under Section 44 of the Children Act 1989.

Parental responsibility is defined under section 3(1) of the Children Act 1989 as meaning all the duties, rights, powers, responsibilities and authority which parents have with respect to their children and their children's property.

Parent Partnership Services: provide advice and information to parents whose children have special educational needs. They provide neutral and factual support on all aspects of the SEN framework to help parents play an active and informed role in their child's education. Although funded by the local education authority they provide a service to parents and are often either run at arms length from the authority or by a voluntary organisation to ensure parents have confidence in them.

Portage: planned, home-based educational support for pre-school children with special educational needs. LEAs usually provide Portage services. The Portage service is named after the town of Portage, Wisconsin, USA. There is an active and extensive network of Portage services in the UK developed by the National Portage Association, which provides a Code of Practice and accredited training.

Physiotherapy: physiotherapy is a health care profession that emphasises the use of physical approaches in the promotion, maintenance and restoration of an individual's physical, psychological and social well-being. Following assessment, a treatment plan is developed in partnership with the client/carers; this plan is constantly evaluated to ensure that it is effective and relevant to the individual's changing circumstances and health status.

Pupil Referral Unit: any school established and maintained by a local education authority under section 19 (2) of the Education Act 1996 which is specially organised to provide education for pupils who would not otherwise receive suitable education because of illness, exclusion or any other reason. Further details are given in DfEE Circular 11/99 Chapter 6.

Responsible Person: the head teacher or the appropriate governor, that is the chairman of the governing body unless the governing body have designated another governor for the purpose. In the case of a nursery school, the responsible person is the head teacher. The LEA must inform the responsible person when they conclude that a pupil at a school has SEN. The responsible person must then ensure that all those who will teach the child know about the child's SEN.

SCE: Service Children's Education. The SCE oversees the education of UK service children abroad. It is funded by the Ministry of Defence and operates its own schools as well as providing advice to parents on SCEA and UK schools.

School Action: when a class or subject teacher identify that a pupil has special educational needs they provide interventions that are additional to or different from those provided as part of the school's usual differentiated curriculum offer and strategies. An IEP will usually be devised.

School Action Plus: when the class or subject teacher and the SENCO are provided with advice or support from outside specialists, so that alternative interventions additional or different strategies to those provided for the pupil through *School Action* can be put in place. The SENCO usually takes the lead although day-to-day provision continues to be the responsibility of class or subject teacher. A new IEP will usually be devised.

SEN coordinator (SENCO): member of staff of a school or early education setting who has responsibility for coordinating SEN provision within that school. In a small school the head teacher or deputy may take on this role. In larger schools there may be an SEN coordinating team.

SEN Tribunal: an independent body which has jurisdiction under section 333 of the Education Act 1996 for determining appeals by parents against LEA decisions on assessments and statements. The Tribunal's decision will be binding on both parties to the appeal.

Special school: a school which is specially organised to make special educational provision for pupils with special educational needs. Special schools maintained by the LEA comprise of community special schools and foundation special schools, and non maintained special schools are approved by the Secretary of State under section 342 of the Education Act 1996.

Speech and language therapy: Speech and language therapy is a health care profession, the role and aim of which is to enable adults and children with speech, language and communication difficulties (and associated difficulties with eating and swallowing) to reach their maximum communication potential and achieve independence in all aspects of life.

Temporary Disapplication: A maintained school must provide access to the National Curriculum for all pupils on the school's register including those being taught temporarily at home, in a hospital school or in a pupil referral unit. Where it is impossible or inappropriate to offer these pupils the full National Curriculum, aspects may be disapplied through a general direction or a special direction if a statement is being considered or amended. Head teachers have considerable discretion over directions for temporary disapplication but should only consider a direction where pupils' present circumstances or conduct mean that they cannot fully participate and benefit from the National Curriculum. Disapplication should be limited to those aspects of the National Curriculum that are inappropriate for the pupil.

Transition Plan: a plan devised following the year 9 annual review and updated at subsequent annual reviews. The purpose of the plan is to draw together information from a range of individuals within and beyond the school, in order to plan coherently for the young person's transition to adult life.

Index